Praise from Job Seekers for the *Knock 'em Dead* Books

"My job search began a few months ago when I found out that I would be laid off because of a corporate buyout. By following your advice, I have had dozens of interviews and have received three very good job offers. Your excellent advice made my job hunt much easier."

—K.C., St. Louis, Missouri

"I've used *Knock 'em Dead* since 1994 when I graduated. It's the reason I've made it to VP—thank you!"

—P.L., Norfolk, Virginia

"My son called me from college last night, desperate to help a friend on her first interview. My advice? Tell her to drop everything and head to the nearest bookstore to get *Knock 'em Dead*. The book is a godsend and helped me obtain the job of my dreams eight years ago. It is by far THE best book on interviewing out there. I highly recommend it to everyone I know who asks me for help. As a Director of HR now, I know. No one should go to an interview without reading, re-reading, and re-re-reading this informative, absorbing, tremendously helpful book. It is utterly amazing. Thank you!"

—S.D., Philadelphia, Pennsylvania

"I was out of work for four months—within five weeks of reading your book, I had four job offers."

—S.K., Dallas, Texas

"I cannot tell you what a fabulous response I have been getting due to the techniques you describe in your books. Besides giving me the tools I needed to 'get my foot in the door,' they gave me confidence. I never thought I could secure an excellent position within a month!"

—B. G., Mountainview, California

"I am very grateful for your *Knock 'em Dead* series. I have read the trio and adopted the methods. In the end, I got a dream job with a salary that is almost double of my previous! By adopting your methods, I got four job offers and had a hard time deciding!"

—C.Y., Singapore

"After reading your book, *Resumes That Knock 'em Dead*, I rewrote my resume and mailed it to about eight companies. The results were beyond belief. I was employed by one of the companies that got my new resume and received offers of employment or requests for interviews from every company. The entire job search took only five weeks."

—J.V., Dayton, Ohio

"Your book is simply fantastic. This one book improved my yearly income by several thousand dollars, and my future income by untold amounts. Your work has made my family and myself very happy."

—M.Z., St. Clair Shores, Michigan

"After having seen you on television, I decided to order the *Knock 'em Dead* books. Your insights into selling myself helped me find opportunities in my field that would not have been attainable otherwise."

—E. M., Short Hills, New Jersey

"I just wanted to say thank you so much for your book. I can really, honestly say that it has influenced my life course!"

—P.B., London, England

"Thank you for your wonderful book! I read it before attempting to secure a position in an industry that I had been out of for fourteen years. The first company I interviewed with made me an offer for more money than I had expected."

—K.T., Houston, Texas

"I got the position! I was interviewed by three people and the third person asked me all the questions in *Knock 'em Dead*. I had all the right answers!"

—D. J., Scottsdale, Arizona

"I followed the advice in *Knock 'em Dead* religiously and got more money, less hours, a better hospital plan, and negotiated to keep my three weeks of vacation. I start my new job immediately!"

—A.B., St. Louis, Missouri

"Thank you for all the wonderfully helpful information you provided in your book. I lost my job almost one year ago. I spent almost eight months looking for a comparable position. Then I had the good sense to buy your book. Two months later, I accepted a new position. You helped me turn one of the worst experiences of my life into a blessing in disguise."

—L.G., Watervliet, New York

"I heard of your book right after I bombed out on three interviews. I read it. I went on two interviews after reading it. I have been told by both of those last two interviewers that I am the strongest candidate. I may have two job offers!"

—B.V., Albuquerque, New Mexico

"I read your book and studied your answers to tough questions. The first interview that I went on after doing this ended up in a job being offered to me! The interviewer told me that I was the best interviewee she'd seen! Thanks a million for writing your book. I am so thankful that I had heard about you!"

—K.P., Houston, Texas

"I just finished writing the letter I have dreamed of writing for three years: my letter of resignation from the Company from Hell. Thanks to you and the book *Knock 'em Dead*, I have been offered and have accepted an excellent position with a major international service corporation."

—C. C., Atlanta, Georgia

"I was sending out hordes of resumes and hardly getting a nibble—and I have top-notch skills and experience in my field. I wasn't prepared for this tough job market. When I read your book, however, I immediately began applying some of your techniques. My few nibbles increased to so many job interviews I could hardly keep up with them!"

—C.S., Chicago, Illinois

"It was as if the interviewer had just put the same book down! After being unemployed for more than a year, I am grateful to say that I've landed the best job I've ever had."

—E. M., Honolulu, Hawaii

"Every time I've used your book, I've gotten an offer! This book is incredible. Thanks for publishing such a great tool."

—W. Z., Columbia, Maryland

"I just received the offer of my dreams with an outstanding company. Thank you for your insight. I was prepared!"

—T.C., San Francisco, California

COVER LETTERS

THAT KNOCK 'EM DEAD

7TH EDITION

Martin Yate, C.P.C.

Adams Media

Avon, Massachusetts

To your good fortune, that intersection of preparation, effort, and opportunity.

Acknowledgments

Knock 'em Dead is now in its nineteenth year of publication, and it has become a staple for job hunters around the world. This is due to the ongoing support of countless people on the team of Adams Media, both past and present.

Published by
Adams Media, an F+W Publications Company
57 Littlefield Street, Avon, MA 02322
www.adamsmedia.com

ISBN 10: 1-59337-747-9
ISBN 13: 978-1-59337-747-2
Printed in the United States of America.

J I H G F E D C B A

Library of Congress Cataloging-in-Publication Data
Yate, Martin John.
Cover letters that knock 'em dead / Martin Yate. — 7th ed.
p. cm.
Includes index.
ISBN-10: 1-59337-747-9
ISBN-13: 978-1-59337-747-2
1. Cover letters. 2. Résumés (Employment) I. Title. II. Title: Cover letters that knock them dead. III. Title: Knock 'em dead.
HF5383.Y378 2004
650.14'2--dc22
2006019729

This publication is designed to provide accurate and authoritative information with regard to the subject matter covered. It is sold with the understanding that the publisher is not engaged in rendering legal, accounting, or other professional advice. If legal advice or other expert assistance is required, the services of a qualified professional person should be sought.
— From a *Declaration of Principles* jointly adopted by a Committee of the American Bar Association and a Committee of Publishers and Associations.

Many of the designations used by manufacturers and sellers to distinguish their products are claimed as trademarks. Where those designations appear in this book and Adams Media was aware of a trademark claim, the designations have been printed with initial capital letters.

*This book is available at quantity discounts for bulk purchases.
For more information, call 1-800-872-5627.*

READ THIS FIRST

THERE'S A CRUEL paradox at work when it comes to writing cover letters.

We strive to excel in our professions, spending our energies to become top-notch accountants, truck drivers, brain surgeons . . . and we spend little or no time learning to promote ourselves on the printed page. When our livelihood suddenly depends on our ability to create a compelling professional profile, we find ourselves in dire straits.

In the technological revolution that brought us computers and e-mail we all started writing once more, but at the same time we found our writing skills have long since rusted. Although packaging our professional selves for evaluation by others has such an enormous impact on all aspects of the quality of our lives, most of us have simply never made the development of adequate written communication skills a top priority. This task is made the more difficult because, when writing a cover letter, we are creating a sales document, and a document where we are the subject. If you are like most people, packaging and pitching yourself to others is both an uncomfortable and difficult prospect.

Sometimes, more senior professionals hire others to craft these messages. As for the rest of us . . . well, we just send these all-important sales documents out into the world far weaker than they could be. The result? We stay longer in that dead-end job, or longer unemployed.

If you find yourself short of writing and self-presentation skills at the most inopportune time imaginable—during your job search—take heart. *Cover Letters That Knock 'em Dead* has helped millions of people around the world craft personal, unique, and hard-hitting job-hunting letters of all types, and it can do the same for you. Use it exactly as I recommend in the pages that follow. If you do, you will reap a number of benefits, the most important of which is this:

- Your job hunt will get a tremendous boost, because your letters will look great, pack a punch, get read, and position you as a mover and shaker worth interviewing, and worth remembering.

This book will enable you to have templates on hand for all kinds of useful letters which you can use in a productive job hunt—not only cover letters of every conceivable type, but letters for every situation, including follow-up letters, acceptance letters, and those oh-so-happy letters of resignation. These letters were all designed to keep your candidacy forefront in the minds of employers. They are real letters written by real job hunters, and also by professional resume and letter writing professionals. They will give you that extra edge in a highly competitive job market, as you will have the advantage of proven tools, customized to your own needs.

There are other advantages:

- You won't waste a moment of precious time conceiving letters from scratch, because you will have a wide selection of templates to rework for your own needs.
- You'll have the satisfaction of knowing that you've made a tough, intricate, and vitally important professional challenge a little easier and more enjoyable than it is for most people in your shoes (your competitors, for example).
- Once settled in a new position, you will be able to adapt the techniques you learn here to other on-the-job written communications that are part of the underpinnings of any successful career.

Employers go through four distinct stages in reaching a hiring decision.

1. *Long-list development.* Advertising and other sources develop the biggest possible field of qualified candidates.

2. *Short-list development.* The long list is screened to rule out also-rans. Those who make the cut are invited in for an interview.

3. *Short-list prioritization.* Through a series of two or three interviews, candidates are weeded out. Those still standing are ranked according to various criteria. (To learn how to successfully make it through the interview process, see the "The Five Secrets of the Hire" chapter in *Knock 'em Dead: The Ultimate Job Seeker's Guide.*)

4. *Short-list review.* After the dust settles, each candidate's strengths and weaknesses are reviewed for one last time before the final decision. The information in the dossier created for every short-list candidate plays a key role here. This dossier will contain all the knowledge the company has about you. This will include your resume, cover letter, and any follow-up letters you have been smart enough to send during the interview process.

In each of these steps, letters have a role to play in taking you to the next level. For example, a resume without a cover letter often gets no further than the trash can. The reader feels you are obviously not interested enough in their specific job to write a cover letter while, on the other hand, your competition is providing concrete evidence of commitment and communication skills.

A "To Whom It May Concern" letter fares little better. A letter with a salutation by name gets read and kept. As will letters following up on meetings that make comments on the discussions and issues addressed.

It's estimated that the average piece of business correspondence initially receives less than thirty seconds of the reader's attention; just a quick scan to reject or save for more careful consideration. A great cover letter will get you much more; it will get a second, more careful, reading, and it will get your resume read with serious attention. In crafting your cover letter, you are not aiming to win a place next to a favorite novel on the reader's bedside table. A powerful cover letter will win that momentary flash of genuine interest and get your resume read carefully. Once that's accomplished, you can use the models in this book for the follow-up letters that will help you to step upward on the four-tiered ladder to the job offer.

Letters help you move through each phase of the hiring cycle by supporting your candidacy and reminding employers of your relevant skills, continued existence, and interest in the job, all the way to the offer. It's a well-known fact, in headhunting circles, that when there is no major difference between two top candidates, the offer will always go to the most enthusiastic; professional follow-through with your letters makes that enthusiasm clear.

In the fourth step (the short-list review), the interviewer recalls what happened in each phase of the interview cycle. All notes and documentation in the applicant's dossier are reviewed for each candidate. This means that as you pass through each step of the cycle, you are presented with a heaven-sent opportunity to advance your candidacy for when that moment of truth finally arrives. You can seize the opportunity to include all manner of pertinent information that will identify you as the unquestioned prime choice when that last, most critical evaluation is taking place.

Your written record (all the different types of letters you can create during the interview cycle to advance your candidacy) demonstrates writing skills, attention to detail, professionalism, and that all-important enthusiasm; each letter adds yet another meaningful plus to your candidacy. And remember that these pluses are being made when you aren't there to speak up for yourself.

I took a commonsense approach to putting this book together: I collected over four thousand successful job-hunting letters from the most cynical professionals in the country: corporate human resources people and professional headhunters. I approached over a thousand of these people and asked them to provide the truly impressive letters they came across—the letters that grabbed attention, advanced someone's candidacy against tough competition, and made a real difference. The cream of the crop can be found within these covers. Over the years, this book has become the standard against which the others in the field are judged, and it is updated on a regular basis to add to its breadth, depth, and efficacy.

From these letters, and from my discussions with professionals in the field, I learned which things work—and which don't—when putting together a cover letter. These qualities are explored in detail later on in the book, but there is one overriding factor that virtually all the successful letters shared, and it's worth exploring here.

All but a handful of the letters were only one page long. Yours probably should be too. Why is brevity so important? My sources on the hiring side of the desk, where I spent a number of years myself, feel that:

1. They don't have time to wade through dense patches of text, and they have a dim view of those who can't get straight to the point.
2. Second pages get detached and often lack sufficient contact information. (For that matter, first pages often fall short in the same category.)

A strong mail dimension to your job-hunting campaign can double and triple your effectiveness. Throughout this book, whenever you read the word "mail" it has a double meaning—regular mail and e-mail. The most effective job-hunting campaign will always use the two mediums in tandem. For maximum impact you will want to follow up each mailing with a telephone call to the recipient; for more information on this part of the job search, my book *Knock 'em Dead: The Ultimate Job Seeker's Guide* will help you with advice on how to turn these calls into interviews, and, where no openings exist, referrals for further opportunities.

If you use the letter samples simply as they are, as noncustomized templates, you may open a few doors. But the "real" you will be so different from the letters that the interviewers will eventually be left with a nagging doubt that you aren't all you appear to be. Besides, when it is so easy to customize these samples, why not make the effort as a gift to your career? Then, with small changes, you'll be able to use them again and again throughout your career.

Browse through the wide variety of letters in the second half of this book. Not all of them will fit your needs at this moment, but take a look anyway. You will see, on every page, proven methods of getting the good word across to potential employers.

This book will also highlight key phrases and wording techniques that caught the eyes of people whose eyes are usually tough to catch. You will discover a "rhythm" to the words and phrases that have real impact. Then you'll be able to incorporate them into your own original work. By sampling a few phrases from this letter, and a few from that letter, you will be able to create powerful communications that reflect the real you.

In choosing the examples for this book, I was pleased to see that the ones that rose to the top were all businesslike, with no gimmickry or cuteness. Some may even seem a little dry to you, but remember: They worked. This collection of successful job-hunting letters includes the best of the best as determined by line managers, human resource professionals, headhunters, and career management professionals who know a winner when they see one. It is just such people who will be evaluating your efforts, and the drawbridge of opportunity will be raised (or lowered) for you depending on their evaluation.

Now let's learn how to put together the jigsaw puzzle pieces. I suggest that you read this book with a highlighter in hand, so you can flag appropriate sections for later reference. That way you'll have a wealth of good ideas you can use after just one read. Then you'll be ready to create your own unique job-hunting letters that will knock 'em dead.

CONTENTS

1. What Is a Cover Letter?

Your cover letter is the personalized factor in the presentation of an otherwise essentially impersonal document, your resume. A good cover letter sets the stage for the reader to accept your resume as something worth serious attention. This chapter examines the component parts of a good cover letter.

2. Four Types of Cover Letters

Your job search is likely to present you with every conceivable challenge to getting that resume read and that interview scheduled. No one type of letter is right for every situation, but there are certain styles of letters that can be adapted to every situation.

3. What Goes In, What Stays Out

Once upon a time, there were just a few set rules for writing a great job-search letter, but the rules of the game have changed. Today, your job skills and professionalism are under closer scrutiny than ever before. The evaluation process starts the moment you make contact—which means that the content and style of your cover letter set the tone for your entire candidacy.

4. Assembling Your Cover Letter

You need solid content to put in your cover letters, and that can take a little thought. The steps in this chapter will probably give you a greater understanding of your selling points than you have ever achieved before.

5. The Final Product

Style—so easy to see but so difficult to define—usually has a distinct look and feel. Here are some of the techniques you should keep in mind when creating your own stylish and professional cover letters.

6. The Plan of Attack

Great cover, broadcast, and follow-up letters won't get you a job by sitting on your desk like rare manuscripts—you have to do something with them. Here's an overview of a sensible plan of attack for your job search.

7. How the Internet Can Help in Your Job Search

The Internet offers you an array of opportunities to get your resume on the desks of thousands of companies and recruiters. This communication medium makes research and contact easier than it has ever been, but you shouldn't rely on the obvious online approaches exclusively.

"Cold" Responses to Employment Industry Professionals
Letters

E-mails

Broadcast
Letters

E-mails

Networking
Letters

E-mails

WHAT IS A COVER LETTER?

DO YOU EVER receive junk mail? We all do. What do you do with the stuff marked "occupant"?

We all receive junk mail and either junk it without reading, or after a quick glance; junk mail never gets the attention a properly focused letter does because it is formulaic. Because we put too little thought into our cover letters, most of them end up being treated the same way.

Your cover letter should be the personalized factor in the presentation of an otherwise essentially impersonal document, your resume. A good cover letter sets the stage for the reader to accept your resume as something worth serious attention. Only if your cover letter and resume work together and do their jobs properly will interviews, and ultimately job offers, result.

When the envelope is opened, your cover letter is the first thing seen. It can make an indelible first impression, it can set the tone for your candidacy, and it can earn your resume the careful examination it deserves.

The higher up the professional ladder you climb, the more important cover letters and the other letters we write during a job search become. For the candidate who must demonstrate written communication skills in the execution of daily duties (and that's just about all of us), these letters become a valuable vehicle for demonstrating critical job skills. If you mess up here, the door to opportunity could well slam shut. On the other hand, if you do a good job here it will help you stand out from the competition.

Step One

There are four basic building blocks to creating a productive cover letter, and the underlying rules of effective written communication embodied in these four steps can be applied to any memo or business letter you ever write.

Your first step is to grab your reader's ATTENTION. You do this with the appearance of your letter: the type is large and legible enough for others to read; it is free of misspellings and it is well laid out so that it is easy on the eye; and if that letter is going by mail rather than e-mail, you grab attention by using quality stationery and matching envelopes. This way your letter and resume will match and give an impression of balance and continuity (see Chapter 5, "The Final Product," for details on paper choice). When your message is crafted with this attention to detail and convenience for the reader, it reflects the kind of professional who just might have something to say.

Step Two

Your second step is to generate INTEREST with the letter's content. The first opportunity you have to do this is by addressing the letter to someone by name. (I explain research approaches to achieve this in *Knock 'em Dead: the Ultimate Job Seeker's Guide.*) The first couple of sentences grab attention, and the rest of the paragraph introduces your candidacy. The secret is to introduce yourself with conviction. Think about it—if you don't believe in the professional product that is you, how can you expect anyone else to believe?

Use research to get your letter off to a fast start; with Google and other search engines, anyone can search the Web for articles and visit the employer's own site. For example:

"I came across the attached/enclosed article in Newsweek *magazine and thought it might interest you. It encouraged me to do a little research on your company. I am now convinced of two things: You are the kind of people I want to be associated with, and I have the kind of qualifications you can use."*

On a company's Web site, you will find lots of eye-opening information, including news and press clippings. You can use search engines to find interesting info about the company by typing in the company name as a keyword. Once you find a relevant article, you can use it in the following ways:

- With an e-mail, you paste the article and attach it
- With a traditional letter, you enclose a copy of the article

Of course, not every company you approach will have been mentioned in *Newsweek.* Even if there is no mention in the press, though, the chances are still good that the company's Web site (or your other research) can give you some insight that can be turned to advantage. Here are some real-life examples that you can adapt to your own needs.

"I have been following the performance of your fund in Mutual Funds Newsletter. *The record over the last three years shows strong portfolio management. With my experience working for one of your competitors, I know I could make significant contributions . . ."*

"Recently I have been researching the local _____ industry. My search has been for companies that are respected in the field and . . . which prize a commitment to professional development. I am such an individual and you are clearly such a company."

"Within the next few weeks I will be moving from New York to _____. Having researched the companies in _____, I know that you are the people I want to talk to . . ."

"The state of the art in _____ changes so rapidly that it is tough for most professionals to keep up. I am the exception, and I am eager to bring my experience to bear for your company."

Step Three

Now, having built a bridge between you and the reader, the intent is to turn that INTEREST into a DESIRE to learn more. First, tie yourself to a specific job category or work area. Use phrases like:

"I am writing because . . ." or *"My reason for contacting you . . ."*

". . . should this be the case, you may be interested to know . . ."

"If you are seeking a _____, you will be interested to know . . ."

"I would like to talk to you about your staffing needs for _____ and how I might be able to contribute to your department's goals."

"If you have an opening for someone in this area, you will see that my resume demonstrates a person of unusual dedication, efficiency, and drive."

You might next call attention to your merits with a short paragraph that highlights one or two of your special contributions or achievements:

"I have an economics background from Columbia and a quantitative analysis approach to market fluctuations. This combination has enabled me consistently to pick the new technology flotations that are the backbone of a growth-oriented technology fund."

Similar statements applicable to your area of expertise will give your letter more personal punch. Include any qualifications, contributions, and attributes that prove you are someone with professional commitment and talent to offer. If an advertisement, or a telephone conversation with a potential employer, reveals an aspect of a particular job opening that is not addressed in your resume, you can use the cover letter to fill in the gaps. For example:

"I notice from your advertisement that A/V training experience would be a plus. In addition to the qualifications stated in my enclosed resume, I have over five years of experience writing and producing sales and management training materials in both these media."

It is through this third step that you want the reader to say, "Wow, this man/ woman really understands the job. I need to read on and learn more."

Step Four

Here's where your letter turns a DESIRE to know more into ACTION. The action you're shooting for is that the reader will dash straight on to your resume, and then call you in for an interview. You achieve this with brevity—always leave the reader wanting more. Offer too much information and you may be ruled out of consideration, so whet the reader's appetite but leave them asking questions.

Make it clear to the reader that you want to talk. Explain when, where, and how you can be contacted. You can also be *proactive* by telling the reader that you intend to follow up at a certain point in time if contact has not been established by then. Just as you worked to create a strong opening, make sure your closing carries the same conviction. It is the reader's last personal impression of you, so make it strong, make it tight, and make it obvious that you are serious about entering into meaningful conversation.

Useful phrases include:

"It would be a pleasure to give you more information about my qualifications and experience . . ."

"I look forward to discussing our mutual interests further . . ."

"While I prefer not to use my employer's time taking personal calls at work, with discretion I can be reached at _____."

"I will be in your area around the 20th, and will call you prior to that date. I would like to arrange . . ."

"I hope to speak with you further and will call the week of _____ to follow up."

"The chance to meet with you would be a privilege and a pleasure, and so to this end I shall call you on _____."

"I look forward to speaking with you further and will call in the next few days to see when our schedules will permit a face-to-face meeting."

"May I suggest a personal meeting where you can have the opportunity to examine the person behind the resume?"

"My credentials and achievements are a matter of record that I hope you will examine in depth when we meet . . . you can reach me at _____."

"I look forward to examining any of the ways you feel my background and skills would benefit [name of organization]. I look forward to hearing from you."

"Resumes help you sort out the probables from the possibles, but they are no way to judge the caliber of an individual. I would like to meet you and demonstrate that I have the professional personality that makes for a successful _____."

"I expect to be in your area on Tuesday and Wednesday of next week and wonder which day would be best for you. I will call to determine. In the meantime, I would appreciate your treating my application as confidential, since I am currently employed."

"With my training and hands-on experience, I know I can contribute to _____, and want to talk to you about it in person. When may we meet?"

"After reading my resume, you will know something about my background. Yet, you will still need to determine whether I am the one to help you with current problems and challenges. I would like an interview to discuss my ability to contribute."

"You can reach me at [home/alternate number] to arrange an interview. I know that your time investment in meeting with me will be repaid amply."

"Thank you for your time and consideration; I hope to hear from you shortly."

"May I call you for an interview in the next few days?"

"A brief phone call will establish whether or not we have mutual interest. Recognizing the demands of your schedule, I will make that call within the week."

Some people feel it is powerful in the closing to state a date—"I'll call you on Friday if we don't speak before"—or a date and time—"I'll call you on Friday morning at 10 A.M. if we don't speak before"—when they will follow up with a phone call. The logic is that you demonstrate that your intent is serious, that you are organized, and that you plan your time effectively (all desirable behavioral traits).

On the other hand, at least one "authority" has said that an employer would be offended by being "forced" to sit and await your call. Frankly, with more than thirty years of involvement in the hiring process, I have never met anyone who felt constrained to wait by the phone for such a call. What sometimes does get noticed, though, is the person who doesn't follow through on commitments as promised. Therefore, if you use this approach, keep your promise.

FOUR TYPES OF COVER LETTERS

PRACTICALLY SPEAKING THERE are four types of cover letters that together address most of the situations you will run into in a job search. The following examples will appeal to you partly based on their relevance to a particular situation, and partly based on your personal preferences.

The General Cover Letter

To show you the nuts and bolts of the Knock 'em Dead way to building effective cover letters, we'll start with an example of a general cover letter. It was created using the sample phrases from the last chapter. You can create powerful job search letters of all types with this same technique, taking a sentence from one sample and a phrase from another; then all you have to do is make the necessary changes to personalize each document.

The following two examples have underlined text to show where I have cut and pasted a phrase from the last chapter. This is the kind of letter you would send with your resume when you do not know of a specific job opening.

James Sharpe
18 Central Park Street • Anytown, NY 14788
(516) 555-1212

October 2, 20—

Jackson Bethell, V.P. Operations
DataLink Products
621 Miller Drive
Anytown, CA 01234

Dear Jackson Bethell,

Recently I have been researching the leading local companies in data communications. My search has been for companies that are respected in the field and who provide ongoing training programs. The name of DataLink Products keeps coming up as a top company.

I am an experienced voice and data communications specialist with a substantial background in IBM environments. If you have an opening for someone in this area, you will see that my resume demonstrates a person of unusual dedication, efficiency, and drive. My experience and achievements include:

- The complete redesign of a data communications network, projected to increase efficiency company-wide some 12 percent.
- The installation and troubleshooting of a Defender IV call-back security system for a dial-up network.

I enclose a copy of my resume, and look forward to examining any of the ways you feel my background and skills would benefit DataLink Products. While I prefer not to use my employer's time taking personal calls at work, with discretion I can be reached at (516) 555-1212 to initiate contact. However, I would rather you call me at _____ in the evening. Let's talk!

Yours truly,

James Sharpe

James Sharpe

JANE SWIFT
18 Central Park Street, Anytown, NY 14788
(516) 555-1212

David Doors, Director of Marketing   January 14, 20—
Martin Financial Group
1642 Rhode Island Way
Anytown, NY 01234

Dear David Doors,

I have always followed the performance of your company in *Mutual Funds Newsletter*.

Recently your notice regarding a Market Analyst in *Investor's Business Daily* caught my eye—and your company name caught my attention—your record over the last three years shows exceptional portfolio management. Because of my experience with one of your competitors, I know I could make significant contributions.

I would like to talk to you about your personnel needs and how I am able to contribute to your department's goals.

An experienced market analyst, I have an economics background (M.S. Purdue) and a strong quantitative analysis approach to market fluctuations. This combination has enabled me to consistently pick the new technology flotations that are the backbone of the growth-oriented mutual fund. For example:

I first recommended Targus Fund six years ago. More recently my clients have been strongly invested in Atlantic Horizon Growth (in the high-risk category), and Next Wave Growth and Income (for the cautious investor). Those following my advice over the last six years have consistently outperformed the market.

I know that resumes help you sort out the probables from the possibles, but they are no way to judge the personal caliber of an individual. I would like to meet with you and demonstrate that along with the credentials, I have the professional commitment that makes for a successful team player.

Yours truly,

Jane Swift

Jane Swift

The Executive Briefing

The executive briefing is a different and dramatically effective form of cover letter whenever you have some information about a job opening from a help-wanted ad, an online job posting, or a prior conversation. This kind of letter gets right to the point and makes life easy for the reader. Why send an executive briefing?

1. It quickly matches stated requirements against the skills you bring to the table, making analysis much easier for the reader.
2. The initial resume screener in Human Resources (HR) might not have an in-depth understanding of the job or its requirements, so the executive briefing helps match an open requirement directly to your abilities. This can be a real help to someone working on fifty or more different openings at a time.
3. Your general resume invariably needs customizing for any specific job. (Overly broad resumes are like "one-size-fits-all" clothes—one size usually fits none.) The executive briefing allows you to fill in the gaps in a succinct and helpful manner.
4. Imagine for a moment that a great opportunity comes your way, but your resume is somewhat (or more than somewhat) out of date and you have to send something out immediately to take advantage of the opportunity of a lifetime. The executive briefing allows you to bring that work history right up to date.

An executive briefing can also help you through a screening and multiple interview cycle. Let me explain. You will be interviewed by a number of people, not all of whom can be expected to have a thorough understanding of the needs of the job—perhaps surprising, but nevertheless true. When this happens, the problems begin.

A manager says, "Spend a few minutes with this candidate and tell me what you think." This means that sometimes other interviewers do not have any way to qualify you fairly and specifically for the needs of the job. While the manager will be looking for specific skills relating to projects at hand, the personnel department will be trying to match your skills to the vagaries of the job-description manual.

Also, by taking multiple copies of your resume and the briefing, carefully stapled together, you guarantee that everyone with whom you interview will have the job's specific requirements and your matching skills front and center when they sit down with you.

The executive briefing, which introduces your resume, as well as customizing and supplementing it, solves the above problems with its layout. It looks like this:

From: top10acct@aol.com
Subject: **Re: Accounting Manager**
Date: February 18, 2005 10:05:44 PM EST
To: rlstein@McCoy.com

Dear Ms. Stein,

I have nine years of accounting experience and am responding to your recent posting for an Accounting Manager on Careerbuilder. Please allow me to highlight my skills as they relate to your stated requirements.

Your Requirements	My Experience
Accounting degree, 4 years exp.	Obtained a C.A. degree in 2000 and have over four years' experience as an Accounting Manager
Excellent people skills and leadership	Effectively managed a staff of 24; ability to motivate staff, including supervisors.
Strong administrative and analytical	Assisted in the development of a base reference skills-library with Microsoft Excel for 400 clients.
Good communication skills	Trained new supervisors and staff via daily coaching sessions, communication meetings, and technical skill sessions.

My resume, pasted below and attached in MSWord, will flesh out my general background. I hope this executive briefing helps you use your time effectively today. I am ready to make a move, hope we can talk soon.

Sincerely,

Joe Black
Joe Black

The executive briefing assures that each resume you send out addresses the job's specific needs and that every interviewer at that company will be interviewing you for the same job. It provides a comprehensive picture of a thorough professional, plus a personalized, fast, and easy-to-read synopsis that details exactly how you can help with an employer's needs.

The use of an executive briefing is naturally restricted to jobs you have discovered through your own efforts or seen advertised. It is obviously not appropriate when the requirements of a specific job are unavailable.

The Broadcast Letter

The broadcast letter is a simple but effective variation on the cover letter. You can use it when:

- You don't have a resume.
- Your resume is inappropriate for the position.
- Your resume is too dreadful to send out.
- Your resume isn't the getting the results you want, and you want to try something different while you are retooling it.

Much of the information will be culled from your resume, because the intent of the broadcast letter is to *replace* the resume as a means of introduction and a tool to initiate conversation. You are well advised to conduct an in-depth analysis of your background, as it relates to a specific target job, in much the same way you do for a resume; you will learn more about this in Chapter 4. Now although a broadcast letter can get you into a telephone conversation with a potential employer, that employer may still ask to see a resume. If this happens, always try to schedule the interview and bring the resume with you; this way you buy a little more time to customize your resume to the employer's specific needs.

If you don't have a resume, you might well have to fill out one of those dreadful application forms. This requires putting your background in the format the employer wants—not the package of your choice, and, if you are like me, in some chicken scratch intelligible only to the ancient Egyptians. Consequently, I do not advise using this kind of letter as the spearhead or sole thrust of your campaign. Rather, you should use it as an integral part of your job search campaign in one of these ways:

- For small, highly targeted mailings to specific high-interest companies, where it can work as an effective customizing technique.

- For small, highly targeted mailings to specific high-interest jobs about which you have enough detailed knowledge that such a letter would supersede the effectiveness of your resume.
- As an initial thrust, but with the more traditional cover letter and resume already in place for a back-up second mailing. In practice, the cold-mailed broadcast letter often results in a request for a resume, and other times it results in a telephone interview and subsequent invitation to a face-to-face interview—with the request that you bring a resume.
- As part of a multiple-contact approach where you are approaching a number of people within a company with personalized letters (see Chapter 6).
- As a back-up approach when your cover letter and resume don't generate the response you want from individual target companies.
- To headhunters, who, if you have the skills they're looking for, will help you package your professional background.

Here is an example of a typical broadcast letter; you can see a whole section of them starting on page 166:

JANE SWIFT
18 Central Park Street, Anytown, NY 14788
(516) 555-1212

October 2, 20—

Dear _____ (name),

For the past seven years I have pursued an increasingly successful career in the sales profession. Among my accomplishments I include:

SALES
As a regional representative, I contributed $1,500,000, or 16 percent, of my company's annual sales. I am driven by achievement.

MARKETING
My marketing skills (based on a B.S. in marketing) enabled me to increase sales 25 percent in my economically stressed territory, at a time when colleagues were striving to maintain flat sales. Repeat business reached an all-time high. I am persistent and pay attention to detail.

PROJECT MANAGEMENT
Following the above successes, my regional model was adopted by the company. I trained and provided project supervision to the entire sales force. The following year, company sales showed a sales increase 12 percent above projections. I am a committed team player, motivated by the group's overall success.

The above was based on my firmly held zero price discounting philosophy, I don't cut margins to make a sale. It is difficult to summarize my work in a letter. The only way I can imagine providing you the opportunity to examine my credentials is for us to talk with each other. I look forward to hearing from you. Please call me at _____.

Yours sincerely,

Jane Swift

Jane Swift

Letters to Employment Agencies and Executive Recruiters

Headhunters appreciate, and deserve, appropriate professional respect. They are, after all, the most sophisticated salespeople in the world—they and they alone sell products that talk back!

A headhunter will be only faintly amused by your exhortations "to accept the challenge" or "test your skills by finding me a job" in the brief moment before he or she practices hoops with your letter and the trash can. They don't have the time or inclination to indulge such whimsical ideas (for a thorough discussion of working with headhunters, see *Knock 'em Dead: the Ultimate Job Seeker's Guide*). So with headhunters—whether they are working for the local employment agency, a contingency, or a retained search firm—bear in mind these two rules and you won't go far wrong:

1. Tell the truth. Answer questions truthfully and you will likely receive help. Get caught in a lie and you will have established a career-long distrust with someone who probably possesses a very diverse and influential list of contacts.

2. Cut immediately to the chase. For example:

   "I am forwarding my resume, because I understand you specialize in representing employers in the _____ field."

   "Please find the enclosed resume. As a specialist in the _____ field, I felt you might be interested in the skills of a _____."

   "Among your many clients there may be one or two who are seeking a thorough professional for a position as a _____."

Remember that in a cover letter sent to executive search firms and employment agencies, you should mention your salary and, if appropriate, your geographic considerations.

Here is an example of a cover letter you might send to a corporate headhunter:

James Sharpe
18 Central Park Street • Anytown, NY 14788
(516) 555-1212

December 2, 20—

Dear Mr. O'Flynn:

I am forwarding my resume, as I understand that you specialize in the accounting profession. As you may be aware, the management structure at _____ will be reorganized in the near future. While I am enthusiastic about the future of the agency under its new leadership, I have elected to make this an opportunity for change and professional growth.

My many years of experience lend themselves to a finance management position in any medium-sized service firm, but I am open to other opportunities. Although I would prefer to remain in New York, I would entertain other areas of the country, if the opportunity warrants it. I am currently earning $65,000 a year.

I have enclosed my resume for your review. Should you be conducting a search for someone with my background at the present time or in the near future, I would greatly appreciate your consideration. I would be happy to discuss my background more fully with you on the phone or in a personal interview.

Very truly yours,

James Sharpe

James Sharpe

JS
resume attached

So these are four basic types of cover letter that you can adapt to just about any job search situation. You can see how they can be assembled, in part, by harvesting suitable phrases from the samples later in the book. However, doing a simple cut and paste could lead to the wrong things going in and the right things being left out. That's what we are going to address next.

WHAT GOES IN, WHAT STAYS OUT

ONCE UPON A time, there were just a few set rules for writing a great job-search letter.

The rules of the game have changed; now more than ever, communication skills are a prerequisite for any job. Saying "I'm a great engineer. Give me a chance and I'll prove it to you" just doesn't cut it anymore. Today, your job skills and professionalism are under closer scrutiny than ever before. The evaluation process starts the moment you make contact—which means that the content and style of your cover letter set the tone for your entire candidacy.

The one overriding objective for your initial cover letter is to grab the reader's attention. With subsequent follow-up letters, your goal is to hold your reader's attention by moving the conversation forward; your letters should work to keep your candidacy foremost in the employer's mind. You achieve this in part by demonstrating your awareness and possession of the learned behaviors that all managers look for when they hire.

Desirable Professional Behaviors

There are a handful of universally admired behaviors that help you become successful in any profession. Each is something you can learn and apply in your career, and collectively their application will contribute a major ingredient to the success of your entire career; they are, in short, your passports to success.

Remember that first day at work on your first job? You got thirsty and went looking for the coffee machine, and there on the wall behind it was a big handwritten sign that read:

Your mother doesn't work here
Pick up after yourself

And this was the moment you realized that working at a job meant that there was a whole new way of behaving that you had to learn, and so you set about watching the successful people in your profession and emulating their behaviors.

When reading your cover letter, interviewers will look for clues to determine what kind of professional you really are and what you will be like to work with. Your cover letter, therefore, becomes a prime opportunity to set yourself apart from the competition. As you read through the following pages explaining each of these universally admired behaviors, you will often recognize that you already possess and apply that particular behavior in your professional life. When this happens, I want you to come up with examples of your using that particular behavior in the execution of your duties. The examples you recall can be used in your letters, and later in your answers to interviewer's questions. Then, for example, when you get asked, "So why are you different?" you will have a meaningful reply, replete with the real world illustrations that give a ring of truth to your answers. If as you read the next few pages, you might also come across behaviors that you realize are not adequately developed. When that happens, don't worry—you have just identified an area for professional growth.

Here, then, are a dozen hallmarks of professional behavior that every employer looks for and values (or should):

Communication & Listening Skills: Your ability to communicate effectively to people at all levels in a company is a key to success, and refers to verbal and written skills along with technological adeptness, dress, and body language. This is an especially important consideration when it comes to your cover letter and resume, because these written documents are the first means an employer has of judging your communication skills. It means you have to take the time to craft, edit, and re-edit your cover letter until it communicates what you want it to, and at the same time demonstrates that you have adequate communication skills.

I recently counseled an executive vice president in the 400K a year range; he was having problems getting in front of the right people. The first paragraph of his resume stated that he was an executive with "superior communication skills." Unfortunately, the other twelve words of the sentence boasting of his communication ability gave the lie to his claims: they contained two spelling errors! In an age of spell checkers this sloppiness isn't acceptable at any level.

Communication embraces *Listening Skills:* Listening and understanding, as opposed to just waiting your turn to talk; there is a big difference between the two. Consciously develop your "listening to understand" skills and the result will be improved persuasive communication abilities.

Goal-Orientation: All employers are interested in goal-oriented professionals: those who achieve concrete results with their actions and who constantly strive to get the job done, rather than just filling the time allotted for a particular task. Whenever possible, you should try to use an example or reference to this behavior in your letters and resume.

Willingness to Be a Team Player: The highest achievers (always goal-oriented) are invariably team players: employers look for employees who work for the common good and always with the group's goals and responsibilities in mind. Team players take pride in group achievement over personal aggrandizement; they look for solutions rather than someone to blame.

Motivation & Energy: Employers realize a motivated professional will do a better job on every assignment. Motivation expresses itself in a commitment to the job and the profession, an eagerness to learn and grow professionally, and a willingness to take the rough with the smooth.

Motivation is invariably expressed by the energy someone demonstrates in their work, always giving that extra effort to get the job done and to get it done right.

Analytical Skills: Valuable employees are able to weigh the short- and long-term benefits of a proposed course of action against all its possible negatives. We see these skills demonstrated in the way a person identifies potential problems and so is able to minimize their occurrence. Successful application of analytical skills at work requires understanding how your job and the role of your department fits into the company's overall goal of profitability. It also means thinking things through and not jumping at the first or easiest solution.

Dedication & Reliability: We are speaking here of dedication to your profession, with an awareness of the role it plays in the larger issues of company success, and of the empowerment that comes from knowing how your part contributes to the greater good. Dedication to your professionalism is also a demonstration of enlightened self-interest. The more you are engaged in your career, the more likely you are to join the inner circles that exist in every department and company, enhancing opportunities for advancement; this dedication will therefore repay you with better job security and improved professional horizons.

Your dedication will also express itself in your *Reliability:* Showing up is half the battle; the other half is your performance on the job. Demonstrating reliability requires following up on your actions, not relying on anyone else to ensure the job is done well, and keeping management informed every step of the way.

Determination: Someone with this attribute does not back off when a problem or situation gets tough; instead, he or she is the person who chooses to be part of a solution rather than standing idly by and being part of the problem. Determined professionals have decided to make a difference with their presence everyday and are willing to do whatever it takes to get a job done, even if that includes duties that might not appear in a job description.

Confidence: As you develop desirable professional behaviors, your confidence grows in the skills you have and in your ability to develop new ones. With this comes confidence in taking on new challenges. You have the confidence to ask questions, the confidence to look at challenges calmly, the confidence to look at mistakes unflinchingly, and the confidence to make changes to eradicate them. In short, you develop a quiet confidence in your ability as a professional who can deliver the goods.

Pride & Integrity: Pride in yourself as a professional means always making sure the job is done to the best of your ability and paying attention to the details and to the time and cost constraints. Integrity means taking responsibility for your actions, both good and bad; it means treating others, within and outside of the company, with respect at all times and in all situations. With pride in yourself as a professional with integrity, your actions will always be in the best interests of the company, and your decisions will never be based on whim or personal preference.

When it comes down to it, companies have very limited interests: making money, saving money (the same as making money), and saving time, which saves money and makes time to make more money. Actually, you wouldn't want it any other way, as it is this focus that makes your paycheck good come pay-day. Developing these professional behaviors and maintaining sensitivity to the profit interests of any business endeavor is the mark of a true professional. To this end, the following three behaviors demonstrate an awareness of the need for procedures, efficiency, and economy; they round out the profile of the con-summate professional:

Efficiency: Working efficiently means always keeping an eye open for wasted time, effort, resources, and money.

Economy: Most problems have two solutions—and the expensive one usually isn't the best. Ideas of efficiency and economy engage the creative mind in ways other workers might not consider; they are an integral part of your analytical proficiency.

Ability to Follow Procedures: You know that procedures exist to keep the company profitable, so you don't work around them. Following the chain of command, you don't implement your own "improved" procedures or organize others to do so.

Together, these twelve learnable behaviors spell long-term career success. As these behaviors are universally admired in all professions and at all levels, it is important that you are able to communicate your awareness of their importance to prospective employers in your written communications and in your conversations. Consequently, your goal is to draw attention to your professional behavioral profile by direct statement, inference, and illustration. *Knock 'em Dead: the Ultimate Job Seeker's Guide*, by the way, will show you how to integrate these behaviors into your answers to hundreds of interview questions.

Writing a cover letter for a job is a bit like baking a cake. In most instances the ingredients are essentially the same—what determines the flavor is the quantity of each ingredient, and how and in what order they are blended and ultimately presented for consumption. There are certain ingredients that go into almost every letter, whether it is a cover, broadcast, networking, follow-up, acceptance, rejection, or resignation letter. There are others that rarely or never go in, and there are those special touches (a pinch of this, a smidgen of that) that may be included, depending on your unique situation and the need your letter will satisfy.

Brief Is Beautiful

Ads and cover letters have a great deal in common. The vast majority of ads in any media can be heard, watched, or read in less than thirty seconds—the upper limit of the average busy consumer's attention span.

It is no coincidence that cover letters adhere to the same rules, as they too compete for attention from distracted consumers, and their initial purpose is simply to grab the reader's attention so that your resume will get read with serious attention—a seemingly easy goal that isn't necessarily so easy in its execution.

Before getting started, advertising copywriters (some of our society's most effective communicators) imagine themselves in the position of their target audience. They understand that their objective is to package and sell the product, so they consider what features their product possesses and what benefits are most likely to appeal to the purchaser.

This is an approach you might find useful in creating effective cover letters. For the next fifteen minutes, imagine that you are a manager in one of your target companies, or perhaps you are in the HR department on "screening" detail. Fortunately, it is a slow morning and there are only thirty resumes and cover letters that need to be read. Go straight to the example sections of this book now and read thirty examples without a break, then return to this page. You will probably feel disoriented, as if your brain has turned to a rather soggy potato salad.

Can you imagine what it would be like to do this every day for a living? Of course, you had it easy: the letters you read weren't attached to resumes, which would have made the task even more mind numbing. The letters you read were demonstrably effective, as they helped land real people real jobs. Even so, you probably felt a little punch-drunk at the end of the exercise, but you learned a very valuable lesson: Brevity, clarity, and punch are beautiful.

This is the environment in which your letters and resumes have to function, and now you have some idea of what it feels like. It also helps to understand the essential criteria applied whenever managers are considering making a hire. When hiring decisions are made, they are made based on five basic criteria, and an awareness of them can inform the structure of your letters and resume, as well as your performance at job interviews. Every hire is made based on a candidate's ability to satisfy these five concerns of the employer.

1. Ability and suitability.
2. Willingness to go the extra yard, and to take the rough with the smooth.
3. Manageability and teamwork: taking direction and constructive input for the good of the team.
4. Problem-solving attitude.
5. A comprehensive and supportive behavioral profile.

Looking at your job from this point of view—that is, how managers make decisions and the behaviors they seek to support their decisions—will enable you to better understand your customer and craft more effective messages.

A Question of Money

Recruitment advertisements sometimes request salary information, either current salary or salary history. With the right letter and work history you will rarely be denied at least a telephone interview, even if you do omit your salary history. I have heard that some HR people consider the word "negotiable" annoying, though they completely understand and accept why it is used, so it is rarely grounds for refusing to talk a candidate. Nevertheless, there may be factors that make you feel obliged to include something.

If you do choose to share information about salary, it should go in the cover letter or be attached to the cover letter, never in the resume itself. This is because your resume may be kept in a database for years and thereby typecast you as, say, an entry-level professional in the eyes of that company's computer. When desired salary is requested, don't restrict yourself to one figure; instead, give yourself a range with a spread between the low and the high end. This dramatically increases your chances of "clicking onto" the available salary range that is authorized for every position. (For more on salary ranges, see the negotiation chapter in *Knock 'em Dead: the Ultimate Job Seeker's Guide.*)

When "salary history" is requested, the prospective employer is usually looking for a consistent progression. Gaps or significant cuts could raise red flags. If you have nothing to hide and have a steadily progressive earnings history, spell it out on a separate sheet. By the way, when background does get checked, salary and dates of employment always get verified.

Many of us have imperfect salary histories for any number of perfectly valid reasons. Consequently, we don't want to release these figures unless we are there in person to explain away any anomalies. In these instances the matter is best skirted in the cover letter itself, with either a range or the word "negotiable."

Here is one way to address the topic of money in your cover letter should you feel it is necessary to do so. You will find other examples later in the book.

"Depending on the job and the professional development environment, my salary requirements are in the $_____ to $_____ range, with appropriate benefits."

Telephone and E-Mail

Once you have determined a primary contact number for your job hunt, you must ensure that it will be answered at all times. There is no point in mounting a job search campaign if prospective employers can never reach you. It's a good idea to invest in a voice mail system such as one offered by your telephone company. Keep the message businesslike and, once recorded, replay it and listen carefully to the message for clarity, tone of voice, and recording quality. Does it present you as a clear-spoken, confident professional?

In your cover letter, you should always list your e-mail address immediately beneath your telephone number, as initial contact is often by e-mail. Under no circumstances should you ever use your company telephone or e-mail for any job search activities, as that can only lead to heartache and regret.

Ingredients: A Basic Checklist

When you examine the sample letters in Chapter 8 you will note that they:

- Address a person, not a title . . . and, whenever possible, a person who is in a position to make a hiring decision.
- Are tailored to the reader of the letter as far as is practical, to show that you have done your homework.
- Whenever possible, include information relevant to the job you are seeking.
- Show concern, interest, and pride for your profession.
- Demonstrate energy and enthusiasm.
- Clearly establish why you are writing and the outcome you hope to achieve.
- Maintain a balance between professionalism and friendliness.
- Ask for the next step in the process clearly and without apology or arrogance.

Now take another few moments to browse through the sample section to examine the variety of types of letters you have to work with—there are enough examples to help you maximize both the volume of interviews you generate and the value of the offers you receive. With the wide range of examples you'll find later in the book, you can create unique letters for any situation. Use that highlighter as you go through the book to flag phrases that seem especially useful to you. It will be a breeze to then customize letters of your own for any circumstance.

4

ASSEMBLING YOUR COVER LETTER

THERE IS A fine line between pride in achievement and insufferable arrogance when listing experiences and behaviors in your work life that will help advance your candidacy.

You need solid content to put in your cover letters, and that can take a little thought. To make this job easier, complete the questionnaire on the next couple of pages. Do not skip this exercise; it will give you a greater sense of what you have to offer employers, and will provide insight and illustrations for your letters. The exercises will also be of real help later, when the time comes to sell yourself at the interview.

Answer every part of every question for every job you have held, starting with the most recent and working backward.

Take some time over this exercise and go back carefully over your past jobs. If you do this it won't going to be necessary to craft *Knock 'em Dead* sentences from scratch; you'll be able to cut and paste from the samples and then insert your questionnaire answers to personalize the content—the end result will be a unique and arresting letter.

The entirely original parts of your letter will be your awareness of the employer and the job, your contributions, and your achievements. That means you need to spend adequate time in this period of preparation. Do not worry about crafting proper sentences now, as whatever you jot down can be polished later on in the editing process. It is easier to do this when you have the whole letter in front of you rather than laboring over every sentence as you write it.

Gather Information

The following set of steps for information gathering and self-analysis was adapted from the comprehensive questionnaire in *Resumes That Knock 'em Dead*. So if you are preparing a resume at the same time as a cover letter, the following steps will help you to work toward that end as well.

Step #1: Identify Your Target Job

Your job search—and the resume and letters that go with it—will be incalculably more productive if you begin by clearly defining a target job that you can land and in which you can be successful. Start by identifying this target job title. Then take out a lined sheet of paper (or open a blank computer document, if you prefer) and write it down.

Step #2: Research the Target Job

Go surf the Web for an hour and collect as many job descriptions as you can with this target job title. Once you have a selection, deconstruct them into a series of bullets, and write them below your target job title as your answer for Step #2.

Any evaluation of your background must begin with an understanding of what potential employers will be looking for when they come to your cover letter and resume.

Step #3: Go Through Your Recent Work History

Once you understand the sort of information your readers are going to be looking for, it is time to start working through your work history. This process is helpful not only for gathering all the information necessary for a resume, but also for reminding yourself of all kinds of data that employers are likely to require at different stages of the selection cycle. Consider carefully the following three elements:

A. Current or Last Employer

Identify your current or last employer by name and location, and follow it with a brief description (5–6 words) of the company's business/products/services.

Note: This includes part-time or voluntary employment if you are a recent graduate or about to re-enter the work force after an absence. Try looking at your school as an employer and see what new information you reveal about yourself.

Write down the following information:

Starting date: _____

Starting title: _____

Starting salary: _____

Leaving date: _____

Leaving title: _____

Reason for leaving: _____

Potential references for this job: _____

Leaving salary: _____

B. Deliverables

Make a bulleted list of the duties/responsibilities/deliverables in this position. Then prioritize that list.

C. Skills and Special Knowledge

Now, for each of your identified deliverables, answer the following questions:

- What special skills or knowledge did you need to perform this task satisfactorily?
- What educational background and/or credentials helped prepare you for these responsibilities?
- What are your achievements in this area?

For each of your major areas of responsibility you should consider both the daily problems that arise and also those major projects/problems that stand out as major accomplishments. Think of each as a problem-solving challenge, and the analytical processes and subsequent actions you took to win the day. There is a four-step technique you will find useful here called **PSRV**:

P. Identify the *project* and the problem it represented, both from a corporate perspective and from the point of view of your execution of duties.

S. Identify your *solution* to the challenge and the process you implemented to deliver the solution.

R. What was the *result* of your approach and actions?

V. Finally, what was the *value* to you, the department, and the company? If you can, define this in terms of time saved, money saved, or money earned. This is not always possible, but it is very powerful whenever you can.

Step #4: Consider Teamwork and Your Professional Profile

Next, ask yourself the following questions:

- What verbal or written comments did peers or managers make about your contributions in each area of your job?
- What different levels of people did you have to interact with to achieve your job tasks? What skills and methods did you get the best out of superiors? Co-workers? Subordinates?
- What aspects of your personality were brought into play when executing this duty?

To help you address that last issue (it's a vitally important one), look over the list of professional behaviors discussed in Chapter 3; these are in demand by all employers for all jobs at all levels. Going through the list, you will probably recognize that you already apply some or many of these behaviors in your work. As you read, come up with examples of your using each particular behavior in the execution of your each of your major duties at this job. The examples you generate can be used in your resume, in your cover letters, and as illustrative answers to questions in interviews.

Step #5: Add in Your Previous Work History

The next step is to do the same things you did in Steps 3 and 4 for your current or most recent job with your previous positions. Do not skimp on this process; all you write may not go into the final version of your resume or cover letter, but all your effort will reward you at some point during the selection process and lead to more and better job offers.

It is not unusual to have held a number of different titles with a specific employer. Such professional progression speaks to your competency and pro-motability; you should repeat Steps 3 and 4 for each successive title, and make sure they are reflected on your resume.

Step #6: Compile Endorsements

Looking at each of your major areas of responsibility throughout your work history, write down any positive verbal or written commentary others have made on your performance that you can find. As you will see in some of the sample letters in Chapter 8, words about you that come from someone else often have a much greater impact than any description you could come up with yourself.

Creating Punchy Sentences

A cover letter is a collection of sequenced sentences organized around a single goal: to get your resume read with serious attention. It is likely that you will need to create more than one type of cover letter, so my best advice is to concentrate on one first, perhaps the one going to postings and help wanted ads. You can then use this letter as a template to cut, paste, and otherwise adapt it to suit cover letters going to specific contacts, headhunters, and so on.

Concise, punchy sentences grab attention.

Ultimately any letter is only as good as the individual sentences that carry the message; the most grammatically correct sentences in the world won't get you interviews because such prose can read as though every breath of life has been squeezed out of it. Your goal is to communicate an energizing message and entice the reader to action. The use of verbs always helps energize a sentence and give it that concise, cut-to-the-chase feel.

For example, one professional—with a number of years at the same law firm in a clerical position—had written:

> *"I learned to manage a computerized database."*

Sounds pretty ordinary, right? Well, after discussion of the circumstances that surrounded learning how to manage the computerized database, certain exciting facts emerged. By using verbs and an awareness of employer interests as they relate to a specific target job, this sentence was charged up and given more punch. Not only that, but for the first time the writer fully understood the value of her contributions, which greatly enhanced her self-confidence for interviews:

> *"I analyzed and determined the need for automation of an established law office. I was responsible for hardware and software selection, installation, and loading all the data. Within one year, I had achieved a fully automated office. This saved forty hours a week."*

Notice how the verbs show that things happened when she was around the office, and put flesh on the bones of that initial bare statement. Such action verbs and phrases add an air of direction, efficiency, and accomplishment to every cover letter. Succinctly, they tell the reader what you did and how well you did it.

As you look through the answers to the questionnaire for information that will impact your cover letter, rewrite the chosen phrases to see if you can give them more depth with the use of verbs. While a cover letter is typically one page, or one screen shot, don't worry about the length right now. The process you go through helps you think out exactly what it is you have to offer and also creates the language and ideas you will use to explain yourself during an interview. To help you in the process, here are over 175 action verbs you can use. This list is just a beginning. Just about every word processing program has a thesaurus; you can type any one of these words into one and get more choices for each entry.

accomplished
achieved
acted
adapted
addressed
administered
advanced
advised
allocated
analyzed
appraised
approved
arranged
assembled
assigned
assisted
attained
audited
authored
automated
balanced
budgeted
built
calculated
catalogued
chaired
clarified
classified
coached
collected
compiled
completed
composed
computed
conceptual-
ized
conducted

consolidated
contained
contracted
contributed
controlled
coordinated
corresponded
counseled
created
critiqued
cut
decreased
delegated
demon-
strated
designed
developed
devised
diagnosed
directed
dispatched
distinguished
diversified
drafted
edited
educated
eliminated
enabled
encouraged
engineered
enlisted
established
evaluated
examined
executed
expanded
expedited

explained
extracted
fabricated
facilitated
familiarized
fashioned
focused
forecast
formulated
founded
generated
guided
headed up
identified
illustrated
implemented
improved
increased
indoctrinated
influenced
informed
initiated
innovated
inspected
installed
instigated
instituted
instructed
integrated
interpreted
interviewed
introduced
invented
launched
lectured
led
maintained

managed
marketed
mediated
moderated
monitored
motivated
negotiated
operated
organized
originated
overhauled
oversaw
performed
persuaded
planned
prepared
presented
prioritized
processed
produced
programmed
projected
promoted
provided
publicized
published
purchased
recom-
mended
reconciled
recorded
recruited
reduced
referred
regulated
rehabilitated
remodeled

repaired
represented
researched
restored
restructured
retrieved
revitalized
saved
scheduled
schooled
screened
set
shaped
solidified
solved
specified
stimulated
streamlined
strengthened
summarized
supervised
surveyed
systemized
tabulated
taught
trained
translated
traveled
trimmed
upgraded
validated
worked
wrote

Varying Sentence Structure

As noted above, your letters will be most effective when they are constructed with short punchy sentences. As a rule, try keeping your sentences under about twenty five words; a good average is around fifteen. If your sentence is longer than the twenty five-word mark, change it. Either shorten it by restructuring or make two sentences out of one. At the same time, you will want to avoid choppiness, so vary the length of sentences when you can.

You can also start with a short phrase ending in a colon:

- Followed by bullets of information.
- Each one supporting the original phrase.

These techniques are designed to enliven the reading process, for readers who always have too much to read and too little time. Here's how we can edit and rewrite the last example.

Analyzed and determined need for automation of an established law office

- *Responsible for hardware and software selection.*
- *Coordinated installation of six workstations.*
- *Trained users.*
- *Full automation achieved in one year.*
- *Savings to company: $25,000.*

K.I.S.S. (Keep It Simple, Stupid)

Persuading your readers to take action is challenging, because many people in different companies will see your letters and make judgments based on them. This means you must keep industry "jargon" to a reasonable level (especially in the initial contact letters—covers, broadcast, and the like); the rule of thumb is only to use the jargon and acronyms necessary to communicate your abilities. There will be those who understand the intricacies and technicalities of your profession—and those who do not.

Within your short paragraphs and short sentences, beware of name-dropping and acronyms, such as "I worked for Dr. A. Witherspoon in Sys. Gen. SNA 2.31." Statements like these can be too restricted to have validity outside the small circle of specialists to whom they speak. Unless you work in a highly technical field, and are sending the letter and resume to someone by name and title whom you know will understand the importance of your technical language, you should be sure to use technical phrases with discretion.

Your letters demand the widest possible appeal, yet they need to remain personal in tone, so obviously you don't want them to sound like they're from Publishers Clearing House. You are not writing a novel, but rather trying to capture the essence of the professional you in just a few brief paragraphs, so short words for short sentences help make short, gripping paragraphs: good for short attention spans!

Voice and Tense

The voice you use for different letters depends on a few important factors:

- Getting a lot said in a small space.
- Packaging your skills and credentials for the target job.
- Being factual.
- Capturing the essence and personality of the professional you.

There is considerable disagreement among the "experts" about the best voice, and each of the following options has both champions and detractors, but whichever voice you use in your letters should be consistent throughout.

Sentences in all types of cover letters can be truncated (up to a point), by omitting pronouns and articles such as *I, you, he, she, they*:

> *"Automated office."*

In fact, many authorities recommend the dropping of pronouns as a technique that both saves space and allows you to brag about yourself without seeming boastful. It gives the impression of another party writing about you. Others feel that to use the personal pronoun—*"I automated the office . . ."*—is naive, unprofessional, and smacks of boasting.

At the same time, some recommend that you write in the first person because it makes you sound more human.

> *"I automated the office."*

In short, there are no hard and fast rules—they can all work given the many unique circumstances you will face in any given job search. Use whatever style works best for you. If you do use the personal pronoun, try not to use it in every sentence; it gets a little monotonous, and it can make you sound like an egomaniac. The mental focus should not be on "I" but on "you," the person with whom you are communicating.

A nice variation is to use a first-person voice throughout the letter and then a final few words in the third person. Make sure these final words appear in the form of an attributed quote, as an insight to your value:

> *"She managed the automation procedure, and we didn't experience a moment of downtime."*
> *—Jane Ross, Department Manager*

Don't mistake the need for professionalism in your job search letters with stiff-necked formality. The most effective tone is one that mixes the conversational and the formal, just the way we do in our offices and on our jobs. The only overriding rule is to make the letter readable, so that the reader can see a human being and a professional shining through the page.

Length

The standard length for a cover letter is usually one page, or the equivalent length for e-mails: typically this is as much as you can see on your screen without scrolling. Subsequent letters stemming from verbal communications—whether over the telephone or face-to-face—should also adhere to the one-page rule, but can run to two pages if the complexity of content demands it.

Generally speaking, job-search letters should be held to one page, and no job-hunting letter should exceed two pages. With conscientious editing over a couple of days, that two-page letter can usually be reduced to one page without losing any of the content, and at the same time it will probably pack more punch; as my editor always says, "If in doubt, cut it out."

Having said this, I should acknowledge that all rules are made to be broken. Occasionally a three-page letter might be required, but only in one of the following instances:

1. You are at a level, or your job is of such technical complexity, that you cannot edit down to one page without using a font size that is all but unreadable.
2. You have been contacted directly by an employer about a specific position and have been asked to present data for a specific opportunity.

3. An executive recruiter who is representing you determines that the exigencies of a particular situation warrant a dossier of such length. (Often such a letter and resume will be prepared exclusively—or with considerable input—by the recruiter.)

You'll find that thinking too much about length considerations will hamper the writing process. Think instead of the story you have to tell, and then layer fact upon fact until your tale is told. Use your words and the key phrases from this book to craft the message of your choice. When *that* is done you can go back and ruthlessly cut it to the bone.

Ask yourself these questions:

- Can I cut out any paragraphs?
- Can I cut out any sentences?
- How can I reduce the word count of the longer sentences?
- Where have I repeated myself?

Whenever you can, cut something out—leave nothing but facts and action words! If at the end you find too much has been cut, you'll have the additional pleasure of reinstating your deathless prose.

Your Checklist

There are really two proofing steps in the creation of a polished cover letter. The first happens now. You want to make sure that all the things that should be included are—and that all the things that shouldn't, aren't. The final proofing is done before printing. Warning: It is easy, in the heat of the creative moment, to miss crucial components or mistakenly include facts that give the wrong emphasis. Check all your letters against these considerations:

Contact Information

- You need contact information—name, address, zip code, personal telephone number, and e-mail address—at the top of the page; if in rare instances you have to run to second page (and avoid this at all costs), remember to include your name, telephone number, and e-mail address.
- Your current business number is omitted unless it is absolutely necessary and safe to include it. This will only be the case if your employer understands

that you are leaving and you have permission to use company time and equipment for your search.

- If your letter is more than one page long, and is going by traditional mail, each page should be numbered "page 1 of 2," etc., and the pages stapled together. Remember the accepted way of stapling business communications: one staple in the top left-hand corner.

Objectives

- Does your letter state why you are writing?
- Is the letter tied to the target company?
- Is it focused on a target job, such as skills that apply from the ad or agenda items addressed during a conversation?
- Does it include references to desirable professional behaviors?
- Is your most relevant and qualifying experience prioritized to lend strength to your letter?
- Have you avoided wasting more space than required with employer names and addresses?
- Have you omitted any reference to reasons for leaving a particular job? Reasons for making a change might be important at the interview, but they are not relevant at this point. Use this precious space to sell, not to justify.
- Unless they have been specifically requested, have you removed all references to past, current, or desired salaries?
- Have you removed any references to your date of availability? If you aren't available at their convenience, why are you wasting their time?
- Do you mention your highest educational attainment if it is relevant, and do you mention your major if it adds credence to the message?
- Have you avoided listing irrelevant responsibilities or job titles?
- Have you given examples of your contributions, your achievements, and the problems you have successfully solved during your career?
- Have you avoided poor focus by eliminating all extraneous information?
- Is the letter long enough to whet the reader's appetite for more details, yet short enough not to satisfy that hunger?
- Have you let the obvious slip in, like heading your letter "Letter of Application" in big bold letters? If so, cut it out.

Style

- When possible, substitute short words for long words, and one word where previously there were two.
- Keep your average sentence to less than twenty-five words. Break longer sentences into two, if they cannot be shortened.
- At the same time, try to vary the length of sentences.
- Keep every paragraph under five lines, with most paragraphs shorter; this leads to more white space on the page and makes your message more accessible to the reader.
- Make sure your sentences begin with or contain, wherever possible, powerful action verbs and phrases.

THE FINAL PRODUCT

STYLE—SO EASY TO see but so difficult to define—usually has a distinct look and feel. Here are some of the basics you should keep in mind when creating your own stylish and professional job-search letters.

Layout

Your cover typically letter arrives on a reader's desk along with many others, all of which require reading. You can expect your letter to get a maximum of thirty seconds of initial attention, and that's only if it's accessible to the reader's eye and speaks to their needs.

The complaints about cover letters that have them nose-diving into the trashcan in record time are:

- They have too much information crammed into the space and are difficult to read.
- The layout is unorganized, illogical, and uneven. (In other words, it looks shoddy and slapdash—and who wants an employee like that?)
- In the age of spell checkers, there are no excuses for misspellings; they are not acceptable.

Fonts

The font you choose has a big impact on the readability of your work, so use businesslike fonts; stay away from script-like fonts. They may look more visually exciting, but the goal is readability for the reader who is plowing through stacks of resumes when he or she gets your message. At the same time, recognize that capitalized copy is also harder to read.

How to Brighten the Page

Once you decide on a font, stick with it. More than one font on a page can look confusing. You can do plenty to liven up the visual impact of the page within the variations of the font you have chosen. For letters going through traditional mail you can, of course, use a different font for the contact information as you create the letterhead.

Most fonts come in a selection of regular, bold, italic, and bold italic, so you can vary the impact of key words with italics, underlined phrases, and boldface or for additional emphasis. For example, when you are sending a cover letter and resume in response to an Internet job posting or recruitment advertisement, you can bold/or italicize those words used by the employer in the recruitment copy, emphasizing your match to their needs.

Another letter writer who wants to emphasize professional behaviors might italicize those words or phrases that describe such behaviors. This is relevant to all professions, and it can be especially useful for people in sales and customer service where dealing with others is a critical skill. That way the message gets a double fixing in the reader's mind. You will also notice powerful letters that employ no typographic pyrotechnics and still knock 'em dead! In the end, it's your judgment call.

Beware if you are crafting a cover letter for mass distribution using the mail merge feature of a word-processing program. What this does is fill in the blanks:

"Dear _____" becomes "Dear Fred Jones." Make sure that the printed letter does not look like this:

Dear **Fred Jones:**

By italicizing or bolding the person's name all you achieve is to state loud and clear that this is a form letter sent, in all likelihood, to hundreds. Why needlessly detract from your chances of being taken seriously?

Another no-no is the use of "clip art" to brighten the page. Those little quill pens and scrolls may look nifty to you, but they look amateurish to the rest of the business world.

Proofing and Printing

It simply isn't possible for even the most accomplished professional writer to go from draft to print, so don't try it. Your pride of authorship will blind you to blemishes you can't afford to miss.

You need some distance from your creative efforts to give yourself detachment and objectivity. There is no hard and fast rule about how long it should take to come up with the finished product; if you think you have finished, leave it alone at least overnight. Then come back to it fresh. You'll read it almost as if it were meeting your eyes for the first time.

Before you e-mail or print your letters make sure that your writing is as clear as possible. Three things guaranteed to annoy cover letter readers are incorrect spelling, poor grammar, and improper syntax. Go back and check all these areas. If you think syntax has something to do with the IRS, you'd better get a third party involved. Here's a practical solution that one job seeker found: She visited the library, waited for a quiet moment, and got into a conversation with the librarian, who subsequently agreed to give her letter the old once-over; everyone loves to show off special knowledge! Another effective technique is to read your letter aloud. If it reads smoothly you did your job well, but if something sounds stilted or clunky it still needs another round of polishing.

With mailed letters, the quality of paper always makes an impression on the person holding the page. The folks receiving your letter see dozens of others every day, and you need every trick available to make your point. Compared to printer paper, good quality paper sends an almost subliminal message about attention to detail. By the way, if an emergency demands you send a letter by fax, remember to follow it up with a copy on regular paper. This is because everything you send is likely to end up in your "candidate dossier," and a fax can have print-out problems.

Although you should not skimp on paper costs, neither should you buy or be talked into the most expensive available. Indeed, in some fields (health care and education come to mind), too ostentatious a paper can cause a negative impression. The idea is to create a feeling of understated quality.

As for color, white is considered the prime choice. Cream is also acceptable, but I reject the opinion that some of the pale pastel shades can be both attractive and effective. These pastel shades were originally used to make letters and resumes stand out. But now everyone is so busy standing out of the crowd in magenta and passionate puce that you just might find it more original to stand out in white or cream. White and cream are straightforward, no-nonsense colors. They say BUSINESS, as should your letters.

It is a given that cover letter stationery should always match the color and weight of your envelopes and resume. Most office supply stores carry packs of matching paper and envelopes for coordinating your letter, resume, and envelope. To send a white cover letter—even if it is your personal stationery—with a cream resume detracts from the statement you are trying to make. In fact, when you print the finished letter, you should print some letterhead sheets at the same time and in the same quantity. You don't need to get too fancy; base your design on other stationery with which you've been impressed.

All subsequent letters (a follow-up letter after an interview, for example) should be on the same paper. Your written communication will be filed in a candidate dossier, then, prior to the hiring decision; the hiring manager will review all the written materials on all the short-list candidates. Your coordinated written campaign will paint the picture of a thorough professional, with the sum of your letters will becoming powerful because they exist as a coordinated package.

Envelopes Send Messages, Too

Throughout this advice I have been differentiating, where necessary, between the considerations for e-mails and traditionally mailed letters, but I'd like to note that approaching employers through both mediums certainly doesn't diminish your chances of getting noticed. With this in mind, what goes on the envelope affects the power of the message inside. Over the years, I've spoken with countless line managers and human resources professionals about the appearance of the envelopes they receive. Did it affect the likelihood of the letter being read and if so, with what kind of anticipation? Here's what I heard:

"I never open letters with printed pressure-sensitive labels; I regard them as junk mail, and I simply don't have the time in my life for ill-targeted marketing attempts."

"I never open anything addressed to me by title but not by name."

"I will open envelopes and read letters or e-mails addressed to me by misspelled name, but I am looking with a jaundiced eye already; and that eye is keen for other examples of sloppiness."

"I always open correctly typed envelopes that say personal and/or confidential, but if they're not, I feel conned. I don't hire con artists."

"I always open neatly handwritten envelopes. What's more, I open them first, unless there's another letter that is obviously a check."

This last comment is especially interesting in an age when just about all correspondence is printed. In fact, over a two-week period every letter I sent out had a hand-addressed envelope, and do you know about 50 percent of the recipients actually commented on not having seen a handwritten envelope in ages.

There are those who recommend enclosing a stamped self-addressed envelope to increase the chances of response. You can do this, but don't expect many people in the corporate world to take advantage of your munificence. I have never known this tactic to yield much in the way of results. On the whole, I think you are better advised to save the stamp money and spend it on a follow-up telephone call. Only conversations lead to interviews. I have never heard of a single interview being set up through the mail, although it will happen through e-mail.

Neat trick department: I once received an intriguing resume and cover letter; both had attached to the top right-hand corner a circular red sticker. It worked as a major exclamation point; I was impressed. I was even more impressed when I realized that once this left my hands, no other reader would know exactly who attached the sticker, but they *would* pay special attention to the content because of it. Nice technique—don't let the whole world in on it, though.

Appearance

Remember that the first glance and feel of your letter can make a powerful impression. Go through this checklist before you seal the envelope:

- Does the paper measure 8½" by 11", and is it of good quality, between 16 and 25 pounds in weight?
- Have you used white, off-white, or cream-colored paper?
- Did you make sure to use only one side of the page?
- Are your name, address, and telephone number on every page?
- If more than one page, have you paginated your cover letter: "1 of 2" at the bottom of the page and so on?
- Are the pages stapled together? Remember, one staple in the top left-hand corner is the accepted protocol.

With e-mail:
- Ditto for spell checks, and so on.
- Do you have an informative and/or intriguing subject line?
- Have you correctly used bold and italics?

THE PLAN
OF ATTACK

GREAT COVER, BROADCAST, and follow-up letters won't get you a job by sitting on your desk like rare manuscripts. You have to do something with them.

Even a company that isn't officially hiring can still be expected (based on national averages) to experience a 14 percent turnover in staff in the course of a year. In other words, every company has openings sometimes, and any one of those openings could have your name on it.

The problem is, you won't have the chance to pick the very best opportunity unless you check them all out. Every intelligent job hunter will use a multi-channel approach to job search, including:

- Internet job postings
- Newspaper advertisements
- Personal and professional networking
- Direct-researched opportunities
- Headhunters
- Business and trade publications

In *Knock 'em Dead: The Ultimate Job Seeker's Guide*, I discuss a dozen different ways to penetrate your target market; your individual plan of attack will use a selection of these twelve approaches most relevant to your unique needs.

Online Job Postings

Here is where the Internet can play an especially useful role. There are thousands of job sites that recruitment advertising or job postings; almost every one of these sites has a resume bank.

Here's how to use them to greatest effect.

Visit the job sites—there's a good selection in Appendix B at the end of this book—and search for appropriate job openings. Most of these job sites have a feature called an "e-mail alert." The alert allows you to identify the type of work you are seeking and receive an e-mail from the site every time a suitable job is advertised by one of their clients. You don't want these e-mails to come to you indiscriminately at work, so be sure to use only your personal e-mail address in any job search.

The on-site resume banks will work well for you too. From an employer or headhunter's point of view, these resume banks are like big fish tanks. The fishing analogy works for you too; your resume in resume banks is like having a baited hook in the water while you go about your business. These resume banks often trash your resume after 90 days (this helps them promote the freshness of the resumes when selling ads), so if you are looking longer than this you will need to go back and reload.

Tip: It is not a bad idea to keep your resume posted online as an ongoing career management tool; it will keep you aware of who is looking for what and how much they are paying and will keep your finger on the pulse of the job market. At the very least you will always know what skills are in demand; beyond that you don't have to interview for those jobs, and if you do, you don't have to accept the offers. Overall, you will be in far greater control of your professional destiny.

If you are writing as a result of an online job posting, you should mention both the Web site and the date you found it on:

"I read your job posting on your company's Web site on January 5th and felt I had to respond . . ."

"Your online job posting regarding a _____ on _____.com caught my eye, and your company name caught my attention."

"This e-mail, and my attached resume, is in response to your job posting on _____."

Recruitment Advertising

A first step for many is to go to the want ads and do a mass mailing. Bear in mind, there should be a method to your madness when you do this. Remember, if it is the first idea that comes to your mind, hitting the want ads will be at the front of everyone else's thoughts, too.

A single help-wanted advertisement, just like an Internet job posting, can draw hundreds of responses. The following ideas might be helpful:

1. Most newspapers have an employment edition every week (usually Sunday, although sometimes midweek) when, in addition to their regular advertising, they have a major drive for help-wanted ads. Make sure you always read this edition of your local paper.

    So-called authorities on the topic will tell you not to rely on the want ads—that they don't work. Rocking horse droppings! Want ads and online job postings don't work if you are too dumb to know how to use them. Look for back issues and when online check for job posting archives. Just because a company is no longer advertising does not necessarily mean that the slot has been filled. The employer may well have become disillusioned and is now using a professional recruiter to work on the position. They may have filled the position, but perhaps the person never started work or simply did not work out in the first few months. Maybe they hired someone who did work out well and now they want another person for a similar position. When you go back into the want ads/postings you'll find untold opportunities awaiting you, and instead of competition from 150 other job hunters and you'll be tapping into the hidden job market of unadvertised positions.

In fact, I received a letter from a *Knock 'em Dead* reader who told me he had landed a $90,000 job from a seven-month-old want ad he came across in a pile of newspapers in his father-in-law's garage! (You see? There is a use for in-laws, after all.)

2. As mentioned above, jobs are often available but just aren't being advertised, in what is referred to as the hidden job market. Likewise, in some high-demand occupations where want ads aren't famous for drawing the right caliber of professional, the employer may only run one or two major "institutional" ads a year for that type of position.

3. Be sure to cross-check the categories. Don't rely solely on those ads seeking your specific job title. For example, let's say you are a graphic artist looking for a job in advertising. You should flag all advertising or public relations agencies with any kind of need. If they are actively hiring at the moment, logic will tell you that their employment needs are not restricted to that particular title. It is arrogant to think that all jobs are advertised where you happen to be looking today.

4. If you are writing as the result of a newspaper advertisement, you should mention both the publication and the date. Do not abbreviate advertisement to "ad" unless space demands, and remember to underline or italicize the publication's title:

"I read your advertisement in the Daily Gotham *on October 6th for a* _____ *and, after researching your company, felt I had to write . . ."*

"Ref: Your advertisement in the Columbus Dispatch *on Sunday the 8th of November."*

"Dear _____:
As you compare your requirements for the above-mentioned position with my attached resume, you will see that my entire background matches your requirements."

"Your notice regarding a _____ *in* _____ *caught my eye, and your company name caught my attention."*

"This letter and attached resume are in response to your advertisement in _____."

Networking

Networking is one of those dreadful words from the 1970s that unfortunately is so entrenched we might as well learn to live with it. I'd prefer, however, that you think of it as professional connectedness, because becoming properly connected to your profession is simply the best approach for ongoing professional growth; it is also the activity that will generate the widest range of relevant contacts for this and future job hunts.

The danger with the traditional concept of networks is that once you are comfortably networking among friends and acquaintances, you might unconsciously derail your job search by ignoring other and possibly more fruitful avenues of exploration for job opportunities. An effective job search requires more than writing to and shooting the breeze with old cronies on the telephone. Besides, you will often discover that your network is not as comprehensive as you might have wished.

The important thing for any professional to grasp is that to have a friend you must be a friend. Just because you worked with someone five years ago and haven't spoken to them since doesn't mean they still regard you as a friend. From personal experience and surveys through my own professional networks, and through your own observations, I think you'll find we both share the following conclusions on connectivity.

- To those requests from people I didn't know, I asked for a resume (of course, if they had an introduction or were fellow members of an association, things would be different). If I received it in good time with a thoughtfully prepared accompanying letter, I would give that person help if I could.
- To those requests from people with an introduction from someone I liked and respected, I gave time and consideration and, wherever possible, assistance.
- To those requests from friends, people I had worked with at one time and who had kept in touch since we had worked together, I stopped everything and went through my Rolodex. I provided leads, made calls on their behalf, and I insisted they keep in touch. I also initiated follow-up calls myself on behalf of these people.
- To those requests from people who regarded themselves as friends but who had not maintained contact, or who had only reestablished contact when they wanted something, I looked through the Rolodex once but for some reason was unable to find anything. I wished them the best of luck. "Sorry I couldn't help you. If something comes to mind, I'll be sure to call."

Nothing works like a personal recommendation from a fellow professional—and you get that best by *being* a fellow professional—by being connected to your profession and the professionals within it. It is no accident that successful people in all fields know each other—they helped each other get that way, because they stayed in touch.

If you are going to use business colleagues and personal friends in your job search, don't mess up and do it half-heartedly. We live in a very mobile society, so you shouldn't restrict yourself to family, friends, and colleagues just where you are looking; if you want to get your networking skills up to speed fast, come to knockemdead.com and take the free networking workshop.

Here are some tips for writing letters asking for assistance; you can also use these guidelines as a structure for networking conversations.

1. Establish connectivity. Recall the last memorable contact you had or someone in common that you have both spoken to recently.

2. Use your common membership in professional associations as a bridge builder to other members. If you're not currently a member of the relevant associations and organizations, you can go to the Internet resources page on the knockemdead.com Web site, and Appendix B in this book, for links and information

3. Let contacts know what you are looking for. They will invariably want to help, but you have to give them a framework within which to target their efforts. At the same time do not get too specific, or allow your ego to get in the way of leads for jobs you could really do. You want to be non-specific: "I'm looking for something in operations within telecom" gives the listener the widest possible opportunity for coming up with leads.

4. Tell them why you are writing: "It's time for me to make a move; my job just got sent to Mumbai, India, and I'm hoping you could help me with a new sense of direction."

5. Ask for advice and guidance: "Who do you think are the growing companies in the area today?" "Could you take a look at my resume for me? I really need an objective opinion and I've always respected your viewpoint." Don't ask specifically, "Can you hire me?" or "Can your company hire me?"

6. By all means ask for leads within specific target companies, but don't rely on a contact with a particular company to get you into that company. Mount and execute your own plan of attack. No one has the same interest as you in putting bread on your table.

7. When you do get help, say thank you. And if you get it verbally, follow it up in writing. The impression is indelible, and it just might get you another lead.

When you write networking letters and make the follow-up calls you might be surprised to find who your friends are: someone you always regarded as a real pal won't give you the time of day and someone you never thought of as a friend will go above and beyond the call of duty on your behalf.

Whether they help you or not, let all your contacts know when you get situated and offer to be a resource for them, and maintain contact in one form or another at least once a year. A career is for a long time, it might be next week or a decade from now when a group of managers (including one of your personal network) are talking about filling a new position and the first thing they will do is say "Whom do we know?" That could be you . . . if you establish professional connectedness now and maintain it.

If you are writing (and calling) as the result of a referral, say so and quote the person's name if appropriate:

> *"Our mutual colleague, John Stanovich, felt my skills and abilities would be valuable to your company . . ."*

> *"The manager of your San Francisco branch, Pamela Bronson, has suggested I contact you regarding the opening for a _____."*

> *"I received your name from Henry Charles, the branch manager of the Savannah Bank last week, and he suggested I contact you. In case the resume he forwarded is caught up in the mail, I enclose another."*

> *"Arthur Gold, your office manager and my neighbor, thought I should contact you about the upcoming opening in your accounting department."*

Direct-Research Contacts

The Internet is a most comprehensive job search resource, although by no means a resource that you can rely on exclusively. There are job sites that provide a wide array of services. Careerbuilder.com is an excellent example of such a site. This site, like many others, features a meta-search tool that allows you to search other job sites' job banks simultaneously, provides descriptions and links to thousands of U.S. companies, has comprehensive salary surveys in all fields, provides free resume posting, and has many other useful tools. Chapter 7 on using the Internet and Appendix B on job search resources will give you plenty of information for making the most of online options.

Most companies are also listed in online or library-based resources. Take the time to do direct research and you will discover job opportunities along with the all-important names and contact information for hiring managers, that 90 percent of your professional competitors never dreamed existed. Just for starters, here are a few useful research resources:

www.harrisinfo.com
www.hoovers.com
www.idexec.com
www.wmich.edu

Research resources exist that will enable you to identify the names and contact information of hiring executives at just about every within the geographic scope of your search. If you use your local library rather than online resources, realize that not every library has every book, so you may not find all of the reference books relevant to your search. However, almost all libraries belong to interlibrary lending systems, so just ask the reference librarian for help if you cannot find the book you need.

Your goal is to identify and build personalized dossiers on the companies in your chosen geographic area, so do not be judgmental about what and who they might appear to be: You are fishing for possible job openings, so cast your net wide and list them all. To this end you should also check out local Yellow Pages, which list smaller local companies. Don't turn your nose up at this option, because the majority of all job growth in America is in companies with 100 employees or less. Only if you present yourself as a candidate for all available opportunities in your geographic area of search will you maximize your chances of landing the best possible opportunity.

Tip: If you are 50 plus and experiencing age discrimination, smaller companies (where most of the job growth is anyway) are far more likely to feel the need for an experienced hand.

Develop electronic docs or paper file folders containing all the relevant information for each company. You'll want to include the names of the company's president and all other management names and titles, a description of the complete lines of company services and/or products, the size of the company, and the locations of its various operations. Of course, if you find other interesting information, copy it down, by all means. For instance, you might come across information on growth or shrinkage in a particular area of a company; or you might read about recent acquisitions the company has made; you can use Google or other search engines to track industry news.

All this information will help you target potential employers and stand out in different ways: Your knowledge will create a favorable impression when you first contact the company; that you made an effort is noticed and sets you apart from other applicants who don't bother. The combination says that you respect the company, the opportunity, and the interviewer; combined, these perceptions help differentiate your candidacy.

All your efforts have an obvious short-term value in helping you generate job interviews and offers. Who would *you* interview and subsequently hire? The person who knows nothing about your company, or the person who knows everything and shows enthusiasm with that knowledge?

Your efforts also have long-term value, because you are building a personalized reference work of your industry/specialty/profession in a specific target geography that will get you off to a running start the next time you wish to make a job change.

E-mail Blasts and Mailing Lists

Posting your resume online is a sensible passive job search technique, although the blasting of your resume across the Internet with one of the resume blasting services doesn't always live up to its apparent promise. In fact, until recently I was pretty much against the approach as I just wasn't seeing the results; however, I've just been working with an executive in international port security who got twenty responses resulting from an e-mail blast to some four hundred executive recruiters. Of course, he is in an in-demand occupation and had an arresting message expressed in his cover letter. And nowadays when everyone is delivering everything by e-mail it might just be the time to think about a serious traditional mail campaign to support (but not as the sole or main thrust of your job search campaign) your other job-hunting activities. You can put together your own lists of people to pitch your resume to or use the services of an online or print broker.

Associations

You're a member of an appropriate professional association, aren't you? If not, you will want to invest in membership just as soon as humanly possible. The professional connectedness you achieve through membership, the skills you will learn, and the contacts you make will pay dividends throughout your career. Not to mention the networking database and directory you get to use immediately. You don't know of an appropriate association? As mentioned previously, you can come to the association page within Internet resources on the *knockemdead.com* site.

Alumni Associations

Most schools—from the Ivy leagues to vocational schools—have an active alumni association. These associations have alumni who post jobs, and most members will offer assistance to someone from their old alma mater. You can usually get mail and e-mailing lists from them, which vary from just names to names and occupations and employers. Every working alumnus is worthy of a networking letter and a call; just check through the networking letter section for examples of what to write. Never, ever, underestimate the power of "the old school tie."

Employment Agencies and Executive Recruiters

There are essentially three categories: state employment agencies, private employment agencies, and executive recruiters.

State Employment Agencies

These are funded by the state labor department and typically carry names like State Employment Security, State Job Service, or Manpower Services. The names may vary, but the services remain the same; they will make efforts to line you up with appropriate jobs and mail resumes out on your behalf to interested employers and will often initiate calls of introduction. It is not mandatory for employers to list jobs with state agencies, but more and more are taking advantage of these free services. Once the bastion of minimum-wage jobs, these public agencies now list positions with salaries reaching $100,000 a year. In fact the job bank that connects them all together—America's Job Bank at *www.ajb.dni.us*—is our country's largest.

If you are moving across the state or across the country, your local employment office can plug you into this national job bank, in case you don't have Internet access at home. The most effective way to use this service is to visit your local office and ask for an introduction to the office in your destination area. Then send them a cover letter (via e-mail and regular mail) with your resume, and follow up with a phone call.

Private Employment Agency Sources

The following are a few sources for employment service listings, from temporary help through local employment agency, contingency, and retained headhunters. Depending on who you are and what you are looking for, any or all of these categories could be of interest to you. Here is some contact data for the most comprehensive lists and directories available.

www.kennedyinfo.com/er/estore.html
www.aesc.org/
www.therecruiternetwork.com/
www.net-temps.com/

Don't restrict yourself to any single category in this area. Executives, especially, should not turn their noses up at contingency search firms without first seeing what they have to offer. Often a local agency has better rapport and contacts with the local business community than the big-name search firms. I have also known more than one "employment agency" that regularly placed job candidates earning in excess of $250,000 a year. Don't get hung up on agency versus search firm labels without researching the firms in question; you could miss some great opportunities.

Online and Print Business Magazines

There are a number of potential uses here. The articles about interesting companies can alert you to growth opportunities, and the articles themselves can provide a neat little entry in your cover letter. Many professional association and trade magazines rely more or less on the contributions of industry professionals. So articles bylined by Bill Edwards, VP of Openings at Sesame Furnaces, could go into a dossier for targeted contacts. It's also a neat idea to enclose the clipping with your letter. These mailings to sometime authors can be tremendously rewarding. Writing is hard, and writers have egos of mythical proportions (just ask my editor), so a little flattery can go a long way.

By the same token, you can write to people who are quoted in articles, again with a clipping or a link. It's great to see your name in print; in fact there is only one thing better, and that is hearing that someone *else* saw your name in print and now thinks you're a genius. Bear in mind that most of these magazines also carry a recruitment section.

These ideas are just some of the many unusual and effective ways to introduce yourself to companies; you'll find more in the latest annual addition of *Knock 'em Dead: The Ultimate Job Seeker's Guide.*

Sending Out Your Cover Letters

Cover letters are more effective when you can find an individual to whom you can address it. As noted earlier, salutations like "Sir/Madam" or "To whom it may concern" says you don't care enough about the company to find out a name. Any reader will pay more attention to a letter addressed by name, and if nothing else it guarantees the letter will opened and read. Additionally, your research pays off because you have someone to ask for by name when you make your follow-up telephone call.

Must you send out hundreds or even thousands of letters in the coming weeks? I once took a call from a woman on a call-in TV show who had "done everything and still not gotten a job." She explained how she had sent out almost 300 letters and still wasn't employed. After I asked her a couple of questions it turned out that she had been job-hunting for almost two years (that equals two or three letters a week), and there were, conservatively, 3,000 companies for whom she could work. This breaks down to a single approach with no follow-up to only one in ten potential employers. Two employer contacts a week will not get you back to work—or even on the track with the kind of job that can help you advance toward your chosen work life goals. Only if you approach and establish communication with every possible employer and follow up properly will you create the maximum opportunity for yourself.

In the world of headhunters, the statistical average is 700 contacts (that's letters, e-mails, making and receiving calls) between offers and acceptances. These are averages of professionals representing only the most desirable jobs and job candidates to each other. When I hear that it takes a white-collar worker about eight months to get a job nowadays, I have a feeling those 700 or so contacts are being spread out needlessly. If you approach the job search in a professional manner, the way executive search professionals and employment agents approach their work, you can be happily installed on the next rung of your career ladder much sooner than the national average—that is, if you really put the advice of the *Knock 'em Dead* books to work for yourself. Just look at the reader endorsements at the front of the book to see what you can achieve if you follow this advice in letter and in spirit.

I am not recommending that you immediately make up a list of 700 companies and mail letters to them today. That isn't the answer. Your campaign needs strategy. While every job search campaign is unique, you will want to maintain a balance between the number of emails and letters you send out on a daily and weekly basis and the kinds of letters you send out. This needs to all be integrated into an intelligent overall campaign that includes other job-search activities; just mailing resumes with none of the other productive job-search approaches is a sad excuse for a job campaign.

The key is to send out a balanced mailing representing all the different types of leads, and to send them out regularly and in a volume that will allow you to make follow-up calls. There are many headhunters who manage their time so well that they average over fifty calls a day, year in and year out. While you may aim at building your call volume up to this number, I recommend that you start out with more modest goals.

To start the campaign:

Source	Number of Letters Per Day
Internet job postings	10
Newspaper ads	10
Networking	10 (5 to friends, 5 to professional colleagues)
Direct-research contacts (online searches, reference works, magazines, etc.)	10
Headhunters	10

Do You Need to Compose More Than One Letter?

Almost certainly, there is a case for all of us having a number of letters and resumes targeted for different specific needs. The key is to do each variation once and do it right. Your computer makes this job many times easier than it used to be, and you can use these letters again and again over the years as your circumstances demand. Sometimes you may find it valuable to send upward of half a dozen contact letters to a desirable target company, just to assure that all the right people know you are available. To illustrate, let's say you are a young engineer crazy for a job with Last Chance Electronics. It is well within the bounds of reason that you would submit a cover letter and resume to any or all of the following people, with each letter addressed by name to minimize its chances of going straight into the trash:

- Company President
- Vice President of Engineering
- Chief Engineer
- Engineering Design Manager
- Vice President of Human Resources
- Technical Engineering Recruitment Manager
- Technical Recruiter

Each of these letters might require a slightly different introductory paragraph, while the body of the letter could remain the same.

The Plan

A professionally organized and conducted campaign should include both an e-mail and a traditional mail dimension. So when I talk about "mail" and "mail campaign," understand that the terms embrace both communication mediums.

Approach #1

A carefully targeted rifle approach of a select group of companies. You will have first identified these "super-desirable" places to work as you researched your long list of potential employers. You will continue to add to this primary target list as you unearth fresh opportunities in your day-to-day research efforts. In this instance you have two choices:

1. Mail to everyone at once, remembering that the letters have to be personalized and followed up appropriately.
2. Start your mailings off with one to a line manager and one to a contact in human resources. Follow up in a few days and repeat the process to other names on your hit list.

With the e-mail dimension of your campaign, you can bookmark target companies and check in on their openings on an ongoing basis. As employers cannot be relied on to keep your resume front and center, you should submit to your target companies on a regular basis, say every six weeks. The worst that can happen is that someone finally pays attention!

Approach #2

A carpet-bombing strategy designed to reach every possible employer, on the basis that you won't know what opportunities there are unless you go find out. (Here, too, you must personalize and follow up appropriately.)

Begin with a mailing to one or two contacts within the company and then repeat the mailings to other contacts when your initial follow-up calls result in referrals or dead ends. Remember, just because Harry in engineering says there are no openings in the company, that's not necessarily the case; always find out for yourself. Even if he doesn't have a need himself, another contact in the same company could know the person who is just dying to meet you.

Once you have received some responses to your mailings/follow-up calls and scheduled interviews, your emphasis will change. Those contacts and interviews will require follow-up letters and conversation. You will be preparing for interviews.

This is exactly the point where most job hunts stall. We get so excited about the interview activity we convince ourselves that "This will be the offer." The headhunters have a saying, "The offer that can't fail always will." What happens is that the offer doesn't materialize, and you are left with absolutely no interview activity.

The more resumes and cover letters you send out, the more follow-up calls you can make to schedule interviews; the more interviews you get, the better your interviewing skills become and the better you feel.

So no matter how good things look with a particular company, continue the campaign—maintain activity with those companies with whom you are in negotiation, and continue to make fresh submissions every week. You must maintain your marketing schedule. Your daily plan now looks like this:

Source	Number of Letters Per Day
Internet job postings	5
Newspaper ads	5
Networking	5 (associations, alumni, colleagues)
Direct-research contacts (online searches, reference works, magazines, etc.)	5
Headhunters	5
Follow-up letters and calls	15–20

Small but consistent mailings have many benefits. The balance you maintain is important, because most job hunters are tempted simply to send the easy letters and make the easy calls (network with old friends), but only doing this will knock your job search out of balance.

Even when an offer is pending, keep plugging—and by "pending" I include all variations on "Harry, you've got the job and you can start Monday; the offer letter is in the mail." Yeah, just like the check in the old saying. Never accept the "yes" until you have it in writing, have started work, and the first paycheck has cleared at the bank! Until then, keep your momentum building.

Following Up: A Cautionary Tale

In theory, your cover letter will generate a 100 percent response, but this is not reality. Although you will get calls from your mailing, if you sit there like Buddha waiting for the world to beat a path to your door, you may wait a long time.

A pal of mine once put a two-line ad in the local paper for an analyst; the ad also appeared on the paper's Web site. By Wednesday of the following week he had received more than 100 responses. Ten days later he was still plowing through them when he received a follow-up call (the only one he did receive) from one of the ad respondents. The job hunter was in the office within two hours, returned the following morning, and was hired by lunchtime.

The candidate's paperwork was simply languishing there in the pile waiting to be discovered. The follow-up phone call got it discovered. The call made the interviewer sort through the enormous pile of paper, pull out the letter and resume, and act on it.

Follow-Up Calls Work

You'll notice that examples in the letter section mention that they will follow up with a phone call. This allows the writer to explain to any inquisitive receptionist that Joe Schmoe is "expecting my call" or that it is "personal," Or, "it's accounting/engineering/customer service business."

I find it surprising that so many people are nervous about calling a fellow professional on the phone and talking about what they do for a living. To help reduce any nervousness, understand that there is an unwritten professional credo shared by the vast majority of successful professional people: You should always help another if it isn't going to hurt you in the process. Because of this, almost everyone you speak to will recognize and be sympathetic to your cause.

If you are not already successful in management, you need to know the principle outlined in my book for managers titled *Hiring the Best*: "The first tenet of management is getting work done through others." A manager's success is based on this single idea. Managers are always on the lookout for competent professionals in their field for today and tomorrow. In fact, the best managers maintain a private file of great professionals they can't use today but want to keep available. I know of someone who got a job as a result of a letter retained in these files. She got the interview (and the job) from the letter and resume she'd sent months earlier.

No manager will take offense at a call from a competent fellow professional. To know exactly how to make the call and what to say, look at the chapter on telephone interviews in *Knock 'em Dead: The Ultimate Job Seeker's Guide*.

Using a Contact Tracker

To ensure that you keep track of your mailings and the follow-up phone calls, I recommend that you create a Contact Tracker on a spreadsheet program like Microsoft Excel. Create columns for the company name, telephone number, e-mail address, and contact name. A mailing loaded in your contact tracker today will allow you to have a follow-up call plan set and ready to go for a few days later. As a rule of thumb, a mailing sent today is ripe for follow-up four to eight days from now. Any sooner and you can't be sure the mail has arrived; much later and it may already have gotten lost or been passed on; with e-mail you will probably want to follow up within a couple or three days. In addition to your Contact Tracker, it may be helpful to use your computer address book to keep track of whom you contact.

You will know that your job search is on track when you are filling in more contacts every day as a result of a mailing, and creating a second Contact Tracker as a result of your follow-up calls.

If you follow the advice in this book, and in *Resumes That Knock 'em Dead* and *Knock 'em Dead: The Ultimate Job Seeker's Guide*, you will get multiple job offers—people do all the time. When you get your first job offer, you will want to read the section on generating multiple offers in *Knock 'em Dead*, which will show you how to turn many of these contacts into additional interviews and competitive offers.

I spoke to a man on a radio call-in show who had been out of work for some months. He had bought the books and followed my advice to the letter and had generated four job offers in only five weeks. I have lost count of the number of similar encounters I've had over the years. Follow my advice in letter and spirit and the same good fortune can be yours. After all, good fortune is really only the intersection of opportunity, preparation, and effort.

CHAPTER · CHAPTER · CHAPTER · CHAPTER · CHAPTER · CHAPTER

7

How the Internet Can Help in Your Job Search

THE INTERNET IS a vital job search tool. Here's a kick-start guide to getting your cover letter and resumes read by human eyes

The Internet offers you an array of opportunities to get your resume on the desks of thousands of companies and recruiters. This communication medium makes research and contact easier than it has ever been, but you shouldn't rely on the obvious online approaches exclusively.

The Internet is especially effective in identifying all the target employers in a specific geography whether it is where you live today or where you want to live as soon as possible. Its usefulness diminishes somewhat when you are only looking for jobs in your immediate area, and that area is a small town, although there are still many useful ways you can use the medium.

From the corporate perspective, Internet recruitment serves a dual purpose: their personnel openings are advertised cost effectively to attract candidates, and the technologically challenged screen themselves out

How can the Internet benefit your job search? It allows you to:

- Research your industry and identify companies
- Create customized electronic documents and communicate with potential employers and recruiters pretty much instantly.
- Find job openings through job banks and employers' job sites.
- Have potential employers find you, whether you are currently looking for a position or just maintaining visibility for career growth opportunities.
- Use database and networking sites to identify names and titles.
- Pick up useful job search and career management advice, especially at *www.knockemdead.com*.

You can post your resume on the Internet so that companies and recruiters can find you; you can surf for job openings and you'll have access to more information about prospective employers, making you a better-informed candidate. The Internet offers you access to millions of job openings, and tens of thousands of companies and recruiters. Of course, they are not all going to be in your town, so the wider your geographical parameters, the more useful the tool will become.

What You Need to Start an Online Job Search

You need computer access from outside the workplace. Using your office computer for writing your resume, sending out e-mails, or surfing the net for job postings is regarded by the corporate world as theft of time and services; it can cost you your job and the reason for termination will make the next one more difficult to find. Studies show that 50 percent of all companies either read their employees' e-mail and/or track their Internet usage. Some companies have assigned IT staff members whose job it is to track inappropriate Internet usage, and they have software packages to help with that tracking. Originating primarily in the high-tech industries, this practice seems to be on the rise in industries across the board. Don't ignore this warning because you feel your boss is computer illiterate, too stupid to catch you, or too trusting to snoop.

Online Privacy and Organization

Personal privacy and confidentiality become serious issues when you use the Internet for job-hunting and resume distribution. It's a good news/bad news situation—with the ease of electronic document distribution comes the fear of prying eyes. So take precautions to protect your privacy. Almost all companies are using the Internet for recruitment purposes; someone in Human Resources could accidentally stumble across your online resume, which lists the company for whom you're currently working.

If you have Internet access at home, it is probably through a local ISP (Internet service provider) such as MSN, AOL, or Earthlink. These accounts typically come with more than one e-mail address, so you can utilize one of the additional addresses for career management activities. If you are currently employed and executing a confidential search, it is a good idea to set up a separate online identity and maintain it exclusively for your job search.

As your experience broadens, your education and professional experience will allow you to pursue a number of different jobs. Therefore, you have the option of creating multiple professional identities online to separate these activities. Setting up separate e-mail accounts for each of these career-specific identities will allow you to keep things organized by job classifications, giving more focus to your search and allowing you to effectively manage your job search activities.

Privacy Is a Concern for Everyone

Don't be afraid to use the Internet in your job search, but be aware that the information that you post is readily available to other users. Be careful about the type of information and the amount of personal data you make electronically available.

Anyone who has an e-mail account is familiar with junk e-mail, commonly referred to as spam. Reverse spamming is when an electronic "spider" (a programmed tool that searches the Internet for any information the "spider owner" specifies) grabs your personal information, e-mail address, or resume, then redistributes it to other sites or a third party . . . so you must be circumspect about the personal information you make available in electronic documents. You put your professional identity at risk when listing professional license or certificate numbers on your resume. Similarly other personal information such as date of birth, driver's license numbers, and social security numbers should never be included on electronic resumes or any publicly available document. With that information alone, someone could steal your identity and ruin your personal or professional credibility.

Don't include too much personal information in an online resume. It could allow unscrupulous people to use your personal or professional identity for their own purposes; at the same time, posting your home phone number or address on the Internet can attract junk mail and telemarketing calls.

Rules to Protect Your Online Privacy

Here are some general guidelines for making online job sites and resume banks work for you rather than against you:

- Look at the site's privacy statement. Read it carefully to understand the extent of protection afforded your personal information. Even without guarantees, this is a security starting point.
- Only post your resume to sites that protect their resume bank with a password (this is the best prevention against those pesky spiders). Password protection means that the site electronically screens all visitors. This helps to ensure that only credible employers and recruiters have access to your resume.
- Know who owns and operates the site. The owner's contact information should be available. If they are unwilling to share their identity with you, don't share yours with them.
- You must be able to update, edit, and remove your posted resume, along with any other personal information whenever you choose.
- Blocked resume bank services supposedly allow you to block access to your information from specifically unwanted viewers, such as a current employer. Do not trust these services to actually do so. Technology is not foolproof, so only post items that you don't need blocked, or create a secure online identity.
- If you decide to build and create your own Web site to post your resume and work samples, you might wish to password-protect it at certain times.
- Never put your social security number, driver's license number, or professional license number on your resume in any format.
- Do not use your company e-mail address, computer, or Internet lines to search for jobs or to access your private e-mail account.

Free E-Mail Accounts

There are dozens of sites that offer free e-mail accounts that take only minutes to set up. While many personal interest sites offering free accounts exist, remember that your career e-mail address shouldn't contain any personal information.

For example, the e-mail address *Martin@match.com* (from a dating site) reveals altogether too much personal information, and obviously isn't appropriate for professional use. Your intent is to create a professional, eye-catching image right from the start; take time in selecting your professional e-mail service and user names.

As an example of the process, let's create a secure online identity for a fictional job search candidate, Susan O'Malley. Go to *www.hotmail.com*, and then select the "New Account Sign Up" icon on the front page of the site. That will link you to a page requesting a user profile. When you complete the profile, you will be directed to the site user agreement. This explains user rules and the site's privacy policy. Read this information carefully; you have to accept the terms of the agreement before your address becomes active. Stick with the larger, more public firms, because they tend to be more reliable and honorable about such terms. Typically, public sites offer paid upgrades to your new account that allow you more control over your e-mail address. Upgrades are unnecessary if you limit the number of messages stored in your mailbox at any given time, or if you don't care to pay to limit spam.

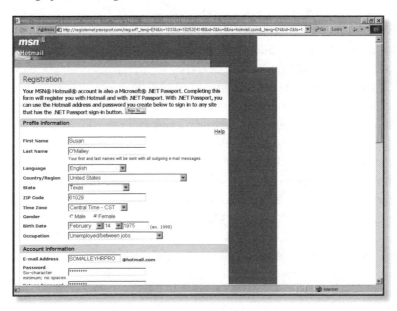

Account signup

You will notice that I chose a professional user name for Susan: SOMALLEY HRPRO—this gives her the e-mail address *somalleyhrpro@hotmail.com*. Remember: this account is set up strictly for job-search purposes.

An appropriately named professional e-mail like this gives immediate focus for recruiters and prospective employers.

Should you run into a situation where the user name you want is not available, choose your alternatives wisely. Most sites will make suggestions, usually by adding numbers to the end of the user name. This is not always the best idea for job search and career management needs. You do not want to be confused with *jsmith118@hotmail.com* when you are assigned the name *jsmith119@hotmail.com*, nor do you want to choose a number that could easily be mistaken for your year of birth. Instead, make it a career-related screen name as we did for Susan.

How to Organize Your Job-Search E-Mail Account

If you use shared or public computers, free accounts such as this one offer a nice security feature at the front door. Susan activated the highest level of security by clicking on the "Public/shared computer" button. At this increased level of security, Susan will be asked for her user name and password whenever she attempts to enter her account from any computer. If Susan always uses her home or private computer, the "Neither" or the "Keep me signed in" option assumes that every time her Web browser links to Hotmail, she is identified as the user and is automatically logged in. This also allows Sue to keep her job search secure on her family computer, so those darling rugrats don't destroy all her work. For your own safety, emulate Susan and set up your account at the highest security level possible.

Whether you use Hotmail, Yahoo!, Outlook, or some other major e-mail program, all of them allow you to create and manage folders. (Do you see the buttons for "Create Folder" and "Manage Folders" in the figures on the following page?)

Think of these as the electronic equivalent of paper folders and filing cabinets. What folders do you need? Let's start with the two major sites where Susan will be posting her resume and searching for jobs: Monster.com and SHRM.org (the Society for Human Resource Management Web site). Like most job sites, both of these offer job delivery service, automatically linking her to relevant jobs whenever those new jobs are posted on the site.

Susan will also create a folder for leads. As the leads mature into communication and contact with specific companies and recruiters, she can create specific folders for them. To get started, Susan's new e-mail account looks like this:

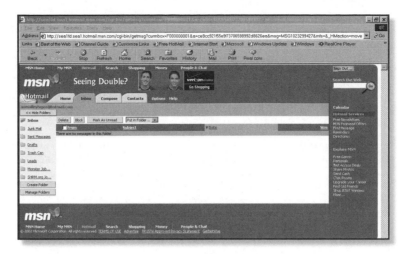

The new e-mail account

You could have folders for different geographic areas, or professional areas of expertise, for headhunters and the like; then, as communications develop with specific companies, said companies might warrant separate folders of their own. Now traditionally we trash much of this info once it has been processed: for example, when that recruiter tells us that she has nothing, or when we come in second at that company, or when we realize that none of those X number of companies are going to interview us. But times have changed and some of the old traditions don't make much sense anymore.

It's pretty much a given that you are somewhere in the middle of a half-century work life, and that in that time you likely to change jobs about every four years and have three or more distinct careers in that time. Given this likely scenario your current job search is not likely to be your last, so why not save all this data and information? A few years down the road, you'll be able to update the resume and retool the cover letters. And you know those companies who were hiring accountants back in 2007? Well, they are still hiring accountants! Even if your contact Jim Smith has since left that one company, the fact that you knew him will ensure that you are given his replacement's name. Organize and save today's work and next time you come to a job search you won't be starting from scratch!

Take another look at the previous screen shot, only this time look up to the right, above the messages. Locate the tab in the middle of the screen labeled "Address Book." This tab sends you to another screen, where you are given additional options. These options allow you to send e-mail, view and edit messages, delete e-mail, and, most important for your organizational efforts: create a new address book.

In creating new address books, you want to organize groups of addresses, and not just add individual ones. Each "group" will contain a separate set or group of addresses, tailored to specific audiences for current or future job searches. Typically, these groups fall into three categories: companies, recruiters, and networking prospects/professional colleagues. By creating an address book group for each of these categories, you create a database for your work life.

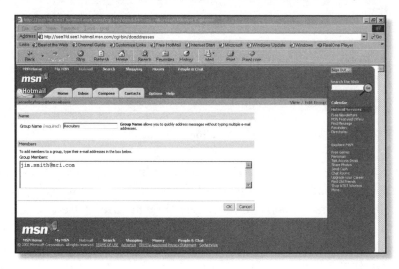

Address book groups

Additions to these groups needn't be based on direct contact, interviews, or job offers. If you see a recruiter working within an industry segment of interest, put that address in the recruiter book. If you find a company in your geographic area or professional field, put that address in the company book. By doing this regularly, you create a vehicle for launching a massive career blitz whenever the need arises. Organize yourself now, and the information you collect along the way can be used throughout your entire work life. You'll have an enormous database loaded and ready to go!

Cover Letters and Online Search

A productive resume plays a significant role in the job search success, but it will often remain unread without a dynamite cover letter to pave the way. In the online world, your cover letter is the e-mail message preceding your resume.

The Internet and subsequent growth of the electronic recruitment process have been both a blessing and a curse for corporate recruiters. Although electronic recruitment can be much more efficient in many ways, it tends to yield more responses from a wider range of candidates. This creates a time management challenge the people who must review the avalanche of resumes the medium generates; consequently, there has been a dramatic growth in resume software capable of scanning resume databases by keywords.

These programs allow companies to store digitally encoded documents such as resumes and letters, saving them for later access using keywords and other criteria to rank their usefulness. Initially, only large companies could afford these services, but with competition and the growth of the Internet, resume scanning and searching capabilities are now available to virtually all companies and recruiters.

With traditionally mailed resumes, a powerful cover letter separates you from the crowd. The same is true with e-mailed resumes; a well-crafted cover letter can save your resume from cursory review and relegation to the company's resume fish tank.

An e-mailed cover letter must adhere to all the same criteria that we have already set out. The message is the same, but at the same time it is smart to be sensitive to the medium through which it is delivered. Think of your e-mail cover letter as an electronic talent agent, the opening act for your resume. The two must complement each other because working together they both play crucial roles in a successful online job search. No matter how well written your cover letters are, inappropriately presented documents will result in wasted effort.

Differences Between Electronic and Print Cover Letters

Today's workplace tends to demand 50+ hours weekly from busy, multitasking employees; I've spoken to corporate executives who base their decisions on listening to voice mail messages depending on the first ten words recorded. Your e-mailed cover letter competes for the attention of this same audience.

The amount of e-mail traffic is growing exponentially, so hit your main points quickly, or lose the reader's attention. A good subject line grabs attention, but if the first two sentences don't succinctly state your purpose and grab the reader's attention, they'll have little reason for wasting any more precious time on the rest of your message.

Cover letters typically consist of three to five carefully constructed paragraphs. Very rarely should they exceed one full page, in most cases as we have discussed, a second page simply won't get read.

Just as you would limit a paper cover letter to one page, you should try to keep an electronic cover letter to one screen view where possible. This can sometimes be less than the length of your original script, so edit as strongly as you can. If you cannot get your entire letter in one screen view, at least make an effort to get the meat of your pitch onto that first full screen.

Before discussing formatting, let's take a minute to focus on cover letter content issues. We've established the fact that e-mail cover letters need to be concise, giving the reasons why the message is being sent and why the reader should move onto your resume. Review the samples below. Look for the ways in which these letters build bridges between writers and readers, use keywords, make points about the writers' suitability for the positions, and then request next step information.

Sample #1

I was excited to see your opening for a Financial Analyst vacancy (job #1854) on the NationJob.com Web site. As my attached resume demonstrates, the open position is a perfect match for my payroll, general ledger, and accounts receivable experience. I welcome the opportunity to discuss my skills and your job requirements in greater detail. Please respond with a time of day I might call you.

Sample #2

While browsing the jobs database on careerbuilder.com, I was intrigued by your Regional Sales Manager job posting (MZ - wj25508). Although I am currently employed by one of your competitors, I have kept my eye open for an opportunity to join your organization. Over the past year I have:

- *Built a sales force of 7 reps*
- *Exceeded my quota-growing revenue to $2.3 million*
- *Implemented a customer service plan that successfully reduced client turnover*

Please review my attached resume and contact me to schedule a time for us to meet.

Sample #3

It was great meeting you Monday for lunch. I enjoyed sharing ideas with a fellow association member, and, as you suggested, I have attached a copy of my current resume. Since our meeting I have given more thought to your company goals and believe they are closely related to my skill set and career objectives. I will call you next week to schedule a time when we can continue our conversation.

Sample #4

Your colleague, Bill Jacobson, suggested that I send you my resume. He mentioned that your department is looking for a Database Administrator with experience in Intranet implementation and management. As my attached resume demonstrates, I have done that type of work for six years with a regional organization on a platform of 15,000 users. I welcome the opportunity to discuss your specific projects and explore the possibility of joining your team.

Sample #5

Although I am currently employed by one of your major competitors, I must admit that I was captivated by your company's mission statement when I visited your Web site. Your dedication of resources within assisted care facilities not only piqued my interest but is also, as my attached resume indicates, precisely my area of expertise. With significant experience in an area of such importance to your firm, I look forward to the opportunity to discuss available positions.

Sample #6

A colleague of mine, Diane Johnson, recommended your recruiting firm to me as you recently assisted her in a strategic career move. I understand that your firm specializes in the consumer products industry. As a Marketing Director with 12 years of experience in consumer products, I have:

- *Doubled revenues in just 18 months*
- *Introduced a new product that captured a 38% market share*
- *Successfully managed a $5 million ad budget*

I have pasted and attached my resume for your review and will call you in the next couple of days to discuss any openings for which your firm is currently conducting searches.

The content of each of these cover letter samples follows a similar format. They all accomplish four goals:

- They identify why you are sending your resume.
- They identify why the reader should read the resume.
- They ask for the interview or next contact.
- They do so succinctly.

Let's examine each of these points more closely:

Identify why you made contact: You probably initiated contact because of a job posting, a colleague, or because your research identified them as a potential employer or suitable recruiting firm. Just state the reason and tell the reader you see a match. When submitting because of a job posting, always indicate the job title or job number if there is one. Likewise, if a friend, associate, or colleague initiated the contact, clearly state their name and your connection. If you found the opening through Internet research, state that as well.

Give them a reason to read your resume: Quickly and concisely, identify why you believe you are a match. Read the job posting again and then repeat the keywords that you share with it. If appropriate, explain the reason why your mutual acquaintance or colleague referred you, as a segue into stating your credentials. This is your chance to whet the reader's appetite. If you are currently employed by, or have worked for ,a competitor, say it here—many companies seek the expertise of their competitors, and love to lure employees away from them.

Ask for the next step: Wrap up this brief but powerful communication by suggesting a meeting, phone call, or interview. Go ahead and state that you will follow up with them, especially if you are currently employed and confidentiality could be an issue. But if you say you are going to follow up, you must make time to do it.

The Need for Multiple Cover Letters

You will be sending your resume and cover letter in response to many different situations (as well as in different delivery mediums). To maximize effectiveness, you will have to tailor your cover letters to specific audiences. Addressees may include:

1. Companies and recruiters in response to online job postings.
2. Companies you've found from research, newspapers, trade publications, and the Internet.
3. In-house recruiters and the all-important headhunters.
4. Friends and professional colleagues as a means for networking.

When sending resumes to each of these types of contacts, slightly different cover letters will be required, and you'll find lots of examples to emulate and customize later in this book. It is best to compose letters in a word processing program, not in your e-mail folder. Even though you are most likely to send the cover letter via e-mail, it is easier to compose and edit them in a WP doc and move them into e-mail when you're satisfied with the general content; then within the e-mail you can do the final polish that customizes the document for a specific employer.

Creating and saving them in a word processing program allows you to use each letter type you create as a template that can be pasted into an e-mail and customized to the unique needs of that particular situation. In the long run, templates make you more time-efficient in your job search campaign, because you will always have a base from which to start.

Go to your "My Documents" or "My Briefcase" folders, and then create a series of new folders for the various documents and relationships you will be building. This is what Susan's initial folder system looks like:

Job search folders

As you can see, she's created a separate section in the "My Documents" folder, then created a series of subfolders for "Resumes," "Cover Letters," "Job Descriptions," "Follow-up Letters," and "Interview Research." She also reserves space for "Job Offers" and "Employment Contracts" folders to handle such responses when her job search gains momentum.

Remember, in each of these folders, you need to name documents appropriately; create additional subfolders like Susan's "Text Cover Letters" subfolder, which is embedded in the "Cover Letters" folder. Get organized now and never worry about it again.

Make Sure Your Cover Letter Templates Are Electronic Transmission Compatible

Let's revisit Susan O'Malley in the process of editing her cover letter template and converting it to an ASCII or text-based document for e-mail distribution.

Susan's cover letter is nicely formatted, matching the layout of her resume. At this point, the letter is one full page in length, listing a dozen bullet points regarding her skill set. It can certainly be shortened and/or customized for a specific opening where she has some idea of the requirements.

Unlike regular business letters, e-mail letters do not always follow typical letter-writing protocols. For example, you do not include your address, because your contact information and the date and time of your communication is entered automatically. Begin your business e-mail messages with a simple salutation: "Dear Tiffany Carstairs," for example. Basic professional courtesies still apply, so don't address the recipient on a first-name basis unless you are already familiar with your contact; use the same courtesy and respect you would in a hard-copy version.

Always end your business e-mails stating your name and a brief summary of your contact information (confidential phone or fax number). Remove the traditional "resume enclosed" statement, and instead note that it is pasted into the body of the e-mail and also attached (the correct term for e-mail communication, as you have just seen in the examples), You would obviously prefer to have your nicely formatted resume in the attachment viewed, but you should always paste in it into the body of your e-mail because many people simply do not open attachments from people they don't know personally.

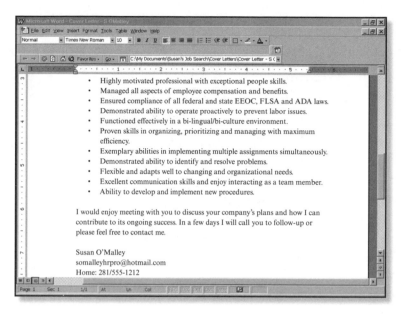

The first edit of the cover letter

Although this letter is still too long, it allows flexibility for specific tailoring. She can edit the bulleted list according to the requirements of any individual position she seeks. At this point, Susan's letter can be altered as needed, so let's ignore the length issue to focus on format. If placed into the body of an e-mail message, this text would develop character and spacing problems. To avoid such problems, convert your cover letters to ASCII or text-based documents before pasting it into an e-mail. This is accomplished by following these simple steps.

Copy the entire document by choosing "select all" from the "edit" pull-down menu. Then, choose "copy" from the "edit" pull-down menu or Ctrl+C for Windows. With a Macintosh you simply choose "save" from the pull-down file menu, click "save" and then, when the dialog box opens up, click on "format" and scroll to "text."

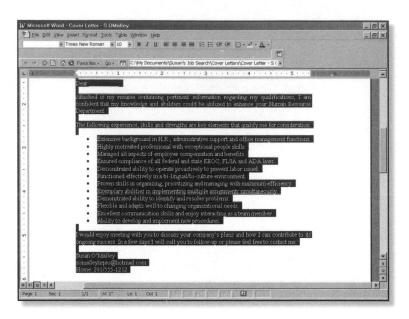

Selecting all text

Sometimes the document will still lose many of its features and the spacing can change dramatically, even when saved as "text," so you need to spend time proofreading your new document before sending. Any tabs, tables, or columns can wreak havoc on new text-based versions. In order to prevent wrapping or flowing issues, you may need to delete empty spaces and tabs to make the document flush left.

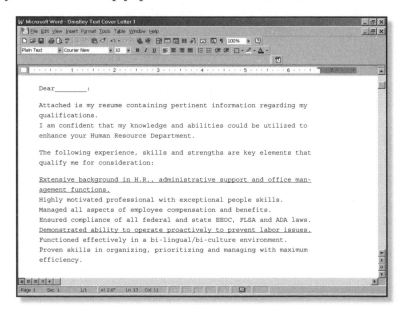

A cover letter with formatting removed

Since the bullets have disappeared in the translation, either adjust the spacing to create a new type of emphasis, or use characters on your keyboard such as "*" to replace the bullets. Additionally, the bullet statements need to be shorter and more concise. If you allow statements to wrap to the next line, your electronic cover letters will be unappealing, less effective, and too long. Save your document to protect all these changes. Keep in mind that this is a template. Once an actual contact or job opening has been identified, customization will be the next step.

E-Mail Subject Lines

The use of a powerful subject line can mean the difference between getting your resume read by human eyes or relegated to the HR resume database. When sending e-mail—not just job-related e-mails but also all e-mails—it is only professional to provide a clear and concise subject line. It should allow the receiver to immediately know who you are and what you want.

The subject line of an e-mail containing your resume needs to be factual, professional, and intriguing. This subject line is like the headline for a newspaper article; its intent is to grab the reader and draw him or her into the body of the e-mail message and your resume. Do not use the subject line to state the obvious, like "Resume" or "Jim Smith's Resume." If you are responding to a job posting, the job title and job posting number are necessary, but just a start. Combine this factual information with a little intrigue such as:

Job #6745 - Top Sales Professional Here
IT Manager - 7 yrs IT Consulting
Financial Analyst #MB450 - CPA/MBA/8 yrs exp
Benefits Consultant - Nonprofit Exp in NY
Posting 2314 - MIT Grad is interested
Referral from Tony Banks - Product Management Job

Do not go overboard with an overly aggressive subject line. Do not think you can trick someone into reading your resume by claiming to be an MIT graduate when you are not, at the same time a funny or whimsical subject line might land your resume right in the delete bin.

How to Customize and Send Your E-mail Cover Letter and Resume

Let's pull it all together and watch Susan, an HR professional, customize her electronic cover letter, pick an effective subject line, and send her resume to a potential employer.

Susan has been using the Society for Human Resource Management career site (*www.shrm.org*) and has found an appealing position in sunny California. A specialty food distributor is seeking a Regional HR Manager.

Job posting

The job posting has requested that correspondence be sent in the following manner:

Qualified candidates send resume, salary history, and cover letter to: *jadariav@gourmetaward.com* or fax *555-555-1234.*

Susan is going to e-mail and mail her customized cover letter and resume to this employer. Since the employer did not provide any additional direction, it is best if Susan attaches the resume to her e-mail message as well as pastes it into the body of the e-mail. Let's start by customizing her electronic cover letter template and then choose a strong subject line.

Since Susan was smart enough to get herself organized, she can quickly find her electronic cover letter template. By comparing this longer template to the actual job description, she can easily spot the "hot points." This position requires 10 years of experience and the job description indicates that knowledge of employment laws such as EEOC, FLSA, and ADA are important. Additionally, Susan is interested in moving to California, so this is a good match.

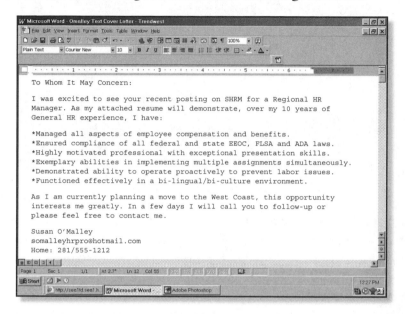

Electronic cover letter for job opening

Susan has customized her cover letter template well: She stated why she is sending the e-mail, hit her "hot points" to get the reader's attention, and asked for the follow-up. In fact, she even renamed the document to reflect the company she will be sending it to and saved it in her cover letter folder.

The next step is to create the e-mail, paste and attach the resume. Susan will go back to her newly established Hotmail account, enter her user name and password, and create a new message by choosing "Compose" from the tabs along the top of the page. By placing her cursor within the message of the newly created e-mail, Susan can then paste the contents of her custom electronic cover letter in the message box. Simply choose "Paste" from the "edit" pull-down menu or Ctrl+V for Windows, with a Mac you'll choose, copy and paste.

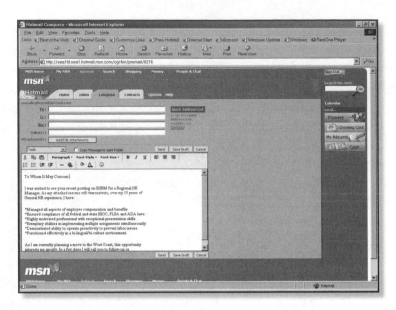

Sending e-mail to employers

With the letter safely pasted in the body of the e-mail, turn your attention to addressing the e-mail to the proper recipient and drafting your subject line. The subject line needs to be factual, professional, yet intriguing: for example, "Your next Reg HR Manager-EEOC, FLSA, & ADA exp" or "EEOC, FLSA, & ADA candidate."

Many people do not realize that the subject line can hold many characters. While a message in your inbox will reveal a maximum of 60 characters, an opened message will show up to 150 characters. To be safe, you should get your headline in the first 30 characters, but do feel free to use all this extra headline space for a subhead; for example,

"Your next Reg HR Manager-EEOC, FLSA, & ADA. 10 years experience in all facets of HR including arbitration, campus and executive recruitment selection, compensation, training, and development." This will only be seen when someone opens the document, but it *will* be seen and noticed. This technique is most effective when you have detailed knowledge of the job and your skills are a good match.

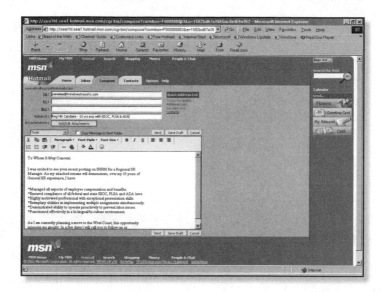

Adding the e-mail address and subject line

It's a smart strategy to keep a copy of all correspondence; in some e-mail programs this is automatic, in others you can do this by selecting that option from virtually any e-mail program. With Hotmail (the example we are using in the illustrations) there is a small box that can be clicked directly above the message box that reads "Copy Message to Sent Folder." This means that a copy of each e-mail you send will be saved in the "sent" folder. This way, you can always refer back to see what was sent, to whom, and when. Additionally, you can always move messages from one folder to another once you have started a communication stream with a particular company, and need to isolate and follow the flow of ongoing communication.

Finally, we need to talk a little about your resume. In Hotmail, under the subject of the new e-mail Susan created, there is a button for "Add/Edit Attachments." In other programs, such as Microsoft Outlook, there is an icon that looks like a paperclip handling the same function; regardless of the program, all the attachment devices work pretty much the same way. Once selected, you will then need to find the document you want to attach. Follow the instructions on the screen. In Hotmail, once you've browsed and found the file you must then select "attach." The name of your file will appear in the attachment box. Continue to follow the instructions and select "OK."

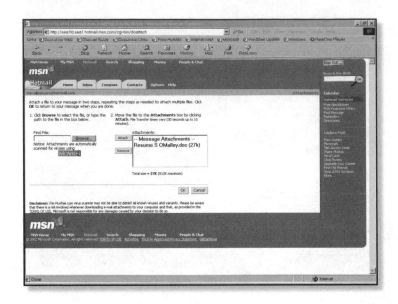

Attaching your resume

Before you send this message, recall two points we addressed earlier when Susan initially found this job posting. First, the employer did not suggest a format in which to send the resume. The most popular is what we have done, but it is not 100 percent effective if the employer does not have Microsoft Word or cannot, for some reason, open the attachment.

Here's a quick solution: Just as you copy and paste your text/ASCII cover letter into the e-mail message box, do the same with your resume. You already have it created—simply go to your "Text Resumes" folder, select the text, copy it, and then return to the e-mail message you just created.

Scroll down through your electronic cover letter. Below your name and contact information insert the word "Resume" (but please not in quotation marks) and then paste in your "Text" saved resume. If the employer has trouble with the attachment, you have sensibly provided a backup solution, which speaks well to your general professional skill sets. Now all that is left to do is hit the "send" button.

Reaching the Right Person

One challenge with the electronic part of your job hunt is to reach human eyes. When the job posting does not list a person's name to contact, you may need to do a little sleuthing to find it. From the contact information, we have an e-mail address and a physical address. Often with company e-mail addresses, the Web site of the company is part of the address that comes after the person's username and the "@" symbol. In this case it is safe to assume that if we break up the e-mail address of *jadariav@gourmetaward.com*, we can probably find the company's home page at *www.gourmetaward.com.*

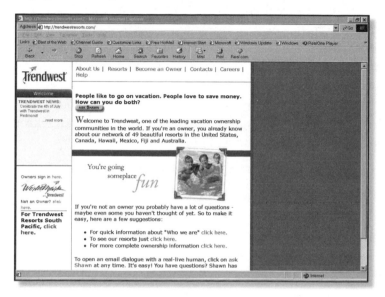

www.gourmetaward.com

Surf the company site and look for a job board, the bios and contacts of company executives, and press releases. Your mission is to find another doorway into this company, perhaps another name to whom you can also send your submission with a slightly different cover letter. With a little extra effort, you could establish a direct connection to your next boss and avoid the corporate resume database altogether. You might also gather other useful information about the company that will help you stand out at the interview.

Electronic Signatures and "Fake" Real Stationery

While most of the free e-mail programs will not support these features, they are available in both Microsoft Outlook and Outlook Express, and in the other deluxe programs. By going to your e-mail program and choosing the "Tools" menu button and then selecting "Options," you will find a box full of many options to customize your e-mail. Under "Options," if you select "Mail Format," you will find both the stationery and signature capabilities.

Although I advise against the use of e-mail stationary or any unusual fonts, I will propose a middle ground on the signature—use the many fonts available in your word processing program. When you receive an e-mail that contains what appears to be a real signature, it makes an impression. However, you should never use your real signature; with the littlest bit of technical expertise, anyone could copy it and electronic signatures can have the same legal validity as a written signature. Don't risk your online security for the sake of style.

Do not think for a moment that you see my signature in the following message. My handwriting has never been that legible, nor would I compromise my identity in this way. It is really just a font, much less effort than scanning in your true signature and risking your credit line.

E-mail with fake signature

Accuracy Is Essential

Maybe your family doesn't mind the jokes with misspelled words, and perhaps your colleagues forgive typos, understanding that you are busy, but this is your career, and you need to put your best professional foot forward. Under "Options" choose "Spelling" as seen on page 89.

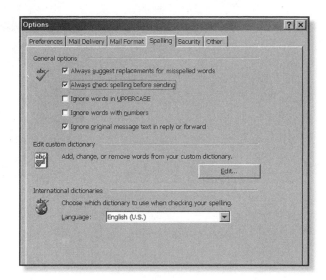

Spell-checking options

Now this is a truly useful little tool. Here you can set your e-mail to check spelling before each and every message is sent. Set this feature to always check before sending, but never forget that automatic spell check is not perfect.

Before you send any online communication, take a deep breath and remember to proof your resumes, cover letters, or any career communication. Practice using your e-mail and send your electronic cover letters and resume attachments to yourself, and friends, family members, and colleagues—make sure that what you think you are sending is received in the way you intended.

You know what it takes to put together a *Knock 'em Dead* cover letter; now it is time to work through all the examples with your highlighter to get a feel for the many different styles that can work for your campaign. Flag the phrases you like and then go to work creating templates for your own *Knock 'em Dead* job search letters.

SAMPLE LETTERS

HERE'S THE REAL meat and potatoes of the book—the sample letters you can use as models for your own.

Now we come to the letters. Apart from the sender's name and address (the personal stationery aspect), all letters adhere to Houghton Mifflin's *Best Writer's Guide* specifications. To those who might notice these things, it is important that we present an impeccable attention to detail.

E-Mail Response to Online Job Posting
(Technical Sales Representative)

From: Joan Carter [jcartersalespro@hotmail.com]
To: mbroome@palmettonetworksecurity.com
Cc:
Subject: Tech sales/key acct/new territory dev/negotiation/customer service

Dear Ms. _____:

Please accept this letter as application for the Technical Sales Representative position currently available with your company, as listed on Monster.com. My confidential resume is attached for your review and consideration, and I believe you will find me well qualified.

Detailed on my resume you will find a solid background in Sales and Marketing, with over two years in technical sales. In this capacity, I have developed an expertise in new and key account acquisition, new territory development and management, contract negotiation, and customer service. I am confident that my experience in these areas will prove to be an asset to ABC Corporation.

Additionally, I am familiar with blueprints, part number breakdowns, and the bidding process of our major accounts, which include _____, _____, _____ and _____ Corp. I have doubled my sales from $40,000/month to $80,000/month in just two years, and I am known for effectively identifying and resolving problems before they affect related areas, personnel, or customers.

I would welcome the opportunity to discuss with you how I might make similar contributions to the success of ABC Corporation. I look forward to hearing from you to schedule a personal interview at your convenience.

Sincere regards,

Joan Carter
(516) 555-1212
jcartersalespro@hotmail.com

E-Mail Response to Online Job Posting (Investment Banker)

From: James Stratton [jsinvest@aol.com]
To: lwilliam@teweles.com
Cc:
Subject: "Can do" administrator

Dear Mr. _____:

In response to your job posting for a _____ on your company's Web site, I have attached my resume for your consideration.

My experience as an administrative investment banker and assistant to a Vice Chairman is, I believe, readily adaptable to your needs. I have spent five years in a position best described as "doing whatever needs to be done" and have capitalized on my ability to undertake a large and widely varied array of projects, learn quickly, find effective solutions to problems, and maintain a sense of humor throughout.

My years as a line and administrative professional have also provided me with an unusual sensitivity to the needs of senior professionals. I have substantial computer experience and am fully computer literate. I have been told my verbal and written communication skills are exceptional.

I believe your firm would provide a working atmosphere to which I would be well suited, as well as one where my diverse experience would be valuable.

My salary requirements are reasonable and negotiable based on the responsibilities and opportunities presented.

Sincerely,

James Stratton
(516) 555-1212
jsinvest@aol.com

E-Mail Response to Online Job Posting (Legal Administrator)

From: Helen Darvik [darviklegalpro@earthlink.net]
To: ggoodfellow@budownoble.com
Cc:
Subject: Administrator/mgmnt/mktg/cmptr/acctg/planning/personnel

Dear Ms. _____:

I am responding to your job posting on Hotjobs.com for a legal administrator of a law firm. I wrote to you on (date) about law administrator positions in the metropolitan _____ area. I have attached another resume of my educational background and employment history. I am very interested in this position.

I have been a legal administrator for two twenty-one-attorney law firms during the past six years. In addition, I have been a law firm consultant for over a year. Besides my law firm experience, I have been a medical administrator for over ten years. I believe that all of this experience will enable me to manage the law firm for this position very successfully. I possess the management, marketing, computer, accounting/budgeting, financial planning, personnel, and people-oriented skills that will have a very positive impact on this law firm.

I will be in the _____ area later in the month, so hopefully, we can meet at that time to discuss this position. I look forward to hearing from you, Ms. _____, concerning this position. Thank you for your time and consideration.

Very truly yours,

Helen Darvik
(516) 555-1212
darviklegalpro@earthlink.net

E-Mail Response to Online Job Posting (Manufacturing)

Shows loyalty, depth of experience in several positions, reliability,
and accomplishments, as well as his well-earned reputation.

From: Murray Danton [manufacturerMD@mindspring.com]
To: resumes@NexPress.com
Cc:
Subject: Warehouse pro committed to productivity

Dear Sir/Madam:

Please accept the attached resume in application for a position with your company that will utilize my extensive background in material handling, shipping, receiving, and warehousing. Throughout my career, I have demonstrated my loyalty, commitment to excellence, and solid work ethic. I am confident that I will make an immediate and long-term contribution to your company.

For the past 26 years, I have been successfully working in manufacturing and warehouse settings. I am a hard-working employee who always looks for ways to improve productivity, efficiency, and accuracy. In past positions, I have identified ways to reduce downtime and waste, as well as methods to increase production.

I am dedicated to the principles of quality, continuous improvement and customer satisfaction. My supervisor has noted my record of "excellent attendance and dependability" and praised me as "reliable and highly motivated."

I would like to meet with you to discuss my qualifications. Please call me at the following phone number, or leave a message, to arrange an interview. Thank you for your consideration.

Sincerely,

Murray Danton
(516) 555-1212
manufacturerMD@mindspring.com

E-Mail Response to Online Job Posting (Production Supervisor)

From: Edwin Pastore [productionpro@yahoo.com]
To: hr@TimesGKielLabs.com
Cc:
Subject: Production Super matches your exact requirements

Dear Ms. _____:

In response to the job posting on your company's Web site, please consider my resume in your search for a Production Supervisor.

With a hi-tech background in *Fortune* 500 companies, I feel well qualified for the position you described. I am presently responsible for the coordination of production in three assembly and test areas which employ 35 union personnel. Maintaining control of work of this magnitude and complexity requires my ability to function independently, and a willingness to make decisions quickly and effectively.

I am accustomed to a fast-paced environment where deadlines are a priority and handling multiple jobs simultaneously is the norm. I enjoy a challenge and work hard to attain my goals. Constant negotiations with all levels of management and union employees have strengthened my interpersonal skills. I would like very much to discuss with you how I could contribute to your organization.

I am seeking an opportunity to excel in a more dynamic company and am looking forward to relocating to the _____ area.

Please contact me at your earliest convenience so that I may share with you my background and enthusiasm for the job. Thank you for your time and consideration.

Sincerely,

Edwin Pastore
(516) 555-1212
productionpro@yahoo.com

Response to Newspaper Advertisement (Health Care Management)

This applicant desires to transition to an administrative position in the field of health care; thus we highlighted her leadership and administrative skills.

REBA WOODWARD

9999 Oracal Ave. • Sunny, Texas 79000
(999) 999-9999 (H) • (999) 777-7777 (C)
r w o o d 5 8 6 @ h o t m a i l . c o m

February 15, 20–

Human Resources Coordinator
Sunny Home Nursing Service
9999 Hospital Ave.
Sunny, Texas 79000

We make a living by what we get,
but we make a life by what we give.
—Winston Churchill

Re: ADMINISTRATOR OF HEALTH CARE SERVICES

Dear Human Resources Coordinator:

Your recent classified ad in the *City-Wide Journal* caught my eye. As an experienced registered nurse, I am currently investigating career opportunities in the field of management in the health care industry where my highly developed skills will nicely transcend. The enclosed résumé reflects an exceptionally viable candidate for the above-named position.

I am a well-established native of this area with a background as program director, school nurse, operating room circulator, and charge nurse in clinic, ER, OR, and hospital floor environments. The following skills and characteristics are reason to take a closer look at my credentials. I am:

- **strong in handling multiple tasks and multifaceted situations while maintaining satisfactory interpersonal relationships with staff, physicians, patients, students, and families.**
- **an expert at ensuring compliance with regulations while keeping costs within budget.**
- **talented in prioritizing issues and tasks and visualizing the "big" picture when considering the long-term effects of my decisions.**
- **an outcome-oriented self-starter with superior organizational and administrative skills.**

After reviewing my résumé, you will discover that my qualifications are a good match for this position. The opportunity for a personal interview to further discuss employment possibilities would be mutually beneficial. You may reach me at (999) 999-9999 to schedule an appointment at your convenience. In the meantime, thank you for your time and consideration.

Sincerely,

Reba Woodward

Reba Woodward

Enclosure: Résumé

Response to Newspaper Advertisement (Adjunct Faculty Position)

A speech therapist in a local school district, this candidate is looking for
an adjunct faculty position with a community college.

Harriette L. Christophorous

585-398-6194   27 Crystal Valley Overlook   harrichris@aol.com
                            Batavia, New York 14020

January 12, 20–

Ms. Alexandra Kinkead
Director of Human Resources
Monroe Community College
1000 East Henrietta Road
Rochester, New York 14623

Dear Ms. Kinkead:

Your recent advertisement for adjunct faculty positions has captured my serious interest. I am confident that my 25 years' experience as a Speech Therapist in the Batavia Central School provides me with the capabilities to fulfill the **Voice & Articulation** position mentioned in the ad. Accordingly, I have enclosed a résumé that briefly outlines my professional history.

Some key points you may find relevant to this opportunity include:

✓ *Experience assessing needs of and providing instruction to the disabled. In my current position, I work one-on-one with students having hearing loss, emotional disorders, ADHD, autism, and other physical disabilities impacting their ability to acquire speech. I also develop IEPs and participate in the CSE process to define students' needs and implement instruction plans.*

✓ *Excellent leadership skills, with experience mentoring co-workers. Currently, I mentor speech therapists and teachers working with hearing-impaired students, as well as direct the activities of two other speech therapists.*

✓ *A master's degree in Speech Pathology, plus NYS Certification as a Speech & Hearing Handicapped Teacher. In addition, I have attended workshops in Phonemic Awareness, Autism, and Pervasive Developmental Disorders.*

In my current role, I am accountable for addressing the needs of approximately 300 elementary and secondary school students with various speech deficiencies. I believe that my knowledge and expertise would allow me to effectively serve your students in this Voice & Articulation instructional role. I would enjoy speaking with you in person to discuss in fuller detail how my qualifications can fulfill your needs. Please contact me via phone or e-mail to arrange a mutually convenient date and time for us to meet.

Thank you for your time and consideration. I look forward to talking with you soon.

Sincerely,

Harriette L. Christophorous

Harriette L. Christophorous

Enclosure

Response to Newspaper Advertisement (Hydrogeologist)

Applying for positions in a newly emerging scientific discipline; her resume requires a heavy emphasis on educational background information.

Aileen Renfro
545 Appleton Street ▪ Houston, TX 77068
(713) 888-9900 ▪ aileenrenfro@msw.com

June 30, 20–

Human Resources Department
CRPH
155 Garner Avenue, Suite 1000
Los Angeles, CA 95496

RE: Position of Hydrogeologist/Groundwater Modeler, Company Job ID: ACHZ4121-234059, AJB Reference Number: 4950495, Job ID #0000BZ/BBBB

Dear Human Resources Representative:

I learned about your position description for a Hydrogeologist/Groundwater Modeler with great interest, as my qualifications match your requirements for this position. Therefore, please accept my resume for your review and allow me to explain briefly how I can contribute to the future success of CRPH.

With an MS Degree in Hydrologic Sciences and over 7 years of research experience, I have developed a strong background in advanced theories of solute transport modeling; consequently, I have developed effective quantitative skills and a practical understanding of the fundamental principles and concepts associated with hydrogeology.

My resume will provide additional details regarding my educational background and professional experience. Beyond these qualifications, it may be helpful for you to know that I have worked successfully in both independent and team project environments, adapt readily to rapidly changing work conditions, and enjoy the prospect of contributing to CRPH's "80-year reputation as a water industry leader" in the advancement of hydrogeologic and groundwater projects.

I would welcome the opportunity to interview for this position and discuss the results you can expect from me as a member of your team. Thank you for your time and consideration.

Sincerely,

Aileen Renfro

Aileen Renfro

Enclosure

Response to Newspaper Advertisement
(Customer Service Representative)

An ad response with requested salary history.

Cassidy Stratton

444 Marks Street • Brentwood, NY 11717 • (631) 435-1879 • cassidy123@custsrv.net

---

February 4, 20–

Mr. Josh Williams
Personnel Director
LI Financial Group
777 Alexander Road
Huntington Station, NY 11746

Dear Mr. Williams:

In response to your open position announcement in *Newsday* for a customer service representative, I am forwarding my resume for your review and consideration. Ideally, this position will make optimal use of my experience working in capacities that require strong interpersonal communication and customer needs assessment skills, an ability to interface effectively with internal/external contacts, and a skill for ensuring the accurate, timely processing of electronic, verbal, and written information.

Since 1994, I have held longstanding positions of increased responsibility for leading financial services organizations, in charge of tracking, monitoring, reviewing, and processing of account and market-related data. In these positions, I have proved and continue to prove myself as a capable, take-charge team player with an ability to coordinate diversified departmental and customer support functions. Combined with my ability to proficiently manage and train others on the complexities of comprehensive databases and improve workflow efficiencies, I am confident that I would be an asset to your customer service organization.

I would welcome the opportunity to meet with you for an in-depth interview. Thank you for your review and consideration. I look forward to hearing from you soon.

Sincerely,

Cassidy Stratton

Cassidy Stratton

Salary Requirement:
$36,000 – $44,000

Salary History:
LI Financial Group. Starting $29,000; Ending $40,000
Credit Checkers: Starting $20,000; Ending $26,000

Response to Newspaper Advertisement (Sales Associate)

An entry-level cover letter to convince the employer that he can tackle a full-time job even though he is still in school.

MARC LOMBARDI

September 3, 20–

Mr. John Relka
Sales Manager
A-Jay Sports Outfitters
226 First Avenue
Ocean City, NJ 99999

Re: Sales Associate Position

Dear Mr. Relka:

If you are searching for a success-driven Sales Associate who is a hard worker and an innovator, look no further. Highlights of my achievements include the following:

- Awarded with three plaques and nominated to President's Club for exemplary sales performance.
- Started a business from scratch and grew customer base using multiple marketing methods.
- Earned most of my own college expenses for the last four years.

Although I will not graduate until December, I am eager to start work as soon as possible—either full- or part-time. I am certain that I can balance the responsibilities of a Sales Associate position with my studies, because I have successfully handled full-time employment with a full course load in the past.

My résumé is enclosed for your consideration. I believe that I can make a positive contribution to A-Jay Sports Outfitters and look forward to discussing my qualifications in detail.

I will call you next week to arrange for a meeting at a mutually convenient time. Thank you for your consideration.

Sincerely,

Marc Lombardi

Marc Lombardi

Enclosure

111 Park Place • Ocean City, NJ 99999 • (555) 555-5555 • mlombardi@dotresume.com

Response to Newspaper Advertisement (Medical Biller)

Emphasizes people skills, which are as important as
technical abilities in a busy medical office.

Doreen Canfield
703 West Pike Street
Valley Forge, PA 00000
(555) 555-5555
doreen&george@dotcom.com

February 27, 20–

Healthcare Associates
P.O. Box 000
Philadelphia, PA 00000

Dear Hiring Manager:

I am very interested in the medical biller position you advertised in Sunday's *Inquirer* and believe I have the qualifications to successfully fulfill your requirements.

As you review my enclosed resume, you will see that I have a solid administrative background, combined with intensive training in medical billing policies and procedures received at Franklin Institute for Allied Health Professionals. My coursework heavily emphasized the international classification of diseases (ICD-9) and complex CPT coding for insurance purposes, and also included instruction in standard billing procedures to produce invoices or superbills within the office, utilization of outside billing services, and electronic billing.

From my prior experience, I had many occasions when I had to deal with confused and difficult clients, not unlike the patients at a doctor's office who do not understand the provisions of their healthcare plans. With my personable manner of interaction and skill in tactfully communicating or clarifying information, I was able to quickly resolve disagreements, answer questions, and retain their confidence. I am equally comfortable in close working relationships with physicians and other professional staff, learning quickly, and adapting easily to any office environment.

I feel confident that I could be a valuable asset to your practice and look forward to an interview to discuss how I may be able to contribute to your profitability and efficiency. May I hear from you soon?

Sincerely,

Doreen Canfield

Doreen Canfield

Enclosure: Resume

Response to Newspaper Advertisement (Skilled Laborer)

This cover letter had to overcome an obvious "overqualification" barrier.

JACK LEVAN
1121 MAILER AVENUE ◆ KNOXVILLE, TENNESSEE 37901 ◆ JLEVAN555@YAHOO.COM ◆ 865.555.5555

Tuesday, 11 November, 20–

Mr. Drake Norris
Lockheed Martin Corporation
1122 Cortland Avenue
Suite 210
Miami, Florida 33101

Dear Mr. Norris:

When I saw your announcement for a skilled laborer at Cudjoe Key, I made writing this letter my first priority. Of course, I've already applied online. But, the more I thought about this opportunity, the more it seemed a perfect match for both of us. And so I wanted you to have a good deal more than the usual, impersonal, application.

I think you deserve to see the contributions I can make to the Lockheed Martin team at once. That's why you'll find my résumé different from others you may have run across. In place of the usual "objective statement," you'll read about four productivity-building capabilities I can bring to the job. And, right below them, are seven examples of the kinds of contributions I've made to my employers.

But I am concerned that you may think I am "overqualified." To put that in plain language, you may feel I will be bored by the job. In fact, your position fits in nicely with my goal of getting my degree in Aerospace Engineering. I can't think of a better opportunity to see the OT&E process at work than being "in the trenches" on a project like yours.

I do best when I can learn about my employer's special needs. May I call in a few days to explore how I might fit best onto your team?

Sincerely,

Jack Levan

Jack Levan

Encl.: Résumé

Response to Newspaper Advertisement (Peace Officer)

As a recent graduate, his education section needed to come first
and have the primary focus; however, he also wanted to emphasize
his experience as a trainer and team leader.

JAMES BURLINGTON
9803 Clinton Avenue
Lubbock, TX 79424

(806) 783-9900
jamesb@door.net

September 13, 20–

Lubbock Police Department
320 9th Street
Lubbock, TX 79416

Dear Hiring Representative:

I am submitting my résumé in application for the position of Peace Officer. I have recently completed necessary educational requirements, and I am enthusiastic about the possibility of interviewing for this position.

My studies at Texas Tech University provided me the opportunity to study and analyze key concepts, principles, and practices associated with human behavior and criminal justice. Subsequently, I demonstrated in-depth knowledge of law enforcement and social science issues through excellent work on class assignments and projects. Of course, I realize that there is a significant difference between academic studies and practical field experience, but I am confident that my strong knowledge in criminal justice will increase my ability to perform effectively within your department.

Additionally, I earned recognition from my managers in my employment positions for my leadership and organizational skills. As a Certified Trainer at Orlando's, I trained a staff of eight bussers and contributed to improved team performance by building great relationships with team members and guests. As a Garden Shop Associate at Sutherland's, I organized the garden area in such a way that made it easy for both employees and customers to find items readily. The additional skills I gained from these positions could transfer readily to your department, as well.

My résumé is enclosed to provide you with additional details concerning my background and achievements. Thank you for your time and consideration.

Sincerely,

James Burlington

James Burlington

Enclosure

Response to Newspaper Advertisement (Assessment Coordinator)

Anna M. Sanchez

123 FORT AVENUE • HUNTINGTON, NY 12752 • (631) 555-2222 • CELLULAR (631) 555-3333

2 PAGES VIA FAX   June 11, 20–
DEPT. HD 212-555-9999

Your advertisement in the *New York Times*, on June 9, 20–, for an **Assessment Coordinator** seems to perfectly match my background and experience. As the International Brand Coordinator for Kahlúa, I coordinated meetings, prepared presentations and materials, organized a major off-site conference, and supervised an assistant. I believe that I am an excellent candidate for this position as I have illustrated below:

YOUR REQUIREMENTS	MY QUALIFICATIONS
A highly motivated, diplomatic, flexible, quality-driven professional on every project.	Successfully managed project teams involving different business units. The defined end results were achieved.
Exceptional organizational skills and attention to detail	Planned the development and launch of the Kahlúa Heritage Edition bottle series. My former manager enjoyed leaving the "details" and follow-through to me. Coverdale project management training.
College degree and minimum 3 years relevant business experience	B.A. from Vassar College. 5+ years business experience in productive, professional environments.
Computer literacy	Extensive knowledge of Windows & Macintosh applications.

I'm interested in this position because it fits well with my new career focus in the human resources field. Currently, I am enrolled in NYU's adult career planning and development certificate program and working at Lee Hecht Harrison.

I have enclosed my resume to provide more information on my strengths and career achievements. If after reviewing my material you believe that there is a match, please call me. Thank you for your consideration.

Sincere regards,

Anna M. Sanchez

Anna M. Sanchez

AS
enclosure

Response to Newspaper Advertisement (Office Administrator)

Mark Stevenson

May 5, 20–
Philip _____
(title)
ABC Firm
1 Industry Plaza
Lansing, MI 48180

Dear Mr. _____:

Your notice for an **Office Administrator** caught my attention because my background appears to parallel your needs. Please refer to the enclosed resume for a summary of my qualifications. I am sure you have been flooded with hundreds of qualified applicants; please allow me to explain why you would want to call me first.

I am very **self sufficient** and able to **work independently with little supervision**. With little formal training, I have taken the initiative to learn about and remain current with my company's products, processes, and expectations. I am looked at as **an information resource** and enjoy sharing my knowledge with others. I also enjoy **managing projects** and **planning meetings, trips, and special events**.

I am always looking for ways to **streamline processes** and become more efficient. I have **developed systems and processes** using available software to automate production reporting, notify customers of changes, and inform the field staff of corporate changes or initiatives. When supervising clerical staff, I always try to **plan ahead** to make the best use of their time.

I **work well with executives, sales representatives, customers, vendors, *and* coworkers, and demonstrate strong interpersonal communication and good judgment**. I always try to listen closely and understand what others need. Then, I look for ways to help solve the problem. I have particularly found that listening, without interrupting, can diffuse a tense situation and allow the issue to be resolved more quickly with a positive outcome.

I am confident that I can deliver similar results for ABC Firm. I would appreciate the opportunity to speak with you to schedule an appointment and provide you with more information. Thank you for your time and consideration; I look forward to speaking with you soon.

Sincerely,

Mark Stevenson

Mark Stevenson
MS
enclosure

200 Westwood Drive • Trenton, MI 48183 • (313) 555-9020 • officeadministrator@hotmail.com

Response to Newspaper Advertisement (Legal Secretary)

Marianne Johnston

293 Hunter's Pointe / Berea, Ohio 44110
216-248-1699 / 440-737-1725 (Cellular)
legalsecretary@earthlink.com

(Date)

Emily _____
(Title)
ABC Bar Association
1 Industry Plaza
Columbus, OH 44119

RE: OBA OFFICE OF BAR COUNSEL LEGAL SECRETARY

Dear Ms. _____:

It is with continued interest and enthusiasm that I respond to your advertisement for Legal Secretary to the ABC Bar Association's Office of Bar Counsel. I believe that my education and experience combine to create a perfect match for the position, and would appreciate careful consideration of my credentials as presented below and within my resume, enclosed.

It has long been my dream to pursue a career in the legal arena, and my goal to associate with the top professionals in the field. Where better to continue my professional development than within the heart of the organization as a provider of administrative support to members of the Ohio Bar Association itself!

Although a relative newcomer to the field, I have earned my degree in Paralegal Studies, graduating in 20– with Magna Cum Laude distinction. With more than two years of experience after graduation providing administrative and clerical support in private practice, I am confident that I possess the expertise and dedication that will make an immediate and significant contribution to the efficiency and organization of the Office of Bar Counsel.

If you are looking for a legal support professional who is committed to the highest standards of performance, relates well with others, is self-directing and highly motivated, and is looking for a long-term employment relationship, please contact me to arrange an interview. I will make myself available at your first convenience.

Thank you for your consideration; I will look forward to the opportunity to speak with you soon.

Sincerely yours,

Marianne Johnston

Marianne Johnston

MJ
enclosure (Resume and Professional References)

Response to Newspaper Advertisement (Accounting Manager)

Paul Anthony

516.555.4844   169 Laure Road   accountingpro@bellsouth.net
Hunt Town, New York 11553

(Date)

Phillip _____
(Title)
ABC Corporation
1 Industry Plaza
Long Island, NY 11551

Dear Mr. _____:

Re: File No. 213

I have six years of accounting experience and am responding to your recent advertisement for an Accounting Manager. Please allow me to highlight my skills as they relate to your stated requirements.

Your Requirements	My Experience
• A recognized accounting degree plus several years of practical experience	• Obtained a C.A. degree in 20– and have over three years' experience as an Accounting Manager.
• Excellent people skills and demonstrated ability to motivate staff	• Effectively managed a staff of 24 including two supervisors.
• Strong administrative and analytical skills.	• Assisted in the development of a base reference library with Microsoft Excel for 400 clients.
• Good oral and written communication skills	• Trained four new supervisors via daily coaching sessions, communication meetings, and technical skill sessions.

I believe this background provides the management skills you require for this position. I would welcome the opportunity for a personal interview to further discuss my qualifications.

Yours truly,

Paul Anthony

Paul Anthony

PA
enclosure

Response to Newspaper Advertisement (International Sales Manager)

Suzanne A. Kennedy
2490 Sierra Ridge Overlook
Colorado Springs, Colorado 80922
719-265-1109

(Date)

Phillip _____
(Title)
ABC Corporation
1 Industry Plaza
Denver, CO 80911

Dear Mr. _____:

Re: International Sales Manager, *Globe & Mail*, September –, 20–

I was recently speaking with Mr. _____ from your firm and he strongly recommended that I send you a copy of my resume. Knowing the requirements for the position, he felt that I would be an ideal candidate. For more than eleven years, I have been involved in international sales management, with seven years directly in the aerospace industry. My qualifications for the position include:

- establishing sales offices in France, Great Britain and Germany;
- recruiting and managing a group of 24 international sales representatives;
- providing training programs for all of the European staff, which included full briefing on our own products as well as competitor lines;
- obtaining 42%, 33% and 31% of the French, German, and British markets, respectively, dealing with all local engine and airframe manufacturers; and
- generating more than $32 million in sales with excellent margins.

My Bachelor of Science degree in electrical engineering was obtained from the University of _____ and my languages include French and German.

I feel confident that an interview would demonstrate that my expertise in setting up rep organizations and training and managing an international sales department would be an excellent addition to your growing aerospace corporation.

I look forward to meeting with you, Mr. _____, and will give you a call to follow up on this letter the week of (date) _____.

Yours truly,

Suzanne A. Kennedy

Suzanne A. Kennedy

SK
enclosure

Response to Newspaper Advertisement (Executive Assistant)

Andrew F. Petersen

387 ROCKINGHAM PLACE • ROCHESTER, NEW YORK 14613

585-287-6981 • EXECUTIVEASSISTANT@LOCALNET.COM

(Date)

Box 9412
New York, NY 01234

Dear _____:

I was very pleased to learn of the need for an Executive Assistant in your company from your recent advertisement in _____. I believe the qualities you seek are well matched by my track record:

Your Needs	My Qualifications
Independent Self-Starter	• Served as company liaison between sales representatives, controlling commissions and products.
	• Controlled cash flow, budget planning, and bank reconciliation for three companies.
	• Assisted in the promotion of a restaurant within a private placement sales effort, creating sales materials and communicating with investors.
Computer Experience	• Utilized Lotus in preparing financial spreadsheet used in private placement memoranda and Macintosh to design brochures and flyers.
	• Have vast experience with both computer programming and the current software packages.
Compatible Background	• Spent 5 years overseas and speak French.
	• Served as an executive assistant to four corporate heads.

A resume is enclosed that covers my experience and qualifications in greater detail. I would appreciate the opportunity to discuss my credentials in a personal interview.

Sincerely,

Andrew Petersen

Andrew Petersen

AP
enclosure

POWER PHRASES

Consider using adaptations of these key phrases in your responses to newspaper advertisements.

I believe that I am particularly well qualified for your position and would like to have the opportunity to meet with you to explore how I may be of value to your organization.

Your advertisement #5188 in the March 25th edition of The _____ *has piqued my interest. This position has strong appeal to me.*

I am confident that with my abilities I can make an immediate and valuable contribution to _____.

I would be pleased if you contacted me for an interview.

I was recently speaking with Mr. _____ from your firm and he strongly recommended that I send you a copy of my resume. Knowing the requirements for the position, he felt that I would be an ideal candidate.

I've had both large and small company experience and it is my preference to work in a smaller operation where goals are measurable, results are noticeable, and contributions really make a difference!

I feel confident that an interview would demonstrate that my expertise in setting up rep organizations, and training and managing an international sales department, would be an excellent addition to your growing _____ company.

I look forward to meeting with you, Mr. _____, and will give you a call to follow up on this letter the week of September 25th.

The opportunity to work with your client is appealing to me, and I would appreciate an opportunity to discuss the position further. I look forward to hearing from you soon.

I believe this background provides the management skills you require for this position. I would welcome the opportunity for a personal interview to further discuss my qualifications.

In response to your ad, please consider my resume in your search for a Sales Service Coordinator.

I look forward to hearing from you in the near future to schedule an interview at your convenience, during which I hope to learn more about your company's plans and goals and how I might contribute to the success of its service team.

I am accustomed to a fast-paced environment where deadlines are priority and handling multiple jobs simultaneously is the norm. I enjoy a challenge and work hard to attain my goals. Constant negotiations with all levels of management and union employees have strengthened my interpersonal skills. I would like very much to discuss with you how I could contribute to your organization.

I am seeking an opportunity to excel in a dynamic company and am looking forward to relocating to _____.

Please contact me at your earliest convenience so that I may share with you my background and enthusiasm for the job.

Your ad captured my attention.

My personal goal is simple: I wish to be a part of an organization that wants to excel in both _____ and _____. I believe that if I had the opportunity to interview with you it would be apparent that my skills are far-reaching.

Although I'm far more interested in a fine company and an intriguing challenge than merely in money, you should know that in recent years my compensation has been in the range of $45,000 to $60,000.

May we set up a time to talk?

What you need and what I can do sound like a match!

Please find enclosed a copy of my resume for your review. I believe the combination of my _____ education and my business experience offers me the unique opportunity to make a positive contribution to your firm.

As you will note in my resume I have not only "grown up" in and with the Operations and Warehousing area of a major (apparel) (consumer products) company,

I have also established my expertise and my value to a discriminating and brilliant employer who depended upon me—on a daily basis—to represent and protect his interests and contribute significantly to his profitability.... I am seeking an opportunity to replicate this situation and again utilize my considerable abilities to dedicate myself to the profitability of my employer.

I am available to meet with you to discuss my qualifications at your convenience. I can be reached at _____. I would like to thank you in advance for your time and any consideration you may give me. I look forward to hearing from you.

Having been born and raised in the _____ area and wishing to return to this area to work as a _____, I have been researching _____ firms that offer the type of experience for which my previous education and work experience will be of mutual benefit. Highlights of my attached resume include: _____.

Please consider my qualifications for the position of _____ which you advertised.

As you will note on the enclosed resume, the breadth of my expertise covers a wide area of responsibilities, thereby providing me with insights into the total operation.

Recently, I saw an advertisement in the _____ for a position as a Technical Trainer. My candidacy for this position is advanced by my experience in three areas: training, support, and a technological background.

I thrive on challenge and feel that my skills and experience are easily transferable.

I would appreciate an opportunity to discuss my abilities in more depth, and am available for an interview at your earliest convenience.

Is the ideal candidate for the position of _____ highly motivated, professional, and knowledgeable in all functions concerning _____? Well, you may be interested to know that a person possessing these qualities, and much more, is responding to your ad in the _____ for this position.

I very much enjoy working in a team environment and the rewards associated with group contribution.

The skills you require seem to match my professional strengths.

I have a strong background in telemarketing small and medium-sized businesses in the _____ District and outlying areas.

I look forward to hearing from you soon to set up an appointment at your convenience. Please feel free to give me a call at my office at _____ or leave a message at my home number, _____.

As a recent MBA graduate, my professional job experience is necessarily limited. However, I believe that you will find, and previous employers will verify, that I exhibit intelligence, common sense, initiative, maturity, and stability, and I am eager to make a positive contribution to your organization.

I read, with a great deal of interest, your advertisement in the October 20, _____, issue of _____.

Please allow me to highlight some of my achievements which relate to your requirements: _____.

I would greatly appreciate the opportunity to discuss this position in a personal interview. I may be contacted at _____ to arrange a meeting.

I would appreciate an opportunity to meet with you. At present I am working as a temp but am available to meet with you at your convenience. I look forward to meeting you.

Thank you for taking the time recently to respond to my questions concerning a _____ position with _____.

I will be in your area Friday, December 5th, and will call you early next week to see if we might schedule a meeting at that time.

This experience has provided me with a keen appreciation for the general practice of _____.

A salary of $30,000 would be acceptable; however, my main concern is to find employment where there is potential for growth.

"Cold" Cover Letter to a Potential Employer (Entry-Level Network Admin.)

Network administrator seeking entry-level opportunity; highlights his certifications to emphasize recent professional development. Good idea when attempting ground-floor position.

ANDREW J. STELLS

P. O. Box 2146 ◆ Buffalo, New York 27893 ◆ (505) 554-9021 ◆ ajs@hotmail.com

Dear Sir or Madam:

I have received my **MCP Certification**, and I am currently working on my **A++ Network Certification**. I am seeking an opportunity that will enable me to utilize my training and hands-on technical exposure within an **entry-level Network Administrator** position. A brief highlight of the skills and values I would bring to your organization include:

- Knowledge of installation, configuration, troubleshooting and repair of sophisticated, state-of-the-art software and hardware developed through recent computer operations training.

- Analytical, research, troubleshooting, interpersonal and organizational skills developed through on-the-job training within an IT environment.

- Proven success in prioritizing time, completing projects and meeting deadlines under time-sensitive circumstances, achieving stellar results.

- An energetic, enthusiastic, and "people-driven" communication style.

Since a résumé can neither fully detail all my skills and accomplishments, nor predict my potential to your organization, I would welcome a personal interview to further explore the merging of my training and knowledge with your **IT** needs.

Very truly yours,

ANDREW J. STELLS

Enclosure

"Cold" Cover Letter to a Potential Employer (Entry-Level Librarian)

Helena, who emigrated from Poland, has completed her master's in library science and is looking for her first full-time position in her career field.

Helena Swenka

(410) 997-5555	555 Chestnut Street Columbia, MD 21044	helenaswen@nsn.com

---

November 15, 20–

Mr. Jeffery Devine, Library Division Director
Columbia Public Library
2774 Swan Point Road
Columbia, MD 21046

Dear Mr. Devine,

Does your library anticipate the need for an **Entry-Level Research or Reference Librarian or Cataloguer?** With my recent MLIS degree from an ALA-accredited program, as well as internship experience in the reference department of academic and state government libraries, perhaps I can be of service.

My résumé is enclosed for your review. You will find evidence of my librarianship training, library database and computer skills, and work history. What you will not immediately see on my résumé are my character traits and achievements—allow me to list some of them for you that I believe are relevant:

✓ *Hard-working, determined achiever – I set my sights high, whether attaining a **3.95 GPA** at University of Maryland in a demanding **MLIS Degree** program, empowering foreign nationals to achieve their goals of US citizenship by teaching them English and Civics (pass rate of 100% over 8-year period with more than 2,000 individuals), or responding to reference requests with a high-level of customer service and promptness (within 1–3 hours).*

✓ *Information technology savvy and fast learner – My references will attest to how quickly I assimilated knowledge of library databases, computer software, and integrated library automation systems. With hands-on experience using **Voyager Module, AACR2r, LC classification scheme, MARC format, and OCLC,** as well as Lexis-Nexis, Dow-Jones, Dialog Web and Classic, I have worked with diverse reference materials such as legal, Maryland State and Federal, genealogy documents, as well as periodicals.*

✓ *Proactive problem-solver and team player – Utilizing my broad foreign language skills (Polish, Russian, Slovak, German, Latin) allowed me to problem-solve with confidence and correctly catalog foreign language materials while serving a **reference library internship** with **The Baltimore County Library.** As an **intern cataloger,** I worked cooperatively with others in serial publication cataloguing and serial control, achieving high rates of daily production.*

Providing high-level customer service and efficiency is my goal in library services and support. My knowledge and practical use of Internet resources and navigational tools, combined with my experience with library databases, affords you the opportunity to hire an entry-level library professional with proven librarianship success. May we meet soon to discuss your needs? I will call your office next week to schedule a mutually convenient appointment, if that is agreeable with you. Thank you for your time and consideration.

Sincerely,

Helena Swenka

Helena Swenka

Enclosure

"Cold" Cover Letter to a Potential Employer (Manager)

Concerned that his company is not doing well financially, William has decided to "test the waters" for another position similar to those he has done in the past.

WILLIAM C. KITE
7271 Foxhill Drive
Livingston, NJ 07039

(973) 740-5555
Wmckite@hotmail.com

December 12, 20–

Mr. Jacob Abernathy
Warehouse and Assembly Services
17 Industrial Way
Livingston, NJ 07039

Dear Mr. Abernathy,

More than ever, good companies need proven performers who can get results in competitive industries and a tough economy, whether working independently or leading teams. If you are in need of a Warehouse Manager, Inventory Control Specialist, Production Manager, or Assembly Order Fulfillment Supervisor, consider my track record:

✓ Efficiently scheduled assembly, material handlers, and warehouse personnel, and closely monitored interplant transfers of raw materials from 20 warehouses. Assembly production and distribution procedures yielded high levels of productivity: 90% on-time delivery, including emergency orders, of up to $1 million in SKUs per week. (Expediter/ Production Dept. Scheduler, Mony-Schaffer Corp.)

✓ Developed cooperative relationships with field sales reps of major corporations, such as PricewaterhouseCoopers, U.S. Healthcare, and UPS, and served as liaison with in-house account executives and customer service reps at The Hibbert Group, to streamline receiving and shipping operations and upgrade quality control. (Warehouse Manager, The Devaney Group)

✓ As final assembly and inspection member of 4-person team, met heavy production schedule (35 to 60 complex, fabricated units per day) with 6% or less error rate. (Order Fulfillment Clerk, Mony-Schaffer)

✓ Working as part of a team, created, tested, packaged, and directed to shipping custom ship sets of complex hose assemblies, meeting deadlines 99-plus percent of the time. Utilized quality assurance testing methods, including pressure testing of assembled units, to ensure highest level of customer satisfaction. (Hose Fabrication Technician, Mony-Schaffer Corp.)

I am confident I can deliver similar results for your company.

With well-rounded experience in assembly, expediting and scheduling, shipping and receiving, order fulfillment, customer service, sales, supervision and training, and a 15-year track record of meeting deadlines in demanding (even emergency) situations, I believe I have the proven skills that can benefit your company.

Page 1 of 2

116

In addition, I realize it is hard-working and cooperative people who deliver results. My focus on teamwork and productivity has proven successful in my past assignments. I am confident I can convince you that I have the technical experience and knowledge that you need, as well as the intangible qualifies—enthusiasm, strong work ethic, dedication and dependability—to get the job done right.

May we meet soon to discuss your needs? I will contact your office next week to schedule a mutually convenient appointment, if that is agreeable with you. Thank you for your consideration.

Sincerely,

William C. Kite
Enclosure

"Cold" Cover Letter to a Potential Employer (Mental Health)

An applicant with a MSW seeking to advance his career.

Dear Sir or Madam:

Throughout my career, I have held increasingly complex positions within the Mental Health Care industry, gaining extensive experience in working both with patients and in administrative functions. My particular areas of expertise are:

- Physical Medicine and Rehabilitation
- Adult Intervention
- Family Counseling
- Legal Issues
- Government Regulations
- Child Evaluation

My greatest strength lies in my ability to communicate with all types of people and different levels of professionals. Being able to work with patients, physicians, legal officers, and family members has enabled me to be a highly effective therapist and an advocate for the patient and the patient's family. As a Veteran's Administration official, I have been inducted into the intricacies of the federal government and have been able to gain a thorough understanding of the workings of various government agencies as they relate to mental health, including the Social Security Administration, Department of Veteran's Affairs, Department of Defense, and other entities.

I feel my knowledge and strengths would be best applied as a consultant or private Mental Rehabilitation Therapist. Further, I desire to return to a more focused health care organization such as yours and would welcome an opportunity to interview with you in person.

I look forward to speaking with you at your earliest convenience and appreciate your time in reviewing my credentials and qualifications. I am confident that my professional knowledge and strengths, combined with my dedication, work ethic, and energy, will add measurable value to your organization. Thank you for your consideration.

Sincerely,

Peter A. Edgewaters
PETER A. EDGEWATERS

Enclosure

....
40 Land Avenue • Plain, New Jersey 05050 • (555) 555-5555 • xxxxxxxxx@msn.com

"Cold" Cover Letter to a Potential Employer
(Senior Customer Service Specialist)

This candidate's most impressive qualifications are summarized in an eye-catching bulleted list.

Maria H. Berretta
111 Creamery Road
Skippack, PA 99999
Home: (555) 555-5555
Cell: (999) 999-9999
berretta@dotresume.com

March 3, 20–

Ms. Jayne Longnecker
Customer Service Manager
Whittier Insurance Company
111 State Road
Blue Bell, PA 99999

Re: Senior Customer Service Specialist

Dear Ms. Longnecker:

Are you looking for a Senior Customer Service Specialist who is:

- A consistent top performer with a strong desire to get the job done.
- A team player, able to achieve results through coordination with employees in all functional areas.
- An effective communicator with excellent writing, training, and telephone skills.
- Able to learn quickly, analyze complex information, and find solutions to problems.
- Organized, thorough, and precise.

If so, you will be interested in my qualifications. I have a bachelor's degree in business administration and seven years of experience in the insurance/financial industry, serving in diverse roles as customer relations advisor and calculations processor. For more than a year and a half, I have consistently received the highest ratings in my unit despite the fact that the difficult cases frequently find their way to my desk. I have also contributed to my team by putting in extra time to clear backlogs and analyzing existing procedures to devise more efficient methods of operation.

My résumé is enclosed for your review. I believe that I can make a positive contribution to Whittier Insurance Company and look forward to meeting with you to discuss my qualifications in detail. Thank you for your time and consideration.

Sincerely,

Maria G. Berretta

Maria H. Berretta

Enclosure

"Cold" Cover Letter to a Potential Employer (Research Professional)

Darrin is a data specialist working for the state, compiling birth/death and census statistics. He wants to enter the private sector to do more consumer/product research projects.

Darrin Wilson

MARKET RESEARCH ANALYST

Dear Sir/Madam:

As a research professional, I understand that success depends on a strong commitment to **customer satisfaction**. Executing the basics and using logic and reasoning to identify the strengths and weaknesses of alternative solutions, conclusions or approaches to problems are key to increasing performance and market share. I believe that my background and education reflect a commitment and ability to find solutions to these challenges. I developed excellent skills in **project coordination and the design and development of research projects** that increased the effectiveness of my organization.

I am considered an energetic, aggressive, and innovative leader who is extremely client-oriented.

My position encompasses multiple tasks and responsibilities that include:

◆ Examining and analyzing statistical data to forecast future trends and to identify potential markets.

◆ Designing and implementing new formats for logging and transferring information while working as part of a team researching data and statistics.

Thank you for your consideration. I approach my work with a strong sense of urgency, working well under pressure and change. I look forward to meeting with you personally so that we may discuss how I may make a positive contribution to your organization.

Sincerely yours,

Darrin Wilson

Darrin Wilson

Enclosure

1124 Liberty Street, 3rd Floor • Chester, PA 18940 • 267.757.5462 • dWilson53@excite.com

"Cold" Cover Letter to a Potential Employer (Personal Trainer)

Transitioning into fitness training after a long and successful career in general management, sales, and customer relationship management.

JAMES J. HUTCHISEN

P.O. Box 901 ▪ Montrose, New Hampshire 58723

(303) 527-9501 ▪ jjhutch@hotmail.com

Dear Sir or Madam:

Reflecting on my professional sales and management experience within the marine industry, it is at this point in my career I am seeking to pursue a long-term personal and professional goal of a challenging opportunity as a **Personal Trainer/Strength Coach** within a health club, physical therapy and/or fitness facility. Let me briefly highlight the skills, values and contributions I will bring to your organization:

- **Certified Personal Trainer/Health Fitness Instructor at leading training facility.**

- Possess over 25 years' health club experience with most types of cardiovascular, plate and free-weight systems.

- Proven ability to plan and implement training programs through experience as a Personal Trainer for a health club.

- Strong general management, sales, marketing and customer relationship management expertise developed through 16 years as an Owner/Operator of a marine business.

- Comprehensive experience in human relations, within the retail/service arena, has characterized me as considerate, dependable, honest, straightforward, hard-working, and personable.

Since a résumé can neither fully detail all my skills and accomplishments, nor predict my potential to your organization, I would welcome the opportunity to meet and discuss the possible merging of my talent and experience with your **personal trainer** needs.

Very truly yours,

James J. Hutchisen

JAMES J. HUTCHISEN

Enclosure

"Cold" Cover Letter to a Potential Employer (Registered Nurse)

An applicant transitioning out of the Navy, where he gained a great deal
of experience with trauma treatment and crisis management.

RICHARD P. ISAACS, RN, BSN
529 Springdale Road • Springwater, New York 14560 • 585-624-6184 • richi@cs.com

January 12, 20–

Ms. Florence Blackwell, RN
Director of Nursing
Long Island Medical Center
1234 Hospital Row
Levittown, New York 11799

Dear Ms. Blackwell:

In anticipation of completing my military service in April, 20–, I am seeking a civilian position that will capitalize on my experience and training as a US Navy Registered Nurse. I believe that my clinical background and specialized training in emergency response and crisis management would make me an asset to your nursing staff. With this in mind, I have enclosed a résumé for your review that outlines my credentials.

Some key points you may find relevant to a nursing position with your facility include:

- **Caring for a broad array of patients, ranging from infants to senior citizens, and including post-operative, medical, infectious disease, oncology, and end-of-life scenarios.**

- **Developing rapport with diverse cultural groups, both in clinical and social settings. The patients I have dealt with cut across the full spectrum of ethnic and socioeconomic strata, from enlisted personnel to flag officers and their dependents. In my current assignment in Tokyo, I have had the opportunity to experience the local culture and interact with the local population.**

- **Completing training and engaging in field exercises that have prepared me for deployment to combat zones. This is relevant to a civilian setting because it encompasses mass casualty treatment, nuclear and biohazard treatment, and field hospital training, all of which relate to disaster response in a civilian community.**

I am confident that my dedication to caring for patients and capacity to function as an integral part of a treatment team would allow me to make a significant contribution to the health and well being of your patients. I would enjoy discussing with you how I can fulfill your needs in a clinical nursing role. Please contact me via phone or e-mail to arrange a mutually convenient date and time for an initial interview.

Thank you for your time and consideration. I look forward to speaking with you soon.

Sincerely,

Richard P. Isaacs, RN, BSN

Enclosure

"Cold" Cover Letter to a Potential Employer (Entertainment Industry)

This letter begins with an attention-grabbing opening followed by statements indicating that she understands the high-energy demands and realities of the entertainment industry. She ends the letter with a call to action.

MARY MANSON

1234 Hillside Drive / Los Angeles, CA 90049
Home (310) 555-5554 / Cell (310) 555-5555
mm@email.com

[Date]

[Name]
[Address]
[City, State Zip]

Dear [Salutation]:

Perhaps your company is in search of a highly motivated recent college graduate who is passionate about the Entertainment Industry and has the energy and drive to "pay my dues," acquire knowledge and advance professionally. If so, then we should talk!!

I offer a combination of creative talents and a strong work ethic as well as the following qualifications:

- BA in Communications from the University of California, Santa Barbara
- Hands-on experience directing, acting in and producing short independent and student films
- Realistic understanding of the demands of the entertainment industry, gained through internships for TV production company
- Operating knowledge of a variety of audio and video equipment

While my enclosed résumé provides a brief overview of my background, I look forward to a personal meeting at which time we can discuss your needs and my qualifications in detail.
I will call you next week to schedule a meeting; in the meantime, you can contact me at the above numbers. Thank you in advance for your time and consideration.

Sincerely,

Mary Manson

Mary Manson

Enclosure

"Cold" Cover Letter to a Potential Employer (Management)

Scott's recent experience with his last employer focused on IT implementation and project management. He seeks to gain a project management position with an IT consulting firm where he can make use of both his technical expertise and his management skills.

SCOTT A. McFADDEN

72 WOODBRIDGE TRAIL • FAIRPORT, NEW YORK 14450
585-223-9899 • SAM@EARTHLINK.COM

January 12, 20–

Mr. Addison Elgar
Director of Client Engagement
Computer Consultants, LLC
1234 Technology Terrace
Rochester, New York 14692

Dear Mr. Elgar:

Capitalizing on a career that encompasses substantial IT project management experience and extensive sales/marketing experience, I am seeking a new professional challenge that will combine these skills in a senior account management, project management, or technical leadership role. With this goal in mind, I have enclosed for your review a résumé that outlines my qualifications.

Some key points that you may find relevant to a position with your firm include:

- *Managing the technical deployment of six different releases of Cannon's SalesTeamXpert sales force automation tool over the past three years. This has involved ensuring that hardware platforms in the field are prepared to receive the latest release and resolving technical issues impacting end-user training for 6,000 users at 34 sites across the US.*

- *Building relationships with key decision-makers at Fortune 500 firms while serving as Marketing Manager for two different firms providing end-to-end transportation solutions for firms importing and exporting materials and products.*

- *Hands-on experience providing desk-side support to end-users; configuring hardware and installing software in the field; and delivering training to end-users and IT specialists.*

I am confident that my knowledge and expertise would allow me to make a meaningful contribution to the success of your firm and its clients. I would enjoy discussing with you in person how my capabilities can match your needs, and will contact you soon to arrange an appropriate time for an initial meeting.

Thank you for your time and consideration. I look forward to speaking with you soon.

Sincerely,

Scott A. McFadden

Scott A. McFadden

Enclosure

"Cold" Cover Letter to a Potential Employer (Physician's Assistant)

This individual has worked as a paramedic and recently finished her Physician's Assistant degree. She is looking to combine her education and extensive practical experience in an emergency medicine position with a large hospital.

Tiffany A. Mitchell
1299 Horseshoe Lane
Henrietta, New York 14467
585-334-1207
tam@frontiernet.net

January 12, 20–

Lara Angleton, R.N., Ph.D.
Director of Medical Human Resources
Clara Barton Memorial Hospital
One Nightingale Parkway
Rochester, New York 14692

Dear Dr. Angleton:

As a Physician's Assistant with nearly two years of clinical experience in an emergency department setting, I hope to utilize my skills in an emergency medicine position at your hospital. With this in mind, I am writing to you regarding potential opportunities, and have enclosed for your reference a résumé that outlines my education and other qualifications.

In addition to a B.S. from Rochester Institute of Technology, I have extensive training and experience in emergency medicine. Some of the highlights of my background include:

➢ Over twenty years' experience as a volunteer and as paid staff for the Henrietta Volunteer Ambulance Corps in suburban Rochester. In addition to logging over 7,600 active duty hours, I served as Vice President/General Manager for this busy service that answers over 4,700 calls each year. In this position, I was responsible for all operational aspects of the services provided.

➢ Three years' experience as a Flight Paramedic for Mercy Flight. I provided critical care to patients being transported by this air medical service that covers an 11-county region, transporting patients to critical care facilities.

➢ Nearly two years' experience in Rochester General Hospital's Emergency Department, treating a wide array of patients from infants to senior citizens, with cases ranging from acute injuries and medical conditions to routine, non-acute cases.

I am convinced that my education, training, and extensive experience have prepared me to effectively contribute to the care of your patients. I would enjoy speaking with you in person about the opportunities that exist and how I can best serve your needs. Please call me at 585-334-1207 to arrange a convenient day and time for us to meet. I look forward to talking with you soon.

Thank you.

Sincerely,

Tiffany A. Mitchell

Tiffany A. Mitchell, R.N., P.A.

Enclosure

"Cold" Cover Letter to a Potential Employer (Radiation Safety Officer)

This highly skilled and highly educated physicist is applying for the post of Radiation Safety Officer, which is his boss's job, as the boss leaves for another opportunity. He is competing with highly qualified external candidates, and his best asset is his familiarity with the institution, based on existing experience.

Michael Z. Ostrowski

2491 Goodman Street, Apartment 12 / Rochester, New York 14620 / (585) 258-6911

michaelzo@earthlink.com

January 12, 20–

Mr. Zachary P. Emerson
University of Buffalo
601 Transit Road, Box 2345
Williamsville, New York 14221

Dear Mr. Emerson:

Please accept this letter and the enclosed résumé as an expression of my interest in the Radiation Safety Officer position you are currently seeking to fill. I am confident that my education, experience, and familiarity with the University of Buffalo Research Center facilities provide me with the necessary skills to meet or exceed your expectations in this role.

For the past year, I have been a Health Physicist with UB, with responsibility for a variety of functions, including:

- Testing & Monitoring Equipment
- Training Medical Staff
- Ensuring Compliance with NYS Regulations
- Monitoring Staff Exposure
- Achieving CRESO Certification
- Supervising Four Technicians
- Serving on Various Committees
- Consulting with Physicians
- Maintaining Updated Technical Knowledge

Earlier, I held a similar position at University of Wisconsin's School of Medicine and Hospital. There I trained and supervised the work of a six-person technical team. I ensured that all equipment, materials, and supplies were in compliance with state regulations. State inspection results were always outstanding. Throughout my career, I have built a reputation for quality, flexibility, and professionalism in all areas. My commitment to health and safety has resulted in a perfect safety record.

I hold two master's degrees, one in Nuclear Engineering from Oklahoma State University, the other in Nuclear Physics from Sao Paulo University in Brazil. I have taught Biophysics at the university level. In addition, I speak three languages (English, Portuguese, and Russian). Having lived and worked in other countries has given me a sensitivity and understanding of diverse cultures and customs.

I have thoroughly enjoyed working at UB, and would welcome this opportunity to make an even more significant contribution to the success of its mission. I would enjoy discussing my qualifications with you in person and invite you to contact me to arrange an initial interview.

Thank you for your time and consideration. I look forward to speaking with you soon.

Sincerely,

Michael Z. Ostrowski

Michael Z. Ostrowski

Enclosure

"Cold" Cover Letter to a Potential Employer (Veterinarian)

This veterinarian practices in an elite niche, treating only competitive horses at racetracks. His goal is to split his time between a track in the Southeast during winter months and one in the Northeast during the summer, allowing him to follow the horses throughout the racing year.

PARKER DOUGLASS, DVM

27 SANTA ANITA CIRCLE ◆ PORT ST. LUCIE, FLORIDA 38291 ◆ 305-934-8816

January 12, 20–

Dr. Amber Morgenstern, DVM
Gainesville Equine Hospital
1218 Shoreline Highway
Gainesville, Florida 34489

FAX: 352-129-6630
E-mail: dramber@juno.com

Dear Dr. Morgenstern:

My extensive experience addressing the health and performance needs of elite race horses at major tracks makes me a strong candidate for the opening you recently advertised on the AAEP website. Accordingly, I have attached my résumé for your consideration and review.

Some key points you may find relevant include:

- **Strong capacity to function independently and make critical decisions without direct supervision. My knowledge of horses and experience at several major tracks means that I will need minimal orientation to "hit the ground running."**

- **An excellent track record of maintaining the health of elite thoroughbreds and quarter horses, as well as assisting trainers in enhancing the performance of horses by improving their respiratory and general health as well as dealing with lameness issues (references can be provided).**

- **The ability to effectively evaluate young horses prior to purchase, through observation and diagnostic testing. I routinely produce quality repository radiographs and review radiographs in a repository setting. I also accompany buyers to auctions (Keeneland, etc.) to assess horses being considered.**

- **Experience assisting trainers setting up effective farm-based training programs, as well as helping breeders address reproductive health issues.**

I believe that I can be an asset to your organization and would enjoy discussing further how my knowledge, expertise, and professional dedication can address your needs. Please feel free to contact me to arrange either a phone or in-person interview at a mutually convenient date and time.

Thank you for your time and consideration. I look forward to speaking with you soon.

Sincerely,

Parker Douglass, DVM

Parker Douglass, DVM

Enclosure

"Cold" Cover Letter to a Potential Employer (Internship)

A cover letter to apply for a competitive college internship in the financial services industry.

Carlos M. Nunez

Current Address
Boston University
45 Bay State Road
Miles Standish Hall Box 1356
Boston, MA 02215-9105

Telephone: (617) 353-0698
Email: nunezc@bu.edu

Permanent Address
3948 Amsterdam Ave.
Apt. 4
Bronx, N.Y. 10453-6613

Telephone: (718) 901-4544

January 13, 20–

Karen Carmichael
Morgan Stanley, Inc.
1690 Broadway
New York, NY 10036
Re: Finance Intern

Dear Ms. Carmichael:

Are you looking for a driven, overachieving intern committed to excelling in business and finance?

As a junior at Boston University, I am pursuing a BSBA with a major in Finance. My passion for financial markets and economics has steadily increased over the last five years and I am committed to developing my career path as a business leader within a major corporation.

I approach all of my work with discipline and focus; as an intern with your organization, I would look forward to effectively contributing to your program goals. Boston University, Cushing Academy, and The Boys Club of New York have acknowledged my academic and leadership achievements for excellence in academic studies, volunteerism, and peer mentoring.

Please feel free to contact me at my campus number in Boston, (617) 353-0698. Thank you for your consideration. I am enthusiastic about working at Morgan Stanley Group. My background, professionalism, and enthusiasm will make me an effective member of your team.

Sincerely,

Carlos M. Nunez

Enclosure

"Cold" Cover Letter to a Potential Employer (Teacher)

A cover letter sent with the resume hard copy as a follow-up to the resume submission via e-mail.

November 14, 20–

Ms. Jennifer Jones
Personnel Coordinator
ABC Language Corporation
555 First Street, Suite 555
Vancouver, BC V9J 5G9
Canada

Dear Ms. Jones:

Although I recently submitted my résumé to your office via e-mail, I am submitting the enclosed hard copy as a follow-up. I welcome any questions you might have.

With this letter, I would like to reiterate my sincere motivation to teach in Japan. My experience as a substitute middle school teacher has helped me to understand methods of student interaction and reach a level of comfort in the classroom. I strive to build relationships with students—as much as a substitute teacher can—to facilitate classroom activities and inspire the learners. It is something I really enjoy.

The ABC web site encourages "all outgoing, dynamic, and flexible people to apply." In my current position as a flight attendant for Hawaii Wings Airlines, I am required to demonstrate these characteristics daily. Communication and quick-thinking skills are a must onboard an aircraft full of passengers. Flexibility is essential in the areas of customer service, in interaction with colleagues, and in work scheduling.

My motivation is indeed genuine, and I look forward to the possibility of discussing the opportunity with you. I will gladly make myself available for a telephone or videoconference interview.

Respectfully,

Jonathan Young

Jonathan Young

Enclosure: One-page résumé

"Cold" Cover Letter to a Potential Employer (Production Supervisor)

Two problems to overcome: transitioning from automotive service manager to production supervisor and a break in employment of more than a year.

FERGUS McLEAN

4040 Wisteria Way
Kalamazoo, Michigan 49001

313.358.7470
FML5505@bellsouth.net

Tuesday, October 28, 20–

Mr. Charles W. Worth
Vice President for Operations
TopLine, Inc.
500 Northridge Parkway
Suite 400
Montgomery, Alabama 36100

Dear Mr. Worth:

How big is that gap between what the TopLine leadership wants from its skilled, semi-skilled and unskilled employees and what the TopLine bottom line gets? If you'd like to shrink that costly mismatch, we should explore adding me to your team as your transportation manager.

On the next pages, you'll see more than a half-dozen contributions I have made in this area. They illustrate the five profit-building capabilities I've listed right at the top of the next page. I'd like to put those advantages to work for you right away.

Over the last year, the health of a family member made the most demands upon me and guided my relocation from Knoxville to Montgomery. Now that problem is resolved and I am ready to return to my first love: helping teams want to do well.

If my approach and philosophy appeal to you, please let me suggest a next step. I would like to hear about your special needs in your own words. May I call in a few days to arrange a time to do that?

Sincerely,

Fergus McLean

Fergus McLean

Encl.: Résumé

"Cold" Cover Letter to a Potential Employer (School Board Seat)

Having retired after thirty years of public service, this applicant decided to target a vacated seat on the Board of Education as a preparation for future political moves.

THOMAS DAVIS
743 Red Fox Road
Dayton, OH 45439
937.423.1258
tdavis@ci.dayton.oh.us

January 13, 20–

Ms. Jillian Laurent, Treasurer
Dayton City Schools Administrative Offices
227 West Florence Avenue
Dayton, OH 45439

Dear Ms. Laurent:

Please let this letter serve as my intent to seek the vacated seat on the Dayton City School Board. My motivation for seeking this position is that of public service. Because I have a deep commitment to community service and an in-depth knowledge of how a community works, I recognize that a public education system is critical to overall community success.

After retiring from law enforcement with thirty years of service, I returned to public service two years ago. I currently work as the Substance Abuse Prevention Coordinator for the City of Dayton Health Department. My expertise in the areas of substance abuse and public health would be beneficial to the school board.

My community involvement is outlined in the enclosed résumé. Since moving to Dayton in 19–, I have continued my life in community service with various organizations. In addition, leadership skills have been honed by coordinating police in-service training sessions, serving as Detective Sergeant for the Dayton Police Department, speaking to students and civic groups as a law enforcement representative, and holding offices in professional associations.

In today's world, we fear for the security of our homeland. Our students and teachers need to be in a safe environment. Parents need to be confident that their children are secure at school and school-sponsored events. From my life experiences and training, I also bring expertise to the school board in this area.

Public service has always been my calling. An appointment to the Dayton City School Board would allow me to use the skills gained from a 32-year career in public service to make a difference in people's lives. Though my children are grown, I look forward to a strong school system for my grandchildren. I have the time to devote to the task and the drive, energy, experience, and vision to make a positive contribution as a board member. I ask you to consider not only my qualifications, but also my desire to serve.

Sincerely,

Thomas Davis

Thomas Davis

Enclosure

"Cold" Cover Letter to a Potential Employer (Sales Professional)

George has two special needs: to show the sales aspect of his previous career as an accountant, and to convince a new employer that his desire to leave his current company was based solely upon having to work in an oversold market.

George Williams

1212 Currie Lane — Montgomery, Alabama 36100
334.555.5555 — 334.555.6666 (cellular) — gwilliams102@charter.net

Thursday, July 20, 20–

Ms. Laura Worth
Sales Manager
TopLine, Inc.
500 Northridge Parkway
Suite 400
Montgomery, Alabama 36100

Dear Ms. Worth:

I want you to get the credit for adding ROI to the TopLine sales team. Specifically, I'd like to become your newest sales professional. And, perhaps the best way to link those two ideas is with this graph that shows how I'm performing right now.

What I do isn't magic. I just work harder and smarter than my competition by finding some profitable way to say "yes" to every customer and potential customer.

My focus on your sales needs starts on the next pages. I wanted you to see a résumé that offers more than the usual recitations of job titles and responsibilities. That's why you'll find six capabilities I want to put at TopLine's disposal at once. Backing them up are a dozen examples of sales that show those capabilities in action.

My company values what I do. And, if I thought our market was growing as fast as yours, I would stay with them. While I cannot control market conditions, I am interested in making even greater contributions to my employer. That's why I'm "testing the waters" with this confidential application.

I do best using the consultative approach to sales. So, as a first step, I'd like to hear about TopLine's sales needs in your own words. May I call in a few days to arrange time to do that?

Sincerely,

George Williams

George Williams

Encl.: Résumé

"Cold" Cover Letter to a Potential Employer (Credit Account Specialist)

Kim wants to affiliate herself with a larger company that offers a more challenging role in analyzing and managing financial accounts; she also seeks to take on more responsibility to allow her to grow professionally.

KIMBERLY A. CARTER
888 West Road ▪ Anywhere, Michigan 55555 ▪ 555.222.2222

December 8, 20–

Marcy Johnson
ABC Accounting Company
333 Capital Avenue
Anywhere, Michigan 55555

Dear Ms. Johnson,

As a well-qualified credit account specialist, I demonstrate my ability to effectively communicate with clients, resolve payment issues, and collect on past due payments. I bring over 18 years of accounts receivable experience in addition to being involved in all processing stages of collections. The scope of my experience includes, but is not limited to, commercial, automotive, and manufacturing environments.

My focus is to deliver results and provide superior service by quickly identifying problem areas in accounts receivable and developing a solution strategy to ensure issues are resolved. My expertise lies in my strong ability to build rapport with clients, analyze accounts, and manage all aspects related to my appointed position and areas of responsibilities. I find these qualities to be my greatest assets to offer employers.

Due to an unforeseen circumstance, I was unable to continue my employment as a cash applications analyst with a well-known automotive industry leader. Since my employment with A-1 Corporation, I have accepted a temporary position as a billing assistant with a local company. My objective is to secure a position in accounts receivable and credit collections with an established company. As you will note, my résumé exhibits a brief review of contributions I have made to my employers and I enjoy challenges.

A complete picture of my expertise and experience is very important. Therefore, I will follow up with you next week. I look forward to speaking with you soon to answer any questions you may have regarding my background.

Regards,

Kimberly Carter

Kimberly Carter

Enclosure

"Cold" Cover Letter to a Potential Employer (Sales)

After "playing around" with part-time and seasonal positions for six years after college, John was ready to combine his variety of sales and customer service achievements into a bid for a serious, high-paying sales career.

JOHN MICHAEL ANDERSON

29 Davison Street • Asheville, NC 28800
(828) 555-0000 (H) • (828) 555-0001 (Cell) • gatehous@aol.com

Dear Hiring Professional:

My competitors were like pesky flies—they kept popping up everywhere, opening with lots of glitz, taking all the customers, and then crashing and burning after six months. But during those six months they were trying to take all my customers! As a newly graduated college student in his first real management position, these were serious challenges to which I responded with all the advertising ideas and new gimmicks I could muster—free pool playing, fruity drinks for girls; I even gave away free beer one night using three kegs we couldn't get rid of.

Today I am the same aggressive, ambitious sales professional I was then. OK . . . these days I wouldn't give away free beer (it might even have been illegal), but I do respond to sales challenges with all the competitiveness, creativity, and customer concern in my heart. In my last sales position, I was quite successful selling vacation packages by telephone for several reasons:

- I qualified my targets well.
- I was very knowledgeable about the product and painted a good picture of the product in the customer's mind.
- I think well and profitably on my feet.
- I'm honest and a natural rapport-builder.

The point of my enclosed résumé is that I would like to talk with you about bringing all the sales, problem-solving, and customer service skills to which it refers to work for your organization. When can we meet?

Sincerely,

John Michael Anderson

John Michael Anderson

enc.

"Cold" Cover Letter to a Potential Employer (Rail Industry)

Bruce wants to pursue his boyhood passion to become a train engineer.

BRUCE PETRELLI
55 Birch Crest Road • Brockport, New York 14420 • (585) 637-1037

January 12, 20–

Mr. Casey Jones
Director of Personnel
Atcheson, Topeka, and Santa Fe Railroad
1234 Railroad Boulevard
Topeka, Kansas 56789

Dear Mr. Jones:

As a mature individual with a life long interest in railroads, I am seeking a job opportunity that will lead to a fulfilling career in the rail industry.

Enclosed for your review is a resume that briefly outlines my relevant qualifications. Some of the key skills that I believe make me a strong candidate for a position with your rail line include:

> - **Significant experience as an Equipment Operator and Truck Driver.**
> - **Experience dispatching for the New York State Dept. of Transportation.**
> - **An excellent aptitude and desire to learn new tasks.**
> - **An enjoyment of and willingness to work outdoors—in all weather conditions.**
> - **Exceptional attention to detail and accuracy in my work.**
> - **Responsible worker who is dedicated to consistently exceeding expectations.**

I understand the structure of the rail industry and am more than willing to accept an entry-level position (and all the challenges that go with it) in order for the opportunity to break in with a railroad line. I would enjoy speaking with you in person about how I could fill a need for your company. Please call me at (585) 637-1037 to arrange a meeting at your convenience. I look forward to talking with you soon.

Thank you.

Sincerely,

Bruce Petrelli

Bruce Petrelli

Enclosure

"Cold" Cover Letter to a Potential Employer (Media)

Letting her professors speak for her and then confirming their words with her own words of commitment is a very effective strategy. The strength of the text is enhanced by the brevity of the letter.

BROOKE M. WELLINGTON

BROOKEWELLI@AOL.COM

6600 BELLESTONE STREET ◆ COLUMBUS, OHIO 43229 ◆ PHONE: (614) 374-6636

"I would rank Ms. Wellington's work in the top 10% of students I have taught; she is not afraid to tackle tough projects; I believe she has the ability to quickly make positive contributions..."

—John Weiss, Ph.D., Chairperson, Department of Communications, Albian College

"Brooke was an exemplary Journalism major. She took charge of the tasks given to her and performed them in a superior manner. I admire her strong enthusiasm and her attention to detail..."

—Stephen M. Ross, Assistant Director of Television Technical Operations, Albian College

Dear Selection Committee:

Tenacious and driven are terms my colleagues have used to describe my work habits. It is with a strong sense of career commitment that I submit my résumé for your review.

Having completed classes in August, I will be granted a B.A. in Journalism from Albian College in December 20–. Sometimes holding two jobs while attending school, I will have completed my degree in three years. It is with the same passion, integrity and energy that I intend to pursue my career.

Like so many, I possess the talent and understanding of how demanding a career in media can be. But unlike most, I am willing to "pay the price" of hard work, rough work schedules and total availability that the industry requires.

Thanks so much for your consideration. I am eager to learn more about the challenges facing your organization and to discuss how I can make a difference.

Best Regards,

Brooke M. Wellington

Brooke M. Wellington

"Cold" Cover Letter to a Potential Employer (Vice President)

Richard T. Carpenter

6 College Drive • San Francisco, California • (921) 784-6306
carpenter_vp@aol.com

(Date)

Emily _____
Title
ABC Corporation
1 Industry Plaza
San Francisco, CA 94162

Dear Ms. _____,

As a Chief Financial Officer, I have built a reputation for my strong ability to provide decisive leadership. For the past several years, my career as a senior-level executive has provided me with opportunities to promote high-level strategic business and financial planning goals for worldwide multimillion dollar corporations. My ability to identify challenges to and capitalize upon opportunities to expand revenue growth, reduce operating costs and improve overall productivity has been one of my strongest assets to my employers.

My strengths in financial and accounting management as well as my thorough understanding of finance operations have vastly contributed to my career and success as a leader. I maintain self-confidence, credibility, and stature to make things happen with colleagues inside and outside the company. Just as significant are my abilities to develop rapport among coworkers and management, build effective teams and promote team effort.

My objective is to secure a position as a CFO or Vice President and to pursue new opportunities with an organization providing new and exciting challenges. Having a complete picture of my expertise and experience is very important. As you will note in my resume, I have made significant contributions to my employers and take my job very seriously.

I appreciate your time and consideration and will be in contact next week to see if we are able to schedule a meeting date for an interview. I look forward to speaking with you soon.

Regards,

Richard Carpenter

Richard Carpenter

RC
enclosure

"Cold" Cover Letter to a Potential Employer
(Pharmaceutical Sales)

Elana M. Carter

1267 Campton Drive • Northville, Michigan 48167

Emily _____   (Date)
(Title)
ABC Corporation
1 Industry Plaza
Dearborn, MI 48120

Dear Ms. _____:

I currently hold a sales management position for a very successful retail company. My talents to achieve high sales volume, work cooperatively with diverse personalities, and focus on providing exceptional customer service has allowed me to excel in customer relations and succeed in sales and marketing.

I have always enjoyed a challenge and have made the decision to extend my experience to the pharmaceutical sales field. Pharmaceutical sales has been an interest of mine for some time and I am confident that my background and skills in customer service, human relations, and product distribution would transition well into pursuing this change. What I may lack in specific experience in your business, I more than make up for with my dedication, energy, and determination.

I thoroughly understand the importance of developing customer relations, generating revenue from sales potential within a designated territory, and maintaining accurate customer information. I have the aptitude and willingness to learn the necessary technical medical materials to promote your products. I am fully capable of projecting a positive and professional image of an organization and its products, and I strongly believe I possess the necessary skills and qualifications your organization seeks to be successful in this field of work.

Your time in reviewing my confidential resume is greatly appreciated. I will follow up next week to answer any questions you may have regarding my qualifications. At that time, I would like to discuss the possibility of setting up a personal interview at your convenience. Please contact me if you would like to speak sooner.

Very truly yours,

Elana Carter

Elana Carter
enclosure

"Cold" Cover Letter to a Potential Employer (Recruiter)

Interested in fast-track career progression, but has reached her peak with her current employer. She is seeking a position in a high-growth global corporation.

BETSY McGILL

256 EAST 73RD STREET – APT. 7M • NEW YORK, NEW YORK 10021 • (212) 895-9045

(Date)

Alice _____
(Title)
Krieger, Skvetney, Howell
Executive Search Consultants
2426 Foundation Road
New York, NY 10025

Dear Ms. _____:

Having spent several years as an executive recruiter, I realize the number of resumes you receive on a daily basis. However, I remember how valuable a few always turned out to be.

The purpose of this communication is to introduce myself and then to meet with you about joining your organization.

When asked which business situations have been the most challenging and rewarding, my answer is the time spent in the search profession.

My background, skills, and talents are in all aspects of sales and sales management. My research indicates that your expertise is in this area.

I have enclosed a resume which will highlight and support my objectives. I would appreciate the opportunity to meet and exchange ideas. I will call you over the next several days to make an appointment. If you prefer, you may reach me in the evening or leave a message at (212) 895-9045.

Thank you and I look forward to our meeting.

Sincerely,

Betsy McGill

Betsy McGill

BM
enclosure

"Cold" Cover Letter to a Potential Employer
(Project Management)

Matthew A. Sims
4545 Oakland
Chicago, Illinois 60671
(224) 555-3513

(Date)
Mr. _____
ABC Company
1 Industry Plaza
Chicago, IL 60675

Dear Mr._____:

Information technology expertise, combined with visionary leadership, the ability to motivate cross-functional teams, and develop cost-effective solutions, are key to creating long-term customer satisfaction and loyalty.

As a seasoned **Project Manager** experienced in providing strategic direction in the design and deployment of technology solutions, I have

- Successfully managed customer accounts from defining project requirements through implementation.
- Engineered e-commerce business solutions for myriad organizations from start-up ventures to *Fortune* 500 companies.
- Completed all of the coursework, including specialized electives to obtain the Microsoft Certified Systems Engineer designation.
- Developed comprehensive RFIs and RFPs; selected the most qualified, cost-effective vendor; and directed cross-functional teams to ensure on-time, on-budget implementation.
- Efficiently prioritized projects, developed realistic timelines, and consistently met deadlines.
- Compiled and driven ratification of product requirements.
- Provided technical expertise to sales teams to assist them in closing the sale.

Could your company use a high achiever with a thirst for growth and new challenges? If so, I would like to discuss how my skills and experience could benefit your organization.

I look forward to speaking with you.

Sincerely,

Matthew Sims

Matthew Sims

MS
enclosure

"Cold" Cover Letter to a Potential Employer (Publishing)

An administrative support person who wants to break into the publishing industry—no actual experience, but an avid reader who volunteers time to edit community fundraising publications and newsletters.

Genevieve Stone
245 The Outlook ▪ Glen Cove, New York 11542 ▪ (631) 236-0965 ▪ genstone@aol.com

(Date)

Phillip _____
(Title)
ABC Corporation
1 Industry Plaza
New York, NY 10021

Dear Mr. _____:

In the interest of exploring opportunities in the publishing industry, I have enclosed my resume for your review.

Over the last two years, I have gained valuable knowledge and experience in many aspects of personnel assistance, office procedures, and administrative operations. Recently I volunteered my time to edit a cookbook and have been responsible for editing the newsletter for my sorority. I consider myself a good writer and an avid reader and have always wanted to get into publishing. With my considerable energy, drive, and ability to work long hours, I believe I could make a positive contribution to your organization, and I would appreciate the opportunity to discuss my qualifications at your earliest convenience.

Should any questions arise regarding the information on my resume, or if you need personal references, please do not hesitate to contact me through the address or telephone number listed above.

Thank you for your time and consideration. I look forward to meeting with you.

Respectfully,

Genevieve Stone
Genevieve Stone

GS
enclosure

"Cold" Cover Letter to a Potential Employer
(International Sales)

JENNIFER DELOREAN

(Date)

Phillip _____
(Title)
ABC Corporation
1 Industry Plaza
Las Vegas, NV 82341

Dear Mr. _____:

I received your name from Mr. _____ last week. I spoke to him regarding career opportunities with _____ and he suggested contacting you. He assured me that he would pass my resume along to you; however, in the event that he did not, I am enclosing another.

As an avid cosmetics consumer, I understand and appreciate the high standards of quality that your firm honors. As you can see from my enclosed resume, I have had quite a bit of experience in the international arena. My past experience working overseas has brought me a greater understanding of international cultures and traditions, as well as a better understanding and appreciation of our own culture. These insights would certainly benefit a corporation with worldwide locations, such as your own. In addition, I have gained first-hand experience in the consumer marketplace through my various sales positions. I have noticed your recent expansion into the television media and am sure that an energetic individual would surely be an asset to ABC in this, as well as other, projects.

I would very much like to discuss career opportunities with ABC. I will be calling you within the next few days to set up an interview. In the meantime, if you have any questions I may be reached at the number above. Thank you for your consideration.

Sincerely,

Jennifer Delorean

Jennifer Delorean

JD
enclosure

529 Caledonia Road • Las Vegas, Nevada 82345 • (701) 984-3690
internationalsalespro@msn.com

"Cold" E-Mail to a Potential Employer (Banking)

Having completed a one-year contract, Matthew had been offered a permanent position. However; he was interested in a position in a company that was more financially stable, and one where he could make use of his diverse technology skills.

From: Matthew Lorenzo [bankerpro@hotmail.com]
To: hr@fleetcareers.com
Cc:
Subject: Financial management/Sales orientation

Dear Mr. _____:

Please include my name in your job search database. As requested, I have attached a copy of my current resume.

Banking today is definitely a sales environment. While my marketing skills will always be useful, my interests lead me now to seek a more distinct financial management position such as Controller, Treasurer, or Vice President of Finance.

Since my CPA will be completed in January 20–, my search may be somewhat premature, but my transcript and results, combined with my practical experience, should offset my temporary lack of an accounting designation. I would therefore like you to begin considering me immediately. As an Account Manager, I saw many different industries, and so would not feel constrained to any one sector.

Including a mortgage loan benefit, I am currently earning $4,500 per month plus a car allowance. This should provide you with an indication of my present job level. Your suggestions or comments would be appreciated. I am available for interviews, and can be reached at (516) 555-1212. Thank you.

Yours truly,

Matthew Lorenzo
bankerpro@hotmail.com

"Cold" E-Mail to a Potential Employer (Software Development)

From: Julie Baxter [softwarespecialist@aol.com]
To: hr@developers.net
Cc:
Subject: Developer with quality, productivity, and commitment

Dear Mr. _____:

ABC Corporation caught my attention recently as I began a search for a new employer in the Phoenix area. ABC Corporation is well known in the software industry for quality products and excellent customer service; it also maintains a strong reputation as a great employer. Your organization has created an environment in which people can excel, which is why I write you today.

I am very interested in joining your software development team. I am confident that my background and experience will meet your future needs. My current position is Application Developer for Ascend Corp. I enjoy it very much as it has provided me with extensive hands-on training in Visual Basic and other languages. However, I am ready to get more into actual software writing, as well as return to the Mesa area. I possess a bachelor's degree in Computer Science as well as training in a variety of programming languages. I am also a fast learner, as demonstrated by my learning Visual Basic quickly after joining Ascend. Additionally, I plan to pursue my master's degree and have begun the application process.

I would appreciate the opportunity to meet with you to discuss your goals and how I can help you meet them. I will call you soon to arrange a meeting at your convenience. In the meantime, please feel free to call for further information on my background and experience.

Thank you for your consideration and reply. I look forward to meeting you in the near future.

Yours truly,

Julie Baxter
(516) 555-1212
softwarespecialist@aol.com

"Cold" E-Mail to a Potential Employer (Internship)

From: David Kent [internationalrelationspro@earthlink.net]
To: hr@internationaljobs.org
Cc:
Subject: Motivated International Relations Intern

Dear Ms. _____:

I am interested in being considered for an internship. I am currently a senior at the University of Denver majoring in International Studies with a concentration in Latin America and a minor in Political Science.

My internships have increased my knowledge of International Relations and have enabled me to make use of my education in a professional environment. I am very serious about my International Relations education and future career and am eager to learn as much as possible throughout my internship. I am interested in working for your organization to gain practical experience and additional knowledge pertaining to my field of study.

My professional and academic background, along with my sincere interest in helping others, has enhanced my sensitivity to a diverse range of cultures. As a highly motivated professional, I enjoy the challenge of complex demanding assignments. My well-developed writing and communication skills are assets to an office environment.

I welcome the opportunity to elaborate on how I could make a substantial contribution to your organization as an intern. I look forward to talking with you soon. Thank you.

Sincerely,

David Kent
(516) 555-1212
internationalrelationspro@earthlink.net

POWER PHRASES

Consider using adaptations of these key phrases in your "cold" letters to potential employers.

My twenty-two-year operations management career with a multibillion-dollar _____ company has been at increasing degrees of responsibility. While I have spent the last five years in top management, I am especially proud of my record—I started as a driver many years ago and, like cream, have risen to the top. I have consistently accomplished all goals assigned to me, particularly overall cost reductions, improved productivity, and customer service. Some of my achievements are:

Your recent acquisition of the _____ chain would indicate an intent to pursue southeastern market opportunities more vigorously than you have in the past several years. I believe that my retail management background would complement your long-range strategy for _____ very effectively.

With the scarcity of qualified technical personnel that exists today, it is my thought that you would be interested in my qualifications as set forth in the attached resume.

In approximately three months, I am moving to _____ with my family, and am bringing with me fifteen solid years of banking experience—the last eight in branch operations management. I would particularly like to utilize this experience with your firm.

I have noticed that you conduct laser exposure testing at your facility. If there is a need for laser technicians in this endeavor, I would like to be considered for a position.

As you can see from my resume, I am a psychology major and was president of our debating society in my senior year. I feel both would indicate a talent for sales. I did some selling in my summer job in 20– (ABC Books), and found not only that I was successful, but that I thoroughly enjoyed it.

The position you described sounds challenging and interesting. After receiving your comments about the job requirements, I am convinced that I can make an immediate contribution toward the growth of _____ and would certainly hope that we may explore things further at your convenience.

The opportunity to put to use my medical knowledge as well as my English degree would bring me great pleasure, and it would please me to know that I was bringing quality to your company.

I feel that the combination of _____'s educational environment and my desire to learn as much as possible about the data processing field could only bring about positive results.

If you think after talking to me and reading my resume that there might be an interest with your client company, I would be very interested. I have been put in many situations where I had to learn quickly, and have always enjoyed the challenge.

My accomplishments include:

As my resume indicates, I have demonstrated commitment to clients and to my employer's goals. That track record is consistent in my career endeavors as well as in my life as a whole. I dedicate myself to whatever task is at hand, marshal my resources, and stay with the project until it is completed—to my satisfaction. Since my goals and demands are even more stringent than my employers' expectations, I consistently exceed quotas and objectives.

You will notice one common thread throughout my career—I am an administrator and a problem solver.

Currently I am considering opportunities in the $65–$85K range.

My confidential resume is enclosed for your review and consideration.

My current salary requirement would range mid to high $50Ks, with specifics flexible, negotiable, and dependent upon such factors as benefit structure and advancement opportunity.

Having spent several years as a _____, I realize the number of resumes you receive on a daily basis. However, I remember how valuable a few always turned out to be.

I would like the opportunity to discuss with you how we could mutually benefit one another. You may leave a message on my answering machine at my home and I will return the call. I look forward to hearing from you very soon.

I'm a clear communicator equally at ease with senior management, governmental officials and control agencies, vendors and contractors, construction/labor force. I'm a hard-driving manager who is project driven and is accustomed to inspiring the best job performance possible from associates and employees. I'm also creative enough to be in compliance with agency requirements without sacrificing profit or deadlines.

This job seems to be the right challenge for me; I know that with my strong Java skills and manufacturing background experience I will be an asset to your company.

Hoping to meet you in person, I thank you for your time.

I will be calling you on Friday, August 15, 20– to be sure you received my resume and to answer any questions you might have.

I have enclosed a resume which will highlight and support my objectives. I would appreciate the opportunity to meet and exchange ideas. I will call you over the next several days to make an appointment. If you prefer, you may reach me in the evening or leave a message at (516) 555-1212.

"Cold" Cover Letter to Employment Industry Professional (Health Care)

Adam has developed strong relationships with HMOs, hospitals, and physicians throughout his career. He seeks to leverage this experience into a position with an HMO, capitalizing on his expertise in preventative health and chronic illness management programs.

ADAM G. STEVENS

934 Sully's Trail
Pittsford, New York 14534
585-248-0917 / FAX: 585-388-9622
E-mail: adams@cs.com

January 12, 20–

Ms. Greta Pederson, President
Hunter, Gatherer & Recruiter Executive Search, Unlimited
1234 Executive Tower
Rochester, New York 14692

Dear Ms. Pederson:

As an accomplished professional with a 20-plus year track record in the pharmaceutical industry, I believe that I have unique talents that could benefit an HMO or a health care management organization. With this in mind, I have enclosed for your review a résumé that briefly outlines my professional history.

Some of the key capabilities that I can bring to a new opportunity include:

- *Design and implementation of health management programs. I have first-hand experience developing programs for asthma management, and direct the implementation of programs that have delivered substantial savings to client firms.*
- *Managing the development and implementation of Web-based services that are new revenue centers for my firm and value-added services to its physician customer base.*
- *Exceptional account relations skills. I currently call on and maintain business relationships with key client contacts at the highest levels.*
- *National certifications from the University of Wisconsin in Quality Management and from the National Heart, Lung & Blood Institute.*

I am confident that my knowledge and expertise would allow me to deliver successful results for one of your clients in the health care industry. I would enjoy speaking with you in person to explore potential opportunities and how I can best serve someone's needs. Please call or e-mail me to arrange a convenient time for us to meet.

Thank you for your time and consideration. I look forward to talking with you soon.

As my employer is unaware of my job search, I trust that you will hold this correspondence in strict confidence and consult with me before releasing my materials to a prospective employer.

Sincerely,

Adam G. Stevens
Enclosure

"Cold" Cover Letter to Employment Industry Professional
(Senior Network Control Technician/Administrator)

Peter's goal is to move from a network administrator/tech to a senior position.

PETER M. GUTIERREZ

9999 9th Street, Cactus Center, Texas 79423 • pmgutierrez@sbcglobal.net • 555-555-5555

January 20, 20–

I regard network downtime as unacceptable, yet realize it sometimes happens due to powers beyond my control. I always have contingency plans. —Peter Gutierrez

Placement Services, Inc.
Cactus Center, Texas

RE: SENIOR NETWORK CONTROL TECHNICIAN/ADMINISTRATOR, Cactus Center Area

Dear Personnel Recruiter:

As I consider career options that offer new and challenging opportunities to expand my growth, I am excited by your job posting for Senior Network Control Technician/Administrator. My qualifications and technical background, as well as fieldwork, marketing, and customer service experience, match your requirements for this position. The enclosed résumé reflects the experience and technical training/expertise to provide customized network and hardware/software solutions to meet remote customer needs.

The following **key strengths** also exemplify highly marketable skills and characteristics. I possess:

- *An accommodating attitude and willingness to work hard at any level to accomplish tasks and meet deadlines.*
- *The ability to effectively prioritize tasks and job assignments to balance customer needs with company goals.*
- *Strategic planning to head off downtime and restructure company systems to realize major improvement.*
- *Aptitude for troubleshooting problems, while respecting customers and explaining problems/solutions in simple, illustrative language.*
- *Consultative, straightforward communication techniques that promote development of strong and lasting rapport and trust.*
- *A work ethic that honors integrity and excellence to enhance company distinction.*
- *A persuasive, take-charge style seasoned with a sense of humor for a pleasant work environment.*
- *Psychological insight and a talent for motivating others to work at higher levels to increase productivity.*

An interview to further investigate your needs and my qualifications would be mutually beneficial. I look forward to hearing from you. In the meantime, thank you for your time and consideration.

Sincerely,

Peter M. Gutierrez

Enclosure: Résumé

"Cold" Cover Letter to
Employment Industry Professional (CPA)

THERESE E. MAYSONET
1915 CEDAR COURT • LANSING, MICHIGAN 48910
MAYSONET_ACCOUNTANT@EMAIL.NET

Emily _____   (Date)
(Title)
ABC Corporation
1 Industry Plaza
Detroit, MI 48723

Dear Ms. _____:

As I am just completing the requirements for my MBA in Accounting at City Institute of Technology, I am exploring potential opportunities with a well-established firm that will lead to a career as a CPA. I hope to join an organization where I can learn and grow within the accounting profession and build a long-term relationship. With these goals in mind, I have enclosed for your consideration and review a resume that briefly outlines my credentials.

Some of the key experiences I can bring to an entry-level position with your firm include:

- **Administering Accounts Receivable and Payroll for an engineering firm that was also engaged in construction and some custom manufacturing.**

- **Preparing individual tax returns as part of a volunteer program in conjunction with CIT.**

- **Serving as Treasurer of a campus organization, Delta Beta Gamma, which encompassed maintaining financial records and providing financial reports to the auditing CPA and to the national organization.**

- **Proficiency with basic Windows and Microsoft Office applications, as well as a keen interest in technology and high-tech businesses.**

I am confident that my education and experience to date provide me with skills that would be beneficial to your firm and its clients. I would enjoy speaking with you in person to discuss the possibilities that exist and how I can best serve the needs of your firm and your clients. Please call me at **(516) 555-1212** to arrange a convenient date and time for us to meet. I look forward to opening a dialogue with you soon.

Very truly yours,

Therese Maysonet

Therese Maysonet

TM
enclosure

"Cold" Cover Letter to Employment Industry Professional (Quality Assurance)

David Jameson
4987 Lubbock Avenue
Centerville, OH 45458
937.555.5264 / cell: 555.555.4652

(Date)

Phillip _____
(Title)
ABC Corporation
1 Industry Plaza
Dayton, OH 45421

Dear Mr. _____:

Reliability. Problem Solving. Attention to Detail. Innovation. These are a few of the many qualities I have developed as a Quality Assurance Technician. If you are looking for a topnotch Quality Assurance Technician, look no further. I have over 15 years of experience in quality assurance and quality control and have not only designed better consumer-friendly products but have improved sales of existing products.

Because delivering solid productivity increases has been the norm throughout my career in the electronics field, I have achieved superior results at Continuum Biomedical, HMT Technologies, Wheco Electronics, 3M Healthcare, Irwin Magnetic, and Xircom Electronics. As a result, you get a Quality Assurance Technician who is productive from day one. My commitment to you would be the same: simplify processes, improve products, develop workforce competencies, and boost output while completing projects ahead of time and under budget.

Qualifications I can bring to your clients are outlined on the enclosed resume. Given my technical skills, familiarity with the product line, and understanding of your clients' needs, I could step into the position and be of immediate assistance.

Please contact me at my home telephone number to arrange a convenient time to meet. Thank you for your time; I look forward to speaking with you soon.

Yours truly,

David Jameson

David Jameson

DJ
enclosure

"Cold" Cover Letter to Employment Industry Professional
(Executive Computer Specialist)

Kelly L. Hillman
225 Springdale Drive ▪ Pittsboro, NC 27312 ▪ (555) 123-4567

(Date)

Emily _____
(Title)
ABC Corporation
1 Industry Plaza
Greensboro, NC 27345

Dear Ms. _____:

My experience installing and maintaining computer networks, hardware, and software, along with my skills in training users and developing cost-saving applications, are the assets I would bring to the position of Executive Computer Specialist.

I am a Certified Novell Administrator. And my technical skills include expertise in Novell Netware, MS DOS and Windows, as well as experience with hardware including Cabletron, and software including the Microsoft Office Suite.

My computer expertise has saved my employers production time and costs. As a Senior Computer Specialist, I installed a Personal Computer LAN utilizing the Novell Netware Networking System. I saved $35,000 and used the savings to upgrade the equipment installation. Also in that position I designed and implemented a system to cut printing costs. The system is projected to save the government $4 million over four years.

I have also developed software packages, including "point of sale" software and mortgage software, which was for commercial sale.

I believe my skills and experience will make me succeed in the position of Executive Computer Specialist. Kindly review my resume, then contact me at your earliest convenience to schedule a professional interview.

Very truly yours,

Kelly Hillman

Kelly Hillman

KH
enclosure

"Cold" Cover Letter to Employment Industry Professional (Vice President)

•• **Thomas J. Flokhart**

(Date)

Mr. _____
(Title)
Krieger, Skvetney, Howell
Executive Search Consultants
2426 Foundation Road
Richmond, VA 62362

Dear Mr. _____:

In the course of your search assignments, you may have a requirement for an organized and goal-directed Vice President. My present position provides me with the qualifications and experience necessary to successfully fulfill a Vice President position. Key strengths which I possess for the success of an administrative position include:

- Direct line operations responsibility improving gross margin to 8.0%.
- Planning and developing over $15 million in new construction projects.
- Reduction of departmental operating expenses to 1.1% below budget.
- Negotiating and developing contractual arrangements with vendors.

I have the ability to define problems, assess both large-scale and smaller implications of a project, and implement solutions.

The enclosed resume briefly outlines my administrative and business background. My geographic preferences are the midwest and southeast regions of the country. Relocating to a client's location does not present a problem. Also, I possess an MBA degree from _____ University, and a BS degree in Business Administration from _____University. Depending upon location and other factors, my salary requirements would be between $130,000 and $150,000.

If it appears that my qualifications meet the need of one of your clients, I will be happy to further discuss my background in a meeting with you or in an interview with the client. I will be contacting your office in the near future to determine the status of my application.

Sincerely,

Thomas Flokhart

Thomas Flokhart

TF
enclosure

"Cold" Cover Letter to Employment Industry Professional (Senior Manager)

Lisa K. Botkin
1003 Farmington Road
Colorado Springs, CO 80031

home: (888) 435-9584
senior manager@yahoo.com

(Date)

Mr. _____
ABC Company
1 Industry Plaza
Los Angeles, CA 90026

Dear Mr. _____:

Mentored by Bob _____, founder of _____, I successfully progressed within his privately held organization for twelve years, serving on the **Board of Directors of 13 separate companies** and holding positions including **Treasurer, Vice President of Finance,** and ultimately **President**. During my tenure the company grew from 7 employees to more than 1,000 while **revenues increased from $3 million to $108 million**. My enclosed resume gives further detail.

My reason for contacting you is simple. I am interested in exploring any senior management opportunities which may be available through your organization and would also be interested in interim or consulting roles. Geographically speaking, I have no limitations and am available for relocation throughout the U.S. and abroad. Due to the level and quality of my performance I feel it pertinent to state that I am only willing to consider positions consistent with my current income level. I have the experience, the talent and the energy to turn around, create or grow a dynamic organization.

I have built my career on my commitment and ability to create open lines of communication between the Board of Directors and senior management to **protect the investments of my organization and to assure the attainment of the target return**.

I look forward to hearing from you in the near future to discuss any mutually beneficial opportunities. If you do not at present have a need for a professional with my experience but know of someone who may, please be so kind as to pass my letter and resume on to that individual, or simply call me.

Sincerely,

Lisa Botkin

Lisa Botkin

LB
enclosure

"Cold" Cover Letter to Employment Industry Professional (International Operations)

Franklin Townsend

5555 Andover Avenue • Los Angeles, California 90025

Residence (323) 555-1234 • Mobile (323) 555-5555 • internationaloperations@email.com

(Date)

Ms. _____
(Title)
ABC Corporation
1 Industry Plaza
San Diego, CA 93725

Dear Ms. _____:

Over the years, I have built a successful career in **international operations and project management** on my ability to quickly and accurately assess situations, identify problems and focus on strategies which obtain results. I am currently seeking a challenging opportunity with an internationally focused, growth-oriented organization. I am willing to explore interim assignments and consulting projects as well as senior management opportunities. My enclosed resume details some of my accomplishments and credentials.

I have extensive experience in **diplomacy and international public affairs** dealing with foreign government officials, Heads of State, and Ambassadors as well as Fortune 100 senior executives. Building effective teams and inspiring others to peak performance are among my strengths. I am particularly adept at living and working effectively in foreign countries and with individuals of various cultural backgrounds. As such I am interested in opportunities both in the U.S. and abroad.

Feasibility studies, crisis resolution, and international risk assessment are areas where I excel. Unit construction and operations, mining/drilling and industrial equipment procurement, sales and distribution are areas where I may be of particular assistance, but my skills are transferable to virtually any industry.

I look forward to hearing from you to discuss any mutually beneficial opportunities that you may be aware of. Please feel free to send my resume to others who may have a need for a professional of my caliber.

Sincerely,

Franklin Townsend

Franklin Townsend

FT
enclosure

"Cold" E-Mail to Employment Industry Professional (IT Professional)

From: Jacqueline Smith [smithITpro@mindspring.com]
To: hr@corptech.com
Cc:
Subject: REF: Project management

Dear Mr. _____:

Capitalizing on my success managing IT design and implementation projects for ABC Design Corporation in Anytown, NY, I am seeking a professional opportunity where my project management, customer relations, and organizational skills can benefit your clients. With this goal in mind, I have attached for your consideration a resume outlining my qualifications.

Some of the experiences I would bring to a position with your firm include:

- *Defining project parameters, including interviewing clients to assess goals and objectives, and developing specifications and project deliverables.*
- *Serving on leadership teams that have managed project budgets of up to $10 million to consistently meet customer timeline requirements and budgetary constraints.*
- *Coordinating activities of programmers, Web developers, software engineers, network engineers, graphic artists, and customer representatives to meet project goals.*
- *Testing and validating applications during development stages and upon completion to ensure client objectives are met.*

I am open to relocation anywhere in the United States and would eagerly accept either contract assignments or permanent employment. I believe that my capabilities would allow me to serve your needs and benefit your clients, and would enjoy meeting with you to discuss my qualifications in greater detail. Please contact me via phone or e-mail to arrange an initial interview at your convenience.

Thank you for your time and consideration. I look forward to speaking to you soon.

Sincerely,

Jacqueline Smith
(516) 555-1212
smithITpro@mindspring.com

"Cold" E-Mail to Employment Industry Professional
(Computer Professional)

From: Sally Winston [computerpro@earthlink.net]
To: mcooper@isculptors.com
Cc:
Subject: Technology guru, plus global experience

Dear Ms. _____:

My broad background in all aspects of computers, from design and installation through user training and maintenance, coupled with my business operations expertise, are the assets I would bring to a position with one of your clients.

Currently I hold a management level position with MainLine Graphics, a firm that designs and builds flight simulators for U.S. and foreign governments. I provide the electronics expertise in completing approximately 12 major projects annually, which means I conceptualize the simulators' computerized mechanisms, direct the design and manufacturing processes, then install and test the systems at clients' sites around the globe.

In addition to providing technical expertise, the other major aspect of my job involves aggressively targeting new business. At a point when MainLine was facing an essentially saturated U.S. market, I designed and implemented an Internet Web site, then had it translated into several languages to target international clientele. The site generated 80% of our new business within one year.

Other assets I would bring to this position include skill in relocating entire company computer systems from existing facilities to new or expanded sites, as well as experience servicing all major brands of PCs. I am extremely familiar with nearly every computer-associated component, program, or operating system on today's market.

Thank you in advance for taking a few moments to review my resume. I am confident that the experience you'll find outlined therein will be valuable to your firm. Kindly contact me at your earliest convenience to schedule a professional interview.

Best regards,

Sally Winston
(516) 555-1212
computerpro@earthlink.net

"Cold" E-Mail to Employment Industry Professional
(Programmer/Analyst)

From: Suresh Gupta [certifiedprogrammer@yahoo.com]
To: hr@techvibes.com
Cc:
Subject: REF: Programming assignments

Dear Ms. _____:

My certification in computer programming, along with my professional background in electro-mechanical engineering, are among the primary assets I would bring to a programmer/analyst position with one of your clients.

As part of my training at Computer Institute in South Fork, NJ, I was required to design, write, code, edit, and modify an e-commerce Web site. The project succeeded not only because of my skill in applying my technical knowledge, but also because of my strict attention to detail.

Currently I'm employed at Dynamic Pharmaceuticals in Price Point, NJ, executing experiments on electrical/mechanical equipment I was involved in manufacturing to ensure conformance to customers' specifications.

I am also committed to furthering my professional education, which is key for success in this field. I plan to augment my knowledge by attending and completing relevant courses.

I am confident this background well equips me for success with one of your clients. Kindly review my resume, then please contact me at your earliest convenience to schedule an interview.

Very truly yours,

Suresh Gupta
(516) 555-1212
certifiedprogrammer@yahoo.com

"Cold" E-Mail to Employment Industry Professional (IT Management)

From: Maria Costas [ITexpert@aol.com]
To: cfloyd@mtechit.com
Cc:
Subject: Top productivity enhancement professional

Dear Mr./Ms. _____:

Leading information technology projects for high-growth companies is my area of expertise. Throughout my career I have been successful in identifying organizational needs and leading the development and implementation of industry-specific technologies to improve productivity, quality, operating performance, and profitability.

In my current position at XYZ company, I have initiated and managed the technological advances, administrative infrastructures, training programs, and customization initiatives that have enabled the company to generate over $3 million in additional profits in the past year. The scope of my responsibilities have included the entire project management cycle, from initial needs assessment and technology evaluations through vendor selection, internal systems development, beta testing, quality review, technical and user documentation, and full-scale, multi-site implementation.

My technological and management talents are complemented by my strong training, leadership, and customer service skills. I am accustomed to providing ongoing support and relate well with employers at all levels of an organization, including senior executives. Most notable are my strengths in facilitating cooperation among cross-functional project teams to ensure that all projects are delivered on time, within budget, and as per specifications.

Originally hired for a one-year contract at XYZ company, I have been offered a permanent position within the company. However, I am interested in greater challenges and would welcome the opportunity to meet with you to determine the contributions I can make to your client. I will call you next week to set up an appointment.

Sincerely,

Maria Costas
(516) 555-1212
ITexpert@aol.com

"Cold" E-Mail to Employment Industry Professional
(Systems Integration)

From: Michael Wilson [systemsintegrationpro@hotmail.com]
To: hr@sap-si.com
Cc:
Subject: Onstar engineer plus more

Dear Company Representative:

My solid background in electrical engineering supported by extensive management and product development experience are key assets that I can contribute to your client's future success.

Throughout my career I have worked with cutting-edge technologies, including **embedded microprocessors, RF, telecommunications,** and **wireless,** in the development and manufacture of products for varied industries. In all of my positions, integrating software, firmware, and hardware to create unique applications has been a key strength. Some of these applications that proved quite marketable include development of custom instrumentation and a PC-based network for tracking vehicles in transit. In addition, I have also played an important role in both the sales and customer support process, helping A+ Corp. win its largest municipal contract with the city of New Orleans.

Currently, I am exploring opportunities in the telecommunications industry where I can contribute significant expertise in systems integration. I welcome the opportunity to meet with you to explore areas of mutual benefit. Attached is my resume for your review.

In order to present my credentials more fully, I will follow up with you to answer any questions you may have. Thank you for your consideration.

Sincerely,

Michael Wilson
(516) 555-1212
systemsintegrationpro@hotmail.com

"Cold" E-Mail to Employment Industry Professional (Systems Administrator)

From: Dae Sung Kwan [systemsspecialist@mindspring.com]
To: gdawson@stokely.com
Cc:
Subject: Sys admin/people skills/military background

Dear Ms. _____ :

If you seek a new Systems Administrator who is more than just technically oriented, but also people oriented, then we have good reason to meet. As you'll find on my attached resume, I possess extensive technical skills and experience. What is more difficult to portray on a brief resume is my people skills.

Several colleagues, supervisors, subordinates, and end-users have commended me for my interpersonal skills. I am dedicated to helping others with their technical issues and sharing my knowledge to help them complete their work more efficiently. My job is to serve as a support person, there to keep the system operating smoothly for end-users, as well as to provide them training. I also understand that most technical projects are a team effort. Again, I have been recognized for my abilities as a team player as well as a team leader. I have a proven track record in taking projects and running with them, but the successes are a result of the combined efforts of the whole team. Whether it's a matter of motivating others, coordinating tasks, or just doing my part, I can do it.

My technical skills speak for themselves. My primary focus has been on Windows NT. In fact, I am currently pursuing my Microsoft Certified Systems Engineer designation. My plans are to attain this at about the time I leave the military. I will be able to bring this added expertise to an employer.

A meeting at your convenience would be greatly appreciated. Please feel free to contact me to schedule a time or to gain further information on my background. I am sure you will agree that I am right for the job after reviewing my resume and meeting with me in person.

Thank you for your time and prompt reply. I look forward to meeting you in the near future.

Best regards,

Dae Sung Kwan
(516) 555-1212
systemsspecialist@mindspring.com

POWER PHRASES

Consider using adaptations of these key phrases in your "cold" letters to employment service professionals.

I am an optimist, thrive on challenges, lead by example, and readily adapt to situations. If your client—international or domestic—would benefit from these kinds of qualities, we should get to know each other. If you will call or write at your convenience, I look forward to telling you more about my background.

As a dedicated listener, I am usually designated for client/customer relations and produce notable results in client/customer retention—even under the least favorable conditions.

An industry association referred to _____ as an active and selective executive search firm, and mentioned your name because of your work in logistics. I liked that referral and think our meeting would be mutually beneficial.

I would like to talk with you personally to further discuss our meeting. I suggest next week, the week of October 13th, when you have a free minute. I have asked my staff to forward your message immediately in case I am unavailable when you call. I look forward to hearing from you.

Please include my name in your job search database.

Including a mortgage loan benefit, I am currently earning $4,500 per month plus a car allowance. This should provide you with an indication of my present job level. Your suggestions or comments would be appreciated.

For 25 years, my family operated one of the most prestigious landmark inn/restaurants on Long Island. From the age of 6, I was a part of the family workforce—I couldn't wait to "help." That attitude pervades my work ethic and I'm grateful for the training that helped me to develop an attitude of service, teamwork and pride in performance and product.

One of your clients is looking for me, if not today then sometime in the near future. I know good people are hard to find because I've had to find them myself.

I have the depth of experience it takes to make a positive contribution.

Income is in the mid-five figures, but the right opportunity is the motivating factor. References and resume are available. With my well-rounded professional background I look forward to a new and interesting career opportunity through your firm.

I'm a natural "enroller" because my enthusiasm is contagious and I personally project credibility—people are inclined to (1) cooperate and participate wholeheartedly on projects with which I'm involved, (2) favorably consider products I recommend, and (3) be open to my efforts on their behalf when they experience problems or dissatisfaction.

The following are some highlights of my track record for your consideration:

I understand your clients frequently ask you to locate senior operating executives with much higher than average ability to accomplish difficult jobs quickly and profitably.

It is my goal to play an integral part in the development, operation and success of a small to mid-sized company where the diversity of my experience and the level of my commitment can be used to their fullest advantage and I can have the satisfaction of seeing the results of my efforts . . . really impacting profitability!

Please call at your convenience this week so we can explore potential opportunities more fully. Use the home number, please; our company's uncertain financial status is stirring up the office rumor mill. Thank you for your time and attention.

I am a motivated and dedicated leader. Many of my staff have worked for me from 10 to 30 years. My enthusiasm for meeting goals and accomplishing objectives has been contagious, and I know how to reward outstanding performance without disturbing a profit and loss balance. My employees and I thrive on a "family" environment with no loss of respect or production.

As a former business owner, I am well aware of the needs, concerns, and challenges facing management. By the same token, I am accustomed to operating with the best interests of the total business in mind and at heart, as well. I operate expeditiously, constantly seeking the best use of time, effort, resources and money . . . for my staff and myself.

My experience as an entrepreneur as well as an employee of a powerful, demanding employer gives me the unique ability to empathize the needs of management as well as the aggressiveness necessary to represent management effectively.

I'm seeking an opportunity to join an employer that can benefit from my expertise and experience while offering me the opportunity for challenge, continued professional growth, as well as commensurate compensation.

I'm a dedicated listener and an accomplished problem solver, always seeking to assist clients in accomplishing their mission. My clients experience and express a sense of trust and confidence in me and my recommendations because my sincerity and my efforts invested on their behalf are evident and consistent. They never have a doubt that I really care and will operate in their best interests.

Broadcast Letter (Faculty Position)

This instructor was awarded the faculty position she aspired to,
and she also was asked to chair the Humanities Department.

SARA ANNE STEEL

9999 OLD MILL ROAD • PAINTBRUSH, NM 77777
(999) 999.9999 • SASTEEL55@MINDSPRING.COM

May 3, 20–

Human Resources Office
RIO GRANDE UNIVERSITY
900 W. Casa Ave.
Yellow Creek, New Mexico 99999

I am interested in ideas,
not merely visual products.

—Marcel Duchamp

Dear Human Resources Coordinator:

An instructor in good standing at Rio Grande University, I am very interested in transitioning from painting, design, and art appreciation instructor to your recently posted **Jewelry Repair and Design Faculty position**. I was thrilled to discover an **exceptional match between your requirements for this opening and my skills and qualifications**. The enclosed curriculum vitae reflects a progressive career path and a credible candidate for this position. Qualifications follow:

Your Requirements:	My Qualifications:
MFA in Metal	MFA in Jewelry/Metalsmithing from Freemont Art University of New York, 20–.
Bench work/experience with jewelry repair practices	Jewelry repair and bench work for local retail jeweler. Experience includes stone setting, soldering, pearl bead stringing, ring sizing, jewelry designing, and riveting. Consider value and safekeeping.
Teaching, jewelry design education, and curriculum development	Two years' teaching experience. Comprehensive knowledge of casting gained through education, freelance, and contract work includes wax carving, wax chasing, and mold making.
Excellent communication skills	Comprehend the English language. Excellent oral and written self-expression. Give clear instructions and relate well to students. Relaxed communication style fosters encouragement and support. Subscribe to open-door policy.
Commitment to working with a diverse population	Successfully teach and interact with physically and mentally challenged individuals, as well as people of all ages from varied backgrounds and cultures.
Ability to manage projects and set specific objectives.	Extremely goal-oriented, giving particular attention to planning and follow up for positive results. Day planner and "to-do" lists spark productivity. Experience coordinating special events such as art shows, parties, and dinners.

Page 1 of 2

166

Besides these qualifications, I am an avid photographer, have an interest in gemology, and produce an average of one large art object a month. Personal qualities include a cheerful, energetic demeanor, positive attitude, dedication, self-sufficiency, and creative/innovative idea generation. I am passionate about art, teaching, and mentoring, and enjoy the two-fold return of the enthusiasm I bring to class.

Additionally, positive feedback from both peers and students precedes me:

- "I have never seen painting so strong from the art department," and "you are raising the bar."
- "I got more from this class (Painting I) than most others I've had."
- "This was the most exciting/stimulating class I've taken in 1½ years."
- "It was nice to see your work and know that it came from someone as normal as the rest of the world."
- "Your help contributed most to my learning. You were not afraid to help in any way you could."

Comments like these are especially fulfilling. Other job satisfaction comes from observing facial expressions when students finally comprehend a theory or concept and helping students discover and expand their creativity.

I am willing to handle the responsibility and safety issues involved in running a jewelry/metals lab and believe properly taught techniques and procedures are of vital importance. The prospect of teaching in my field and being on the ground floor of future jewelry department development energizes me. I am confident I will continue to offer a fresh perspective to course and curriculum development at Rio Grande University and look forward to a personal interview to further discuss your needs. Thank you for your time and consideration.

Sincerely,

Sara Anne Steel

Sara Anne Steel

Enclosure: Résumé

Broadcast Letter (Assistant Director of College Housing)

Used a side-by-side comparison to effectively illustrate her qualifications for the position.

BRENDA YOUNG

254 Dunhill Lane • Brentwood, NY 11717 • (631) 999-8866 • studentlife@college.edu

Miss Christine Timmons   January 12, 20–
Assistant Director for College Housing
State University of New York at Long Island
777 North College Road
Brookhaven, NY 11724

Re: Reference Code: TC-E-5556E2

Dear Miss Timmons:

In response to your ad for an Assistant Director of College Housing advertised in Sunday's *Newsday*, I have enclosed my resume for your review. To further illustrate my qualifications, the following outlines the scope of my experience as it pertains to the position's requirements.

Your requirements	My qualifications
• Bachelor's degree or four years of experience in lieu of degree.	• Master's degree in Clinical Counseling; • Eight years of combined experience in resident hall administration and counseling capacities.
• Promote and develop educational programming and maintain extensive budget.	• Plan, develop, and implement educational programs, and manage an operational budget.
• Administration of three to five residence halls housing approximately 1,000 students.	• Administration of residence halls housing up to 500 college students.
• Supervise, develop, and evaluate three to five full-time resident hall directors.	• Supervise, develop, and evaluate 26 Resident Advisors with direct responsibility for four RAs and a Head Resident Advisor (HRA).
• Develop departmental policies and procedures, manage area office including billing, occupancy, and facilities records.	• Direct all aspects of front desk management and facilities maintenance operations.
• Assist in the development and leadership of departmental committees, and serve as manager for student conduct cases.	• One year as VP of Committees and Organizations for the Student Government with the State University of New York at Suffolk.

Thank you for your review and consideration. I look forward to hearing from you soon.

Sincerely,

Brenda Young

Brenda Young

Broadcast Letter (Financial Planning Professional)

The employer was so impressed with the detail of the cover letter that he offered a position to this applicant at the initial interview.

David Meyers

310 E. 127th Terrace ▪ Kansas City, MO 64141

Phone: 816-555-6226 ▪ Cell Phone: 913-555-3588 ▪ E-mail: meyerstown@juno.com

September 19, 20–

Prudential Financial
David Borgrum, Manager
347 W. 47th Street
Kansas City, Missouri 64164

Dear Mr. Borgrum,

The Rock. Prudential is known internationally by this symbol of security and permanence, the assurance to their clients the company will always be there. The corporate slogan "Growing and Protecting Your Wealth" can only be accomplished through principled management, effective investment strategies, and ethical financial planners.

The relationship. With corporate scandal and financial malfeasance perceived to be the norm, now, more than ever, a relationship built on integrity and mutual respect is paramount to success in the financial services industry. As a goal-oriented financial planning professional who possesses strong marketing and communication skills, I am confident upon review of my qualifications you will find I have the solid combination of experience and achievement that Prudential looks for in its representatives.

My qualifications include:

- ✓ Series 7 and 66 Licensing.
- ✓ Registered Investment Advisor.
- ✓ B.A. in Economics.
- ✓ Commitment to client satisfaction and quality service through needs assessments.
- ✓ Demonstrated results in business development and execution of marketing strategies.
- ✓ Effective communication and presentation skills necessary to articulate product benefits clearly and accurately to clients.
- ✓ Outstanding time management and organizational ability.
- ✓ A willingness to "go the extra mile" for client and corporation.

The consultation. Inherent to every successful consultation, is my obligation to obtain a comprehensive financial background in order to meet the clients' future needs and objectives. Performing an effective client needs assessment, gives me the decisive edge when the client makes their financial planning decisions. Furthermore, I am skilled at new business development, cold calling and seminar presentations. Employers and colleagues have consistently praised my attention to detail, hard work ethic, and ability to deal with the most complex client engagements.

Please contact me at your earliest convenience to set up an interview concerning employment opportunities within your company. I look forward to hearing from you.

Sincerely,

David Meyers

David Meyers

Broadcast Letter (Heavy Equipment Operator)

Relocating to Northern Florida and wants to secure a position that could capitalize on his diverse range of skills.

JACK L. CROUTHER

Dear Sir or Madam:

Please accept the enclosed resume in application of your Heavy Equipment Operator position advertised in The Times Journal.

My diverse range of experience includes over ten years of experience operating and maintaining heavy equipment. In my current position, I operate backhoes, loaders, lulls, Gallion cranes, Ditch Witch trenchers (large and walk-behind), fork lifts, street sweepers, and bucket trucks. In addition, I supervise the troubleshooting, maintenance, and repair of all of the department's equipment.

Of equal importance are my supervisory and leadership skills where I have managed multiple crews of up to 40 employees. Being extremely diligent, I have assumed responsibility for overseeing and monitoring various projects and issues which affect the daily operations, efficiency, and profitability of the company. I am recognized by senior management for consistently completing projects on time and within budget.

My transition through several trades during my career has developed my strong multi-tasking abilities which have proven to be an asset in my current position. Additional areas of experience include plumbing, irrigation, landscaping, electrical work, fiber optics, and carpentry. In each of these areas, I have received training and have worked independently.

If you are in need of a person with my skills, I would welcome the opportunity to meet with you to determine the contributions I can make to your company.

Thank you for your consideration.

Sincerely,

Jack L. Crouther

Jack L. Crouther

11 Oaklawn Boulevard • Orlando, Florida 33082
Phone: (386) 749-2430 • Cell: (386) 147-5874 • jlcrouther@yahoo.com

Broadcast Letter (Executive Chef/Hotel/Restaurant Manager)

Michael started as a chef and went into the management side of the restaurant.
He is now looking to work for a multi-restaurant chain in a management capacity.

Michael J. Fisher C.M.C.

56 Madison Avenue
Summit, New Jersey 07901
(908) 277-8796

Dear Sir/Madam:

I am confident that my extensive experience as an executive chef and hotel/restaurant manager would serve as an asset to a position in your organization. My career began 23 years ago as an apprentice training under several notable internationally known chefs. Since that time I have been involved extensively in the area of food services management and marketing.

I am currently General Manager and Corporate Executive Chef of Hague Nieuw-York. In 20–, I was hired to start up this 225-seat restaurant. The casual dining establishment is part of Avanti Brands, Inc., USA. I am responsible for all financial reporting and instituted key control systems to meet the standards of the parent company. Additional achievements include gaining excellent media publicity, creative menu development, and directing on- and off-site catering for many New York City premieres. I was asked to coordinate all aspects of our new construction and assist in the design aspects of the kitchen.

As Director of Operations for Town Square Katering and Times Square Restaurant in Hoboken, New Jersey, my staff and I expanded the business to accommodate parties ranging from 10 to 4,000 people and grossed over $1.5 million in sales.

Working as Vice President of Operations and Executive Chef for Pine Ridge Country Club, I oversaw all profit and loss functions for a 165-seat à la carte restaurant and a 1,000-seat banquet facility. The club had an 18 hole Championship Golf Course that I managed, with an active membership of 1,000 members.

I gained extensive international experience working as Executive Chef for Ordini's, a five-star-rated restaurant in New Zealand, I prepared food for the Prime Minister, various heads of state, and visiting dignitaries. I obtained my New Zealand Master Chef's Certification. In addition, I served as an Executive Pastry Chef and Chef for a Hawaiian hotel owned and operated by the Sheraton Corporation.

Thank you for your consideration. I look forward to speaking with you personally regarding my qualifications and how I can contribute positively as a member of your management staff.

Sincerely yours,

Michael J. Fisher

Michael J. Fisher C.M.C.

Broadcast Letter (Maintenance Mechanic)

Elizabeth was a school bus driver who transitioned into a warehouse position, and eventually into a higher-paying maintenance mechanic position. After a downsizing, she wishes to continue her career as a mechanic.

ELIZABETH DENTON

1814 TAYLOR DRIVE ~ NORTH BRUNSWICK, NJ 08902
(732) 821-7227 (H) ~ (732) 406-1927 (C) ~ E-MAIL: LIZDENT3@MSN.COM

RE: Maintenance Mechanic

Dear Sir/Madam:

As a professional **Facilities** and **Maintenance Mechanic**, I understand that success depends on several factors. These include timely upkeep of machinery maintenance and repair, supervision of maintenance programs, and monitoring outside contractors. My extensive hands-on experience as a mechanic has allowed me to ensure timely completion of projects and adherence to corporate safety requirements.

Throughout my career I have been promoted and have acquired increasing responsibilities within every position. In my latest position as a Mechanic for Heinz Foods, I had the reputation for excellent machinery knowledge and a keen attention to detail.

Heinz Foods is downsizing the plant in Edison, NJ, and I have accepted a voluntary separation package from the company. I would like to continue my career with a new company offering me new challenges.

Thank you for your consideration. I possess excellent hands-on knowledge as well as supervisory expertise, and I look forward to meeting with you personally so that we may discuss how I may make a positive contribution to your team.

Very truly yours,

Elizabeth Denton

Elizabeth Denton

Enclosure

Broadcast Letter (Database Engineer)

Edward Kumamoto
kumamotoed@islandnet.com

P.O. Box 775
Mililani, Hawaii 96789

Home: 808-555-4563
Cellular: 808-555-5457

(Date)
Phillip _____
(Title)
ABC Corporation
1 Industry Plaza
Honolulu, HI 96772

Dear Mr. _____:

Empowering your employees with the information and tools necessary to make better strategic business decisions is very likely to improve your company's competitive advantage and profitability. I can do this through insightful strategic planning and the delivery of superior data warehouse and decision support systems.

My extensive career experience in data warehousing, database administration, and business systems development, coupled with my commitment to exceed customer expectations and my focus on achieving sustainable strategic competitive advantage, are the primary assets I would bring to your Director of Database Engineering position. I have successfully delivered numerous data warehouse projects that were effectively aligned with company strategic objectives. I am also highly skilled at directing teams on complex initiatives and improving processes, communication, teamwork, and quality.

As a senior-level employee of R & M Information Technology, Inc., I have established an excellent track record for successfully managing large complex projects. Notably, I managed a $10 million development project for Management Source One, building and implementing their first enterprise data warehouse and certain downstream divisional data marts. So successful was this project that within three months after implementation it established itself as the recognized supreme source of accurate company data for all of Management's North American business units. Additionally, it met tight service level commitments over 97% of the time and experienced no downtime due to programming error.

As a Project Leader/Manager for Churchman's Business Systems, Inc., I also managed the development of a large data warehouse. I led the design and development efforts for this data warehouse of sales information for their Specialty Products division. This was the first data warehouse developed at Churchman's that successfully met user expectations.

An additional asset I would bring to your organization is competency in correlating data warehousing functions with overall company goals. I am skilled in providing counsel to senior managers and executives and adept at monitoring data warehouse systems to continually ensure their value and usefulness to an organization as a whole.

I am confident that this experience well equips me for success as your Director of Database Engineering. Kindly review my resume, then please contact me at your earliest convenience to schedule a professional interview.

Sincerely,

Edward Kumamoto

Broadcast Letter (Senior Technical Sales)

STEPHANIE PAIGE NEWMAN

15 Jasper Loop ▪ Ft. Thomas, Kentucky 91075 ▪ (859) 386-2276
techsales@aol.com

Emily _____   (Date)
(Title)
ABC Corporation
1 Industry Plaza
Louisville KY 91057

Dear Ms. _____:

As a seasoned Technical Sales and Marketing Consultant, I've generated considerable new business for my previous employers, and now I'd like to do the same for you. For the past 15 years I have pursued an increasingly successful career in telecommunications sales and marketing. Among my accomplishments are:

SALES
Qualified to spearhead the entire sales cycle management process, from initial client consultation and needs assessment through product demonstration, price and service negotiations, and final sales closings.

MARKETING
Success in orchestrating all aspects of developing a gainful marketing strategy, from competitive market intelligence and trend analysis, product development, launch, and positioning to distribution management and customer care.

TELECOMMUNICATIONS & NETWORK SOLUTIONS
Recognized for pioneering technology solutions that meet the needs of complex customer service, logistics, and distribution operations. Able to test operations to ensure optimum systems functionality and availability, guide systems implementation across multiple platforms, and deliver user training and support programs that outpace the competition.

I hope you will contact me in the very near future. You'll find my address and telephone number listed above. I would welcome the opportunity to contribute my skills to the success of your marketing team and look forward to learning about any available opportunities in your corporation.

Very truly yours,

Stephanie Newman

Stephanie Newman

SN
enclosure

Broadcast Letter (Telecommunications)

Tom Clancy

444 55th Street • Springtown, TX 77333 • telecompro@aol.com
Home: (281) 000-0000 • Work: (281) 000-0000 • Cell: (713) 000-0000

(Date)

Emily _____
(Title)
ABC Corporation
1 Industry Plaza
Houston, TX 77521

Dear Ms. _____:

If you need someone with proven international success who will really listen to your
clients' needs and has leaped over cultural barriers to forge some of the most profitable technical opportunities in the telecommunications field, I am your #1 choice for
any opportunity in international or domestic sales or marketing.

For the last ten years, my work in strategic partnering, developing alliances, creating new opportunities, and exceeding multinational clients' expectations has helped
my employers more than double their sales. However, follow-up, tenacious attention
to detail, and my ability to listen have critically solidified longstanding relationships
with major players worldwide.

With a global leader in telecommunications, I received 3 promotions in 4 years due
to my success in managing contacts, motivating staffs, and implementing marketing
campaigns that delivered ROI threefold.

Since 20– I have ...

- Marketed a full range of data and voice communication services to multinational
  corporations and Internet service providers in Japan, Southeast Asia, Canada,
  and Western Europe.
- Brought in 28 new global accounts representing up to a 250 percent increase
  in business—currently handle brand management efforts for DWDM on pace to
  exceed annual goal; managed 20 accounts requiring broadband connectivity to
  international locations.
- Created the first transcontinental ATM circuit and earned one of the most prestigious awards in the company.
- Trained technical associates in ATM and employed knowledge of DWDM, SONET,
  SDMS, and TCP/IP technology to create some of the most cost-effective networks
  on the planet.

If these proven successes sound like the work of a go-getter you need on staff ...

- Consider that, in just 2 years with a system software developer, I added $1.5M in
  new business, trained an all-Japanese staff in direct marketing principles, and
  launched direct sales campaigns that increased client awareness of our services.

Page 1 of 2

175

Additionally, my efforts with an international contractor ...

- Partnered the parent company with Japan-based joint venture interests that enabled the first US-built airport in Japan.
- Kept Japanese executives and high-ranking government officials apprised of progress—and landed 2 additional opportunities for a total of $10M in business in just a year.

Technically speaking ...

- I have worked with ATM, Frame Relay, Private Line, SONET, DWDM, SNA/SDLE, SDMS and IP, and managed networks and a diverse array of hardware and software packages—in addition to holding numerous Novell and Windows specialized certifications.

I love calling on clients who have been abused by other reps, because I know my negotiating skills, ability to cross cultural barriers and generate win-win opportunities will get the decision-maker to sign every time.

Reviewing my attached resume, you will note doctoral, master's, and bachelor's degrees—and a host of quantifiable results and technical training that serve only to enhance my drive and enthusiasm. I will gladly set aside time to meet with you and discuss how my knowledge of technology, client relations, and strategic partnering can become your biggest asset.

I will take the liberty of contacting you on Monday at 10 a.m. If you need to reach me, please feel free to contact me at 281-000-0000. Thanking you in advance for the opportunity to meet with you, I am,

Sincerely yours,

Tom Clancy

Tom Clancy

TC
enclosure

Broadcast Letter (Senior R&D Engineer)

Samantha Robinson

11825 Rambling Rose Lane • Valley Glen, California 91405
(818) 555-5555 • R&Dpro@email.com

**SENIOR R&D ENGINEER ... patent holder ... launched x# new products...
recognized worldwide ... created win-win alliances ... cornered global markets...**

(Date)

Phillip _____
(Title)
ABC Corporation
1 Industry Plaza
Sacramento, CA 91401

Dear Mr. _____:

If your R&D-to-market time needs a sense of urgency, creativity, and a seasoned coordinator of people and priorities, I am one individual you need to discuss the ABD POSITION with. Here's why:

- STRATEGIC PLANNING: Etched long- and short-term technological plans that kept a $2B manufacturer ahead of its competition since 20–

- COORDINATED RESOURCES: 20+ years in planning, reviewing, and benchmarking technical performance, meeting budgetary goals, and coordinating interlaboratory and interdepartmental efforts

- IGNITED STAFFS' CREATIVITY: Led efforts and piqued an in-house multidisciplinary R&D staff's synergy; got x# new products to market

- ENRICHED KNOWLEDGE: Trained sales, marketing, and technical staffs since 19–; well-known for abilities to communicate new ideas, selected for numerous assignments in product training worldwide

- MOVED THE MARKET TO OUR PRODUCT: Recognized expert—created the need for cutting-edge technology in the cutting tool market by featuring results in technical articles for leading publications

- INTEGRATED OPERATIONS: 1 of 2 individuals to integrate a newly acquired company's R&D with parent company's

- IGNORED STIGMAS: First person to involve marketing with R&D-created pathway between R&D and marketing, bringing projects to market in record time; landed $10 million+ in new accounts—only non-salesperson to get a one-of-a-kind annual sales award

- IMPECCABLE RECORD: Achieved 70 to 80 percent first-time success rate in field testing for all products developed; hold x# US patents; consulted worldwide by engineers and scientists; published; presenter at technical conferences since post-doctoral fellowship

Reviewing my credentials and past results, you will note they occurred in the XYZ field. However, I am confident the core *technical, interpersonal, and organizational expertise I bring to your staff and customers would easily retrofit* at ABC CORPORATION.

If you need *a driven problem solver who can get your people moving to the work*, I am readily available to discuss how I can channel my more than two decades of success as your ABD POSITION at ABC CORPORATION. I will be in the area next month, and would prefer to meet with you then.

I am in a position to move to the Bay area, and *am ready to demonstrate how I can reignite your R&D efforts and create a flurry of opportunity*. Should you need added information, please do not hesitate to contact me at 818-555-5555 or R&Dpro@email.com.

Sincerely,

Samantha Robinson

Samantha Robinson

SR
enclosure

Broadcast Letter (Multilingual Sales Manager)

Robert Rodriguez

555 15th Street Apartment, 5A ~ Hoboken, New Jersey 07030
Cell: 201-555-5555 ~ Pager 201-555-4444 ~ E-mail: robrodriguez@hotmail.com

Fluent in Spanish . . . time management skills . . . 8 years front line experience . . . service-oriented positions . . . trainer . . . presentation expertise . . .

(Date)

Emily _____
(Title)
ABC Corporation
1 Industry Plaza
Trenton, NJ 07028

Dear Ms. _____:

If you know your *customers and operations deserve attention to detail*, as well as a high-energy individual who is *fluent in Spanish and makes people a #1 priority,* I am one individual you need to interview for an ZYX position at ABC Corporation.

Reviewing my credentials, you will note I have taught high school for the past eight years. This exposure to *daily planning, keeping people motivated and moving to the work* can be an immediate asset at ABC, and here are some areas up-front that align with your needs . . .

—SUCCESS IN DIRECT COMMUNICATION: Whether with students, decision-makers or the general public, my presentation skills kept people interested, involved and properly served . . .

—MULTILINGUAL ABILITIES: Fluent in Spanish, Japanese, and Russian—despite having a Spanish-only background, mastered the dialects of Russian and Japanese and was teaching classes upon hire at a school district . . .

—ALWAYS LOOKING FOR IMPROVEMENTS: Successfully integrated technology with additional conversational strategies . . . working for a distributor as an undergraduate, took initiative to revamp routing—increased productivity and service . . . increased a student's competency from 31 percent to 100 percent while an undergrad . . .

—FOCUS ON SERVICE: Made individual needs a priority as a teacher—adept in varying approach per individual personalities and priorities . . .

—MOTIVATED: Worked up to 30 hours weekly while pursuing degree . . . proven abilities to juggle diverse assignments opened door for additional assignments and leadership roles . . .

I seek to channel my communication, presentation, customer service, training and organizational skills, and the ZYX opportunity at ABC Corporation matches my goal for a transferable opportunity. *You would benefit from someone with a proven track record in front line positions, and your customers and operations will have a team player who knows how to set goals, meet goals, and keep customers' needs at the forefront.*

Page 1 of 2

179

I will take the liberty of contacting you on _____ at _____ to confirm your receipt of my information and briefly discuss how my energy and talents could be your asset. I would also like to arrange our meeting at that time. Should you need to reach me sooner, I can be contacted at 201-555-5555 or robrodriguez@hotmail.com.

Best regards,

Robert Rodriguez

Robert Rodriguez

RR
enclosure

Broadcast Letter (Management)

LORI PAULEY

···

6777 ELGIN STREET • MIAMI, FL 99844 • (555) 555-5555

(Date)

Phillip _____
(Title)
ABC Corporation
1 Industry Plaza
West Palm Beach, FL 99831

Dear Mr. _____:

People will only give you what you're willing to accept. That's why my staffs employed "The Golden Rule" every day, treating customers the way they themselves would like to be treated.

If you need someone with a technical background who has hired and kept top talent challenged and on their toes to deliver exemplary service, then consider that in 20+ years...

—I translated my knowledge of physics and business into profits and operational success—for my staffs, my employers, and myself.

—I took on the lead engineering position in my second year with an industry giant, skipping over the traditional 12-year career path—I simply outworked everyone and never said I couldn't do something or get it done on time or within budget.

—I earned full latitude in decision making after proving my team's understanding of a new target market's needs—I introduced more products than my successors, improved processes, and cut manufacturing and warranty costs by roughly $1M the first year.

—Operations I had an impact on experienced extremely low employee turnover—and employees met or exceeded customer expectations 100 percent of the time.

I've made sure my staffs are so service-oriented that the customer doesn't have to ask for warranty repairs or "the next step"—they have the answers or already have performed the warranty work.

And when my name is on a project, it always is on schedule within budget—and is a winner...

—When a relationship with a specialty manufacturer ended, I spearheaded development of an intake manifold line, analyzed and negotiated manufacturing costs, and selected vendors—and launched an 18-unit product line in 18 months that led the industry.

—The first race manifold we developed took the first 5 Chevrolet finishes in the 19– Daytona 500 without prior testing by participating teams.

Page 1 of 2

If you seek someone with the work ethic of a business partner, then I am your top choice for the _____ opportunity with the ABC Corporation. I fully understand the nuts-and-bolts of customer service, and certainly can combine my financial know-how with proven success in the field at ABC.

Right now I'm ready to step down from entrepreneurial management, simplify my role, and do "one or three things" well for an organization that values integrity, hard work, and creativity.

If I sound like the person you need at ABC, then contact me right away to discuss the _____ opportunity. I can be reached at 555.555.5555 after 6 p.m. Monday through Friday, or at my place of business at 555.555.1212 during regular business hours. I will take the liberty of contacting you on Monday at 10 a.m. to briefly screen my qualifications and arrange our interview.

Yours truly,

Lori Pauley

Lori Pauley

LP
enclosure

Broadcast Letter (HR Generalist)

Elliott Davidson
744 Haven Road
Millertown, NH 55599
(555) 555-5555 • davidsonhrpro@msn.com

HR GENERALIST
9 years advising senior decision-makers on employee matters...
5 years in benefits administration for $1B company and 5 affiliates...
15 years delivering HR presentations...
Open enrollment/benefits processing for professional employees...
13 years grievance/disciplinary meeting involvement...
10+ years training/development, entry through professional levels...
Worked through mergers and reorganizations...
Created award-winning concept for enrollment booklet...
Earned highest ratings throughout career...

(Date)

Phillip _____
(Title)
ABC Corporation
1 Industry Plaza
Concord, NH 55587

Dear Mr. _____:

If your organization seeks someone to advance your human resource programs, consider my proven track record. I am ready for a challenge with ABC Corporation, as your recent growth needs someone acclimated to working with new subsidiaries and maintaining the bottom line. I absolutely am ready to step in as your Human Resource Director at ABC Corporation, as my commitment extends to all areas you seek to address.

I bring you and your employees objectivity, knowledge of policy/procedure implementation and interpretation, and hands-on work in an ever-emerging climate. Here are some highlighted abilities that can be put to work immediately at ABC Corporation...

MET THE CHALLENGE: With little notification, stepped in and was an asset in a HR Directorship capacity; administered $20M in health and welfare benefits; initiated multi-tier health care plan to better suit regional product needs

BENEFITS: 5 years working with open enrollment for all levels of employees—restructured benefits during 3 internal reorganizations

Page 1 of 2

REMAINED FLEXIBLE: Adapted to the needs of entrepreneurial organizations while continuing a career with conservative major utility company

LEADERSHIP: Entrusted to step in for superiors due to track record in HR; #1 person consulted by senior managers of a $1B parent company and its 5 affiliates regarding HR or benefits; met with bargaining unit leadership, discussed and resolved grievances and complaints

COMMUNITY INVOLVEMENT: Accepted leadership role in United Way Campaign, keynote speaker for regional fundraising appearances

TRAINING/DEVELOPMENT: Delivered HR and benefits presentations since 1995, safety training, 2 years

OVER/ABOVE: Traveled over 3-year period to help a newly formed company whose explosive growth took it to 2,000 employees in 3 years (coordinated staffing and benefit enrollment while maintaining existing workload); singled out for HR support for special finance division structure, took on policy making/interpretation and HR

If you need someone seasoned in policy making who can interface with decision-makers and keep you 100 percent compliant with federal regulations, I am one individual awaiting your call for an interview.

I prefer to take the lead in contacting you, so I will call on Monday at 10 a.m. to brief you on how my background can be an immediate asset and arrange our meeting. I can forward a resume for your review immediately. Should you need to reach me sooner, I am at 555-555-5555.

Sincerely,

Elliott Davidson

Elliott Davidson
ED

~ Benefits Enrollment ~ Multi-Tier Coverage ~ Labor Relations ~ Grievances ~ Arbitration ~ Job Bidding ~ HCFA, HIPAA, COBRA Regulations ~ EEOC/PHR Compliance ~ Unemployment Compensation ~ Sexual Harassment ~ Safety Training ~ Background Investigations ~

Broadcast Letter (Operations Manager)

A downsized environmental operations manager trying to get back into a tight job market after 9/11.

Diane Baldwin

897 Station Street ▪ Brookfield, OH

330.555.4888 ▪ operationsmanager@alphone.net

(Date)

ABD Corporation
1 Industry Plaza
Cleveland, OH 44429
Attention Ms. Emily_____

Dear Ms._____:

Do you need an experienced, versatile individual who can improve bottom-line profits? I can offer innovative ideas to the position of Operations Manager—ideas that can benefit a service-driven, quality-oriented company like yours. No one has money to burn in a tough economy, which is why adding an already-skilled manager to your staff can reduce time and money.

The match between your needs and my talents is ideal. Why? Because my strengths lie in understanding the labor and manufacturing operations that design, build, install, and manage equipment for environmental and production improvements. I am a leader both by example and through effective management of individuals and teams. In short, I have the drive and vision to make a positive difference in any organization.

Dozens of proposed projects have been successfully implemented due to my established reputation for the quality of work completed. The work performed under my direction has come in at, or below, budget and we meet project deadlines.

The enclosed resume summarizes my qualifications and achievements. I would be glad to discuss any of this information with you as an opportunity of employment. Because "proven skills" are best explained in person, I look forward to our conversation and will call early next week to schedule our meeting. Thank you for taking the time to review my resume and for your consideration.

Sincerely,

Diane Baldwin

Diane Baldwin

DB
enclosure

Broadcast Letter (Pharmaceutical Sales)

.... **Rebecca Marks**

(Date)

ABC Laboratories
1 Industry Plaza
Philadelphia, PA 16175

Ladies and Gentlemen:

ABC Laboratories is one of the fastest-growing companies in the United States. Your achievements are impressive, and I am eager to make a contribution to your professional team as a Pharmaceutical Sales Representative. Given a chance, based on my enthusiasm and desire to excel, **I can make a positive difference in your company!**

As a recent graduate, my professional job experience is limited. However, I believe that you will find that I exhibit intelligence, common sense, initiative, maturity, and stability. Various jobs over the last ten years have required a good attitude and keen interpersonal skills. These jobs, along with my education, life's experiences and extensive travels, have not only enlightened me intellectually, but have also given me a totally different paradigm compared with other candidates.

Analyzing an audience is of utmost importance as a sales representative. As the daughter of a physician, I had great exposure to the medical environment. I strongly believe this gives me insight into the way physicians think—that patients' needs come first. Therefore, effective presentations of products must be made in a timely, succinct, and caring manner for successful sales in this industry. My desire is to stay close to the medical field, and working in a pharmaceutical company is exactly where I aspire to be!

After reviewing the enclosed resume, please contact me at (724) 555-9821 to arrange an interview. Because "proven skills" are best explained in person, I look forward to discussing how my qualifications can meet your personnel needs and contribute to your company's important mission.

Sincerely,

Rebecca Marks

Rebecca Marks

RM
enclosure

....
298 Jefferson Street • Wheatland, Pennsylvania 16161 • 724-555-9821

Broadcast Letter (Information Technology Program Manager)

DARRYL C. WARREN

51 Plantation Road, Apt. 7-C

Durham, NC 27706

(444) 555-4444

ITpro@yahoo.com

(Date)

Mr. Philip _____

CIO

ABC

1 Industry Plaza

Winston-Salem, NC 27561

Dear Mr. _____:

May I ask your advice and assistance?

As a result of J.P. Morgan's merger with Chase Manhattan Bank, I am confidentially exploring my opportunities. Although I am confident that I will be offered a role in the new organization, I am currently assessing where I can make the optimal contribution.

I am an Information Technology Program Manager. In this role, I have led the development of key financial systems and strategic business plans, co-managed the seamless migration of two divisions to another state and founded the PeopleSoft Wall Street Networking Group— delivering noteworthy cost savings and productivity gains. For the past 11 years, I've had dream jobs with leading firms like J.P. Morgan and Andersen Consulting. I have been entrusted with the direction of large scale, global projects. Many times, I learned "on my feet"—to implement new systems, design testing methods, manage resources, repair damaged vendor relations for mutual gain and to meet a wide array of challenges. My career has accelerated based on the results, as you'll note from the accomplishments in my enclosed resume.

I'm considering transferring my skills and experience to an organization where I can continue to be a team player and visionary leader for state-of-the-art technology programs, and where I'll also continue to learn new functional and technical areas. My expertise and interests are in the financial service industry.

I would greatly appreciate a few minutes of your time to discuss my options and glean any suggestions you can offer. I'll phone you in a few days to see if we can schedule a brief meeting.

Thanks very much.

Regards,

Darryl Warren

Darryl Warren

DW

enclosure

Broadcast Letter (Vice President of Operations)

A retiree in his late fifties, Barry is still interested in full-time employment and wants to communicate this to his contacts without giving the impression that he is "old" and "set in his ways." The tone of the letter is intended to be energetic and full of youthful enthusiasm.

Barry D. Hargrove

781 Forest Lane • Palmdale, CA 93591 • (447) 447-4477 • operationsvp@yahoo.com

(Date)

Philip _____, (Title)
Artesia Drilling Equipment
1 Industry Plaza
Modesto, CA 95354

Dear Mr. _____:

Problem - Action - Results. It is a simple formula, and one that I have implemented successfully throughout my long career in manufacturing. A former business associate passed your name on to me after commenting that my business philosophy and style reminded him of a CEO he had heard speak at a conference in Houston. That CEO was you.

It has been several years since I took my first job as a machinist back in Watertown, New York, but I have never lost my enthusiasm for finding faster and better ways to accomplish goals while cutting costs. I have worked my way up through the ranks from Foreman, to Plant Supervisor, to Manufacturing Engineer, to Director of Operations, and finally Vice President of Operations. Taking a swing at every new idea that came my way, I may have missed a few, but overall my batting average has been good:

- led a $340M manufacturing firm to earning ISO9002 certification on first attempt;
- revitalized operations at a plant site in Mexico by implementing a comprehensive employee training program;
- increased profits by 200% by identifying and rectifying problems with production and delivery at a Seattle manufacturing facility.

I believe strongly in teams and am comfortable working with R&D, engineering and marketing professionals. My colleagues have expressed appreciation for my direct and honest approach to people and problems.

Between jobs now, I am planning a fishing excursion on the Gulf. I will be arriving in Galveston on March 20th and would like to get together with you to explore potential opportunities with Artesia Drilling Equipment. It would be great to meet over lunch. I will give you a call the morning of the 22nd to see if that can be arranged.

I'm sending along my resume to lay a foundation for our meeting. I look forward to meeting you and exchanging ideas.

Sincerely,

Barry Hargrove

BH
enclosure

Broadcast Letter (Consultant)

A retired executive who wants to approach companies directly
and offer her unique expertise on a contract or consulting basis.

Elizabeth H. Jameson

49 IVANHOE COURT ◆ MONROE, NJ 08831 ◆ HOME: 732.658.6762

(Date)

Philip _____, (Title)
ABC Company
1 Industry Plaza
Ewing, NJ 08812

Dear Mr. _____:

- **Is your organization fully prepared to safeguard its technology services, information, and facilities in the event of a disaster?**

- **Are you taking full advantage of high-value and cost-effective vendor agreements?**

- **Do you benefit from high team performance and low turnover?**

If you have answered "No" to any of the above questions, then allow me to introduce myself and the expertise I can offer your organization. With a proven and award-winning track record of achievement, I offer a unique combination of expertise in disaster recovery/business continuity planning, vendor management/negotiations, and team leadership. I am currently offering my services to organizations within the Durham region, and would like to draw your attention to the value I offer.

Put simply, my expertise is delivering results. In previous positions, I have designed, implemented, and optimized comprehensive enterprise-class disaster recovery and information security procedures, saved millions in vendor negotiations and third-party service agreements, and led a variety of cross-functional teams to consistently achieve and exceed organizational mandates.

If the following interests you, I invite you to review the attached resume which further illustrates my experience, achievements, and expertise:

- **Expert in Disaster Recovery, Information Security, and Business Continuity**— expertise includes planning, protection, and off-site recovery of technology services, databases, and facilities

- **Superior contract procurement, negotiation, and vendor management capabilities**—proven record for negotiating agreements that improve service quality and save millions in vendor costs

- **Strong, decisive, and motivating leader**—reputation for building and leading high-performance teams to breakthrough achievement

- Available for **full-time, part-time, contract, and consulting opportunities**

Page 1 of 2

If you believe that you could benefit from a highly motivated and talented professional with a reputation for generating results, then I would welcome the opportunity to meet and discuss the specific value I can offer your organization.

I thank you for your consideration and I look forward to speaking with you soon.

Sincerely,

Elizabeth Jameson

Elizabeth Jameson

EJ
enclosure: resume

Broadcast Letter (Project Manager)

MICHAEL J. SALINGER

1 COLONIAL DRIVE • METROPOLIS, LA 70114 • (504) 123-4567

(Date)

Dear Employer:

Because of current market conditions and high unemployment, I am sure you have many candidates and few **Project or Training Manager** positions to fill. With this letter and resume, please allow me to add to your cadre; but, may I also give a few reasons why you might want to call me ahead of other qualified candidates should an appropriate position become available?

You will note that my educational and professional **background is broad** and includes experience in post-secondary organizations, community colleges, business, and the military. Because of this range of experience, I am able to bring **insight and the ability to relate well to individuals at all levels and from diverse backgrounds**.

Working within for-profit organizations has enabled me to develop an **eye for the bottom line**. Whether it be budgetary or profit-enhancing, I am continually evaluating systems and methods to make them more efficient and productive.

Incredulous as it may sound, I appreciate and welcome change. I am **known for my abilities as a change agent**. However, while I may embrace change—technologically or otherwise—I recognize that many do not. Therefore, from a management standpoint, I look for ways to make transitions more tolerable for the people in my charge.

While my resume is comprehensive, it does not fully demonstrate the manner in which I have achieved success. My character, personality, and the ability to effectively lead a project or team could be evidenced in a personal meeting. Therefore, I would welcome an interview to further discuss your needs and my qualifications. Thank you for your time and consideration.

Respectfully,

Michael Salinger

Michael Salinger

MS
enclosure

Broadcast E-Mail
(Senior Buyer/Purchasing Agent/Purchasing Manager)

From: Kalista Jabert [purchasingpro@earthlink.net]
To: humanres@aeiusa.com
Cc:
Subject: Smart Purchasing Choice

Mr./Ms. _____:

SENIOR BUYER * PURCHASING AGENT * PURCHASING MANAGER

Do you cringe at the high costs your company incurs for goods and services?

Do you need someone who will maximize vendor resources, working hard to secure lower-cost, longer-term contracts?

Do you need someone on board who will immediately slash supply costs and streamline purchasing operations?

With more than 20 years in purchasing, retail sales management, store expansions, and new product research and market launch, I believe I may offer just what you're missing.

In my esteemed career with Major Company, a premier auto parts and accessories distributor, I have:

- Directed procurement of over $200M of goods and services, accounting for 60% of MC's total purchasing budget.
- Launched 3 private label programs, garnering $500K in additional profits during the first year of distribution.
- Recouped $300K in stolen merchandise and prosecuted the employees responsible.
- Generated $3M in savings by cultivating partnerships and negotiating long-term contracts with key suppliers.

With the right opportunity, I'd be perfectly willing to relocate. With regard to salary, I understand that flexibility is essential and would consider a compensation package appropriate for a person with my outstanding qualifications and dynamic track record of accomplishments. If you're tired of seeing your company's profits slip through your fingers, call me today to schedule a business meeting. I can't wait to discuss how I can benefit your purchasing operation right away. I can be reached at (516) 555-1212 to arrange our interview.

Very truly yours,

Kalista Jabert
(516) 555-1212
purchasingpro@earthlink.net

Broadcast E-Mail (New Product Marketing)

From: Elizabeth Stettin [marketingexpert@aol.com]
To: bmathis@planetrecruit.com
Cc:
Subject: Real Marketing Savvy

Dear Mr. _____:

If you are looking for a successful executive to take charge of new product marketing, you will be interested in talking to me.

Ten years of experience in every aspect of marketing and sales in different industries gives me the confidence to be open to opportunities in almost any field. My search is focused on companies that innovate, because I am particularly effective at new product marketing. I have successfully managed new product-marketing research, launch planning, advertising, product training, and sales support, as well as direct sales. In my current position with XYZ Company, I created several products and marketing approaches on which other operating divisions in the company based their programs.

My business education includes a Marketing MBA from _____ University's School of Management, and provides me with a variety of useful analytical tools in managing problems and maximizing opportunities. My superior sales track record guarantees that I bring the reality of the marketplace to each business situation; I know what sells and why.

Currently, my total compensation package is in the low seventies; I am looking for a company that rewards performance consistently.

Since I am currently weighing several interesting opportunities, please contact me immediately if you are conducting any searches that might be a good fit. Relocation is no problem.

Thank you in advance for your consideration.

Sincerely,

Elizabeth Stettin
(516) 555-1212
marketingexpert@aol.com

Broadcast E-Mail (Senior Marketing Executive)

From: Joshua Michaels [marketingexec@yahoo.com]
To: hr@quantumcorp.com
Cc:
Subject: Ref: Your Marketing Executive Search

Dear Mr. _____:

I recently learned of your firm's excellent record of matching senior marketing executives with top corporations. I also have learned that you have an officer-level marketing assignment in process now—I am a serious candidate for your client's vacancy. Please consider some successes:

- After joining _____ as Marketing Director, I revitalized a declining processed-meats product category in less than a year, introducing better-tasting formulas and actually reducing product costs by over $100,000. Dramatic new packaging enhanced appetite appeal, and fresh promotion strategies doubled previous sales records.

- I have carefully crafted and fine-tuned many new product introductions and line extensions, such as _____ turkey, _____ processed meats, and _____'s deodorant maxi-pads.

- My sales/marketing experience dates from 199–, when I formed a direct sales company to pay for my _____ MBA (now the top-rated program in the U.S.A., I'm proud to say). Much of my subsequent success springs from strong working relationships with sales management and joint sales calls with field reps and marketing brokers. I have designed events like the _____ program, and _____'s sponsorship of the Indy 500 Williams racing team.

- I have a strong personal and professional interest in consumer electronics. I consult professionally and have successfully adapted marketing techniques for home and commercial satellite systems, "high-tech" audio/video, and radio communications equipment.

Please inform your client that I am fluent in French and I quickly absorb other languages. If your client challenges executives with the greatest of responsibilities and rewards them for remarkable performance, please contact me as soon as possible. I'll quickly repeat my past successes.

Sincerely,

Joshua Michaels
(516) 555-1212
marketingexec@yahoo.com

Broadcast E-Mail (Logistics)

From: Leonard Curtis [logisticspro@earthlink.net]
To: careers@ryder.com
Cc:
Subject: A logical choice for your client

Dear Mr. _____:

An industry association referred to your organization as an active and selective executive search firm, and mentioned your name because of your work in logistics. I liked that referral and think our meeting would be mutually beneficial.

I have a successful career of using logistics to cut costs and improve profits, usually in concert with other parts of the business. For example:

- I supervised the start-up of several remote offices to assist our plants in improving their distribution operations. By offering customized service, and through sharp negotiations, we saved over $500 million in various operations and warehouse costs.

- I directed the efforts of sizeable computer resources in the design and installation of a major application that saved $2.5 million in carrier costs. The application became the standard throughout the company's forty-six locations.

- Working with International Sales, I have established various Quality Control programs that have improved the timeliness and accuracy of product and paperwork delivery. Customer complaints plummeted to virtually zero, and remain there today.

A recent reorganization has reduced the number of senior management positions available within my company. I have concluded that another firm may offer a position and career advancement more in line with my personal expectations.

I would like to talk with you further. I suggest next week, the week of October 29, when you have a free minute. I have asked my staff to forward your message immediately in case I am unavailable when you call. I look forward to hearing from you.

Sincerely,

Leonard Curtis
(516) 555-1212
logisticspro@earthlink.net

Broadcast E-Mail (Vice President Asset Liquidation)

From: Gene Harrison [assetliquidationpro@mindspring.com]
To: cklause@cmaauctions.com
Cc:
Subject: Asset liquidation challenge? Get this guy!

Dear Mr. _____:

In recent years, as the Vice President of Lease Asset Liquidation with XYZ U.S.A., I successfully engineered the recovery of $23 million in assets, almost three times the original buyout offer of $8 million. Throughout my career I have been instrumental in developing and implementing workout and liquidation strategies and as such I have earned a strong reputation as a professional who gets the job done.

My reason for contacting you is simple. I am interested in project opportunities that will serve both to challenge and to utilize my abilities in asset liquidation management. My current project will be completed within the next four to six weeks. I am currently considering offers and intend to make a decision by February 1st.

The attached summary details some of my accomplishments. I look forward to hearing from you to discuss any mutually beneficial opportunities. Please feel free to pass along my resume to others who may have a need for my professional assistance.

Sincerely,

Gene Harrison
(516) 555-1212
assetliquidationpro@mindspring.com

POWER PHRASES

Consider using adaptations of these key phrases in your broadcast letters.

I hope this summary describes my experience and provides you with a better understanding of my capabilities. Thank you for your help.

If you feel that any of the strengths outlined in my resume could make a valuable contribution to your organization, please contact me to let me know of your interest.

Recently I read about the expansion of your company in the _____ Sun. As the _____ industry is of great interest to me, I was excited to learn of the new developments within ABC Corporation.

I feel confident that a short conversation about my experience and your growth plans would be mutually beneficial. I will be calling you early next week to follow up on this letter.

Currently, my total compensation package is in the low $70s; and I am looking for a company that rewards performance consistently.

I'm a responsive and responsible listener, maintaining a gracious and empathetic attitude, creatively troubleshooting, thoroughly researching options and making well-thought-out recommendations designed to establish and enhance customer/client relationships.

I am available for relocation and travel and am targeting compensation in the $50K range.

I fervently request more than your cursory consideration; I request your time to verify my claims. YOUR TIME WILL NOT BE WASTED.

Superior recommendations from industry leaders as well as verifiable salary history is available.

I hope you will not think me presumptuous in writing directly to you; however, in view of your position, I am led to believe that you are more aware of your organization's telecommunications personnel requirements than anyone else.

I am confident that with my experience I can make a significant contribution to your organization.

Throughout my career, I've been fortunate to represent quality merchandise and services and have learned just how to present them in their most favorable aspects. I know how to evaluate competition, to assess consumer/market needs, exploit a market niche, maximize profit margins, create and maintain a reputation for dependability and excellent service.

I am a self-starter looking to join a reputable firm, one that could benefit from an individual who is ready to give 110 percent. With over three years of sales experience, I have developed excellent interpersonal, organizational, and communication skills. I am a hard-working individual who is motivated by the knowledge that my earnings are directly related to the time, energy, and effort that I commit to my position.

I am personable, present a highly professional image, and deal effectively with both peers and clientele. I am confident you will agree that I should be representing your firm and not your competition. My salary requirements are negotiable. I will call you this week to set up a mutually convenient time for an interview.

Since beginning with ABC Company, my average commission has progressed from $400 to $650 weekly. My current salary or commission requirement would range upward of the mid-$20Ks, with specifics flexible and negotiable.

I look forward to hearing from you in the near future to schedule an interview at your convenience, during which I hope to learn more about the position, your company's plans and goals, and how I can contribute to the success of your team.

I am grateful for that environment and the faith that was demonstrated in my capabilities. I automatically moved into the role of Executive Assistant, constantly seeking ways to limit expenses, cut costs and generate additional profit for the company. I was exceptionally successful in that endeavor—while managing 5 operations, 3 warehouses, 6 Warehouse Managers and a staff of 60.

I am appreciative of the time you've spent reviewing this letter (and the accompanying material). I hope to hear from you in the very near future to arrange to meet in person and discuss just how my qualifications may be of value to your organization.

Networking Letter (Managerial/Administrative Position)

A colleague that Maurice hasn't spoken to in several months has been nominated for a prestigious award. He decides to capitalize on an opportunity to renew the acquaintance and enlist her help in his job search.

Maurice DuMaurier
1360 French Court
Rochester, New York 14692
585-555-5555

January 12, 20–

Ms. Philippa Consodine, President
Rochester Regional Industrial Management Council
1000 Main Street
Rochester, New York 14600

Dear Philippa,

Congratulations on your nomination for the Athena Award. Even though you were not the ultimate winner, the nomination itself demonstrates the high degree of professional excellence you have achieved.

It's been a while since we've chatted, and I wanted to bring you up to date on what I've been doing. After leaving The Highlands, I explored several options before accepting a position as Director of Human Resources for Jefferson County. Unfortunately, the daily drive to Port Charles, among other factors, proved to be untenable—particularly during the winter months—and I have left that position.

This puts me back in the job market, and I am writing to inquire if you are aware of any managerial/administrative positions that would capitalize on my skills. I have enclosed for your reference an updated résumé that includes my recent experience.

Reiterating some of the key capabilities that I can bring to a position, consider the following:

- ◆ **Excellent team building and leadership skills**
- ◆ **Superb interpersonal skills and supervisory experience**
- ◆ **Developing and implementing human resource policies**
- ◆ **Extensive knowledge and experience in the healthcare arena**

I am convinced that my experience and professional diligence could be an asset to one of the IMC's member firms, and would appreciate any referrals you may be able to give me for potential employment opportunities. I will contact you to arrange a convenient date and time when we might renew acquaintances. In the meantime, feel free to pass my résumé on to anyone who may have an appropriate opportunity, or give me a call at 585-555-5555.

Thank you in advance for your assistance. I look forward to talking with you soon.

Sincerely,

Maurice DuMaurier

Enclosure

Networking Letter (Administrative Assistant)

This "insider" networking letter positions well for an administrative assistant, especially since this firm values foreign language proficiency in German and French.

Susan Jacobsen
43 Beacon Court, Robbinsville, NJ 08691 ▪ (609) 371-2324

April 26, 20–

Mr. Tom O'Kane
Head of Human Resources
Firmenich Incorporated
P.O. Box 5880
Princeton, NJ 08543

Dear Mr. O'Kane,

Kirsten Alexander of Human Resources suggested that I contact you in regard to applying for a position as an **Administrative Assistant**. If you have need of a well-qualified professional with German and French language skills and experience in office administration, customer service, sales, training, and marketing, then we have good reason to meet.

My resume is enclosed for your review. Highlights include:

✓ Over eight years' experience in organization, coordination, communication, and customer service. Consistently focus on creating and maintaining excellent client relationships, and training others in successful techniques to do the same.

✓ A resourceful problem-solver with a track record of getting positive results, such as a 75% collection rate on accounts 90 days past due.

✓ Ability to build confidence and trust at all levels, and demonstrated experience in supporting cooperative, results-oriented environments.

✓ Proven communication skills, including fluency in French and German.

My career success has been due in large part to supporting teams, as well as internal and external customer relationships, and tackling persistent problem areas with creative approaches. I am seeking the opportunity to transition my experience, skills, and enthusiasm into a new organization where I can continue to contribute to bottom-line results while growing professionally.

Should my qualifications meet with your needs, I would be available to schedule a meeting immediately. I will call your office next week to answer any questions you may have and to set up a mutually convenient appointment. Thank you for your consideration.

Sincerely,

Susan Jacobsen

Susan Jacobsen

Enc. RESUME

Networking Letter (Internship/Employment)

A letter from a Japanese exchange student pursuing either an internship
or employment in a new program on campus.

.... **MOTOSHI MORI**

November 14, 20—

Ms. Deborah Marks
Chairman, Creative Media Academy
University of the Northwest
6543 Campus Road, Jones Hall 322
Seattle, Washington 98155

Dear Ms. Marks:

Since meeting you earlier this year at the Korean Film Festival we have
exchanged e-mails and met several times. We have discussed our mutual interest
in the Japanese movie industry and its future in the global entertainment business. You know well my vision of integrating Japanese gaming and animation
technologies into filmmaking.

Over the course of our conversations, you have mentioned that there might be
an opportunity for an internship or, possibly, employment in the Creative Media
Academy. I am very interested.

I offer negotiation, persuasion, and liaison abilities; and management, leadership,
and communication skills. I have also proven that I can use my bilingual proficiency to enhance international relations. Please see my résumé for examples of
how I have used these abilities in the past.

I believe that my unique strengths can contribute to the growth of the Creative
Media program, particularly if you are able to secure departmental status. I welcome the opportunity to discuss my continued involvement in your program.

Sincerely,

Motoshi Mori

Motoshi Mori

Enclosures: 2-page Résumé
             Addendum of Completed Coursework

....
1234 First Avenue, #460 • Seattle, Washington 98155
(206) 555-5555 • motoshi@hotmail.com

Networking Letter (Computer and Information Systems Manager)

A letter sent to follow up a meeting with a medical school dean.

DAVID KENT

1623 St. Louis Way • Honolulu, Hawaii 96813
808-555-6256 • dkent@alohanet.com

January 14, 20–

John Jones, M.D.
Dean, School of Medicine
University of Hawaii
1234 East-West Circle
Honolulu, Hawaii 96822

Dear Dr. Jones:

Perhaps you remember our chance meeting at the Bio Asia-Pacific Conference at the Sheraton Waikiki on August 18 and 19, 20–. In our brief conversation, I shared with you the idea of utilizing Web Development as an administrative tool. You expressed interest in the possibility of implementing such a system within the School of Medicine.

May I suggest a formal meeting to explore the idea?

I have some exciting and creative ideas, which may encourage you to take the next step toward realizing the positive impact a content management system would have in the School of Medicine. This would also be a great opportunity for us to discuss your goals and how an administrative intranet would help you reach them in a more timely and cost-effective manner.

In addition, there has recently been spirited discussion within the IT community on the topic of organizational continuity and its potential vulnerability due to advances in technology. I think you'll find the specific strategies I have to share with you worthy of consideration.

If you recall, my background is in Web Planning and Development, with specific skills in developing administrative intranets and public web sites, and designing Web-based software to address the internal and external reporting needs of organizations.

Enclosed is my résumé attesting to my experience and specialties. I will contact you within the next few days to discuss the possibility of meeting with you.

Respectfully,

David Kent

David Kent
Computer and Information Systems Manager

Enclosure: Résumé

Networking Letter (Management)

SHARI T. MALSCH

717-755-1369 (Cell) • 717-845-5856 (Home) • managementpro@email.com
202 Mason Street • Atlanta • GA • 30605

(Date)

Philip _____, (Title)
ABC Company
1 Industry Plaza
Atlanta, GA 30601

Dear Mr. Harmond:

It has been said, *"in today's world there are two kinds of companies—the quick and the dead."* I propose the same is true of managers. I am a dynamic management professional with extraordinary team building and interpersonal skills, and thrive in a fast-paced environment that is constantly moving and producing solid bottom line results. I relish a challenge and will never run from a difficult situation. In fact, if you want a successful completion, you can count on it, accurately, timely, and right the first time.

In addition to solid people skills, I posses an extensive management background in International Affairs. While living in Germany for five years, I had the opportunity to study the language and culture. Bilingual with excellent comprehension of both German and English, my translation skills are strong in both languages. I also have conversational knowledge of French. Having held direct responsibility for commercial dealings with the UK, Ireland, and Germany, my knack for capturing key client relations with diverse cultures and people is intense. I would like to bring my business savvy and management/marketing skills to your firm.

My experience spans industries such as Real Estate Development, International Affairs and Procurement; however I am an ideal candidate for a company that values a well-rounded staff who can step in wherever needed and isn't afraid to learn. Dedicated to doing whatever it takes to achieve outstanding results, I will lead your team to meet tight deadlines. In short, I will not let you down.

My resume is enclosed for your consideration. I look forward to meeting with you to discuss your needs and the immediate impact I will make to your organization.

Best regards,

Shari Malsch

Shari Malsch

SM
Enclosure

Networking Letter (Chief Financial Officer)

Primarily a treasury executive, Paul was seeking a broad-based
senior finance assignment and was offered a CFO position.

PAUL A. GERARDI

16 MAIN STREET • ST. PAUL, MN 55401 • 612-624-2817

Dear _____:

Perhaps your company could benefit from a strong chief financial officer with a record of major contributions to business and profit growth.

The scope of my expertise is extensive and includes the full complement of corporate finance, accounting, budgeting, banking, tax, treasury, internal controls, and reporting functions. Equally important are my qualifications in business planning, operations, MIS technology, administration, and general management.

A business partner to management, I have been effective in working with all departments, linking finance with operations to improve productivity, efficiency and bottom-line results. Recruited at The Southington Company to provide finance and systems technology expertise, I created a solid infrastructure to support corporate growth as the company transitioned from a wholesale-retail distributor to a retail operator. Recent accomplishments include:

- **Significant contributor to the increase in operating profits from under $400K to more than $4M.**

- **Key member of due diligence team in the acquisition of 25 operating units that increased market penetration 27% and gross sales 32%.**

- **Spearheaded leading-edge MIS design and implementation, streamlining systems and procedures that dramatically enhanced productivity while cutting costs.**

A "hands-on" manager effective in building teamwork and cultivating strong internal/external relationships, I am flexible and responsive to the quickly changing demands of the business, industry, and marketplace. If you are seeking a talented and proactive finance executive to complement your management team, I would welcome a personal interview. Thank you for your consideration.

Very truly yours,

Paul Gerardi

Paul Gerardi

Enclosure

Networking Letter (General)

Linda Brown
310 Hickory Valley Avenue
Nashville, Tennessee 37201
(615) 555.3471

(date)

Mr. Philip _____
1 Industry Plaza
Memphis, TN 37259

Dear Philip,

Congratulations on your re-election. I hope this letter finds you and your family well and that you have an enjoyable holiday season.

I am writing to update you on my job search. You may recall from our last discussion that I am now focusing on obtaining an hourly position with basic benefits that will sustain me until such time as I am ready for retirement (in three to five years).

As you recommended, I have applications on file with the Town of Anytown for various hourly positions and have corresponded with various department heads, in each case indicating my flexibility and strong interest in making a meaningful contribution to smooth operations within one of their departments.

Philip, I genuinely appreciate the advice and assistance you have offered to date. Once again, I am requesting that if you are aware of any other avenues I should be pursuing, please let me know. I believe I have skills and experience to offer and can be an asset to someone in just about any position requiring maturity, reliability, and dedication.

Thank you, again, for all your help, and Merry Christmas.

Sincerely,

Linda Brown

Linda Brown

Networking Letter (Accounting)

ROBERT A. DOWNEY

24 Autumn Drive ▪ Seattle, Washington 98101 ▪ (206) 730-2187
accountingpro@aol.com

(date)

Mr. Philip _____
ABC Manufacturing
1 Industry Plaza
Olympia, WA 98501

Dear Mr. _____:

As a motivated accounting professional with proven capabilities in financial analysis and accounting management, I believe that my education and experience could benefit your company. For this reason, I have enclosed a resume for your review, which outlines my relevant experiences.
Some key qualifications that may be of interest to your firm include:

- Extensive experience in providing timely and accurate financial reports utilizing a variety of applications and procedures. I have managed accounting functions for a manufacturing firm with over $100 million sales. I advanced quickly in the finance department and have gained a wide range of experiences, primarily focusing my efforts on analyzing, reporting, and planning.

- Absolute reliability and dedication to efficiency. As key financial analyst, I have worked closely with controllers and managers in monitoring financial input/output, streamlining financial reporting processes, and meeting aggressive deadlines for delivering information and analyses. I am also knowledgeable and current on legislative and regulatory requirements.

- Long-term vision. I have participated in both strategic planning for long-term marketing, and in annual budget preparation. My analyses and input have contributed to the successful outcomes of external audits, annual reviews, and budgeting processes in domestic operations.

- Proficiency in current business applications, including CODA, DCS, 4TH Shift, FAS1000, MP 2, FOCUS, and Microsoft Office.

I have a strong desire to move into a business environment where my skills can be fully utilized in effectively furthering a leading firm's business objectives. I am confident that my knowledge and expertise, along with my dedicated professionalism, would allow me to make a significant contribution to your company's ongoing success. I would enjoy meeting with you to further discuss the possibilities. Please contact me to arrange a convenient date and time for an interview.
Thank you for your time and consideration. I look forward to speaking with you soon.

Sincerely,

Robert Downey

Enclosure

Networking E-Mail (Employee Benefits Administration)

From: Angela Sullivan [benefitsspecialist@hotmail.com]
To: awilliams@tcm.com/hr-careers/
Cc:
Subject: Great to talk to you again!

Dear _____:

It was a pleasure to speak with you on the telephone recently and, even more so, to be remembered after all these years.

As mentioned during our conversation, I have just recently reentered the job market and have ten years of experience with a 3,000-employee retail organization in the area of employee benefit administration. My experience includes pension plans, and dental, life, and disability insurance. I have been responsible for all facets of management of the company plan, including accounting, maintenance, and liaison with both staff and coverage providers.

My goal is to become a Benefits Manager in a larger organization with the possibility of advancement in other Human Resources areas. My preference is to remain in the Metropolitan _____ area.

For your information, attached is my resume. If any situations come to mind where you think my skills and background would fit or if you have any suggestions as to others with whom it might be beneficial for me to speak, I would appreciate hearing from you. I can be reached at the telephone number listed below.

Again, I very much enjoyed our conversation.

Yours truly,

Angela Sullivan
(516) 555-1212
benefitsspecialist@hotmail.com

Networking E-Mail (Publishing)

From: Robert Render [publishingpro@aol.com]
To: hr@pennwell.com
Cc:
Subject: Thanks for all the help ;-)

Dear _____:

It was a pleasure to meet with you for lunch today. I am grateful for the time you took out of your busy schedule to assist me in my job search.

It was fascinating to learn about the new technology which is beginning to play a major role in the publishing field today. I have already been to the bookstore to purchase the book by _____ which you highly recommended. I look forward to reading about his "space age" ideas.

I will be contacting _____ within the next few days to set up an appointment. I will let you know how things are progressing once I have met her.

Thanks again for your help. You will be hearing from me soon.

Yours sincerely,

Robert Render
(516) 555-1212
publishingpro@aol.com

POWER PHRASES

Consider using adaptations of these key phrases in your networking letters.

It was good talking with you again. As promised, I am enclosing a copy of my resume for your information. If any appropriate opportunities come to your attention, I would appreciate it if you would keep me in mind.

After you have had a chance to look over the resume, please give me a call.

I am beginning to put some "feelers" out in advance of the completion of my degree in December.

I do not intend to target any specific type of job. I am open to most anything that my qualifications will fit. My only criteria are the following:

I would appreciate any advice and/or referrals you might be able to give me.

I am looking for a position in management and would appreciate any assistance you could provide.

As always, it was good to talk with you. Your positive outlook is catching. I've been called the eternal optimist, but I always feel more upbeat after a conversation with you.

Many thanks for the words of encouragement and taking the time from your busy schedule to help me. It truly is appreciated. I have never faced an unemployment situation like this before.

It was a pleasure to speak with you on the telephone recently and, even more so, to be remembered after all these years.

For your information, enclosed is my resume. If any situations come to mind where you think my skills and background would fit, or if you have any suggestions as to others with whom it might be beneficial for me to speak, I would appreciate hearing from you. I can be reached at the telephone numbers listed above.

He assured me that he would pass my resume along to you; however, in the event that it has not reached you yet, I am enclosing another.

Perhaps you know of a company that could use this scope of experience. In this regard, I enclose a copy of my resume outlining a few of my more significant accomplishments.

My objective is to find a _____ level position at a marketing driven company where my skills can contribute to the firm's growth and profitability.

I am not limited by location and would consider the opportunity wherever it presents itself.

First of all, let me sincerely thank you for taking the time and trouble to return my call last Monday. I found our conversation informative, entertaining, and (alas) a little scary. Needless to say, I genuinely appreciate your prompt response and generous, helpful advice.

Again, a thousand thanks for your time and consideration. If I might ask you one last favor, could you please give me your opinion of the revision? A copy is, as usual, enclosed.

I am writing to you in response to our recent conversation over the telephone. I thank you for your time and your advice. It was most generous of you and sincerely appreciated. Please accept my apologies for invading your privacy. I anticipated an address for written correspondence from an answering service.

I look forward to hearing from you on your next visit to _____.

I hope you'll keep me in mind if you hear of anything that's up my alley!

I recently learned that your firm is well connected with manufacturers in the _____ area and does quality work. We should talk soon, since it's very likely we can help each other. I'll be in the office all next week and look forward to hearing from you. I have alerted my secretary; she'll put your call right through.

_____ suggested that I contact you regarding employment opportunities.

After many years in the _____ community, I have decided that a career change is due in order to use my interpersonal skills to their fullest.

Follow-Up Letter (after telephone contact) (Fundraising Consultant)

From an applicant who has had too many jobs in too few years, this letter
was designed to get two competing "partners" to bring her on board.

··· **Lanina Crowne**

Wednesday, 02 May 20–

Ms. Patty Martineau
Vice President
O'Neill & Associates
Three Peachtree Avenue, NE
Atlanta, Georgia 30305-3001

Dear Ms. Martineau:

Thank you for making time to explore how I could help O'Neill & Associates as
your newest Fundraising Consultant.

I've already starting thinking about how I might be most productive—right from
the start. Of course, my ideas must be preliminary; I don't know exactly how
your organization works. Nevertheless, I would value your reactions to the preliminary thoughts you'll find in the next paragraphs.

I want each of your clients to see the tailored solutions we provide as a rapid,
seamless, continuing operation that guides them through the complex world of
modern fundraising. In fact, I want them to think of us as their "sole source"
for the resources they must have to grow financially and operationally. If we are
to speak with the one voice the clients should demand, then our business model
requires close teamwork between Ms. O'Neill, you, and me.

In the meantime, I am modifying my own continuing professional development
program to concentrate on fundraising from a consultant's perspective. I've begun
to look through the literature and contact professional organizations to hear about
the latest trends directly from industry leaders. Later, I'll use what I learn to re-
evaluate my own successes in campaigns done with and without consultants.

I appreciate your vote of confidence in recommending that I meet with Ms.
O'Neill. And I want to make that interview just as useful for her as possible.
Toward that end, may I call in a few days to get your reactions to the prelimi-
nary thoughts I've outlined above?

With many thanks for all your help...

Sincerely,

Lanina Crowne

Lanina Crowne

···

1000 New College Way • Cumming, Georgia 30041
[678] 555-5555 (Home) • lcc@randomc.com

Follow-Up Letter (after telephone contact) (Adjunct Faculty)

STEPHANIE A. MONACO

862 Lafayette Parkway
Rochester, New York 14625
(585) 555-5555

EDUCATOR/ADVOCATE/MENTOR
"Every leader a teacher, every teacher a leader, every student a success."

Emily _____   (Date)
(Title)
ABC Community College
1 Industry Plaza
Princeton, NJ 08540

Dear Ms. _____:

I enclose my resume in follow-up to our conversation last week regarding the adjunct adult education position currently available at Anytown Community College. I appreciate very much your offer to forward my credentials to the appropriate individual.

With a master's degree in Education Administration, Principal of Administration and Supervision certification through the state of New York, plus four years of cumulative experience in the classroom, I believe I possess the expertise and qualifications that are critical to leading your organization's adult students to successfully achieve their educational goals.

What do I offer your students?

- Effective listening and communication skills—a demonstrated ability to provide individualized instruction based on students' interests and needs.
- Encouragement and motivation—a creative, inviting atmosphere of interaction and participation.
- Sincere desire to reach them on a level they can understand, no matter what age, skill level, or cultural background.

I am excited at the opportunity to work with adult students, because I recognize that they are in that classroom because they want to be there. The adult population brings a unique flavor of enthusiasm and motivation that energizes and inspires me as an instructor and makes me eager to go above and beyond expectations to help them reach their goals.

In terms of salary, I realize that flexibility is essential and am therefore open to discussing your organization's compensation package for an individual with my distinctive talents. If you believe that I could play an important role on your educational team, please call me at (585) 555-5555 to arrange for an interview.

Sincere regards,

Stephanie Monaco

Stephanie Monaco

SM
enclosure

Follow-Up Letter (after telephone contact) (Legal Assistant)

JAMES PENSON
2279 Reynolds Road, Ocala, Florida 33739
(352) 796-4476 legalpro@aol.com

(Date)

Phillip _____
(Title)
ABC Corporation
1 Industry Plaza
Orlando, FL 33576

Dear Mr. _____:

Thank you for returning my telephone call yesterday. It was a pleasure speaking with you, and as promised, a copy of my resume is enclosed. As I mentioned, I have been working in law firms since the end of February, as well as working on weekends and in the evenings for over one year. At present, I am looking for a second or third shift to continue developing my word-processing and legal skills.

Although the majority of my positions have been more managerial and less secretarial, I have developed strong office skills over the years. While I was attending both undergraduate and graduate school, I worked as Administrative Assistants to Deans and Department Heads, in addition to working in other professional capacities.

_____ speaks very highly of me, and if you need to confirm a reference with him, please feel free to contact him at _____. In addition, I would be happy to furnish you with names of people I have worked for within law firms over the past year.

Within the next day, I will be contacting you to arrange a convenient meeting time to discuss the position you now have available. However, if you would like to speak with me, feel free to contact me at 352-796-4476.

Thank you again for calling yesterday. I look forward to speaking with you on the telephone, and meeting you in person.

Sincerely,

James Penson

James Penson

JP
enclosure

Follow-Up Letter (after telephone contact) (Purchasing)

CHERYL BLOOM
....
89 PINE ROAD • OMAHA, NE 68117 • (555) 555-5555

(Date)

Bob _____ - (Title)
Krieger, Skvetney, Howell
Executive Search Consultants
2426 Foundation Road
Lincoln, NE 68154

Dear Mr. _____:

In reference to our telephone conversation, enclosed is my _____ resume. I believe the one you have is written toward a sales and marketing position.

Since we last spoke I have been working as a business consultant for the _____ group of companies on projects in a number of different areas outlined below.

- Elected to serve as the Vice Chairman of the _____ Chapter 11 bankruptcy creditors committee including the two primary subcommittees reviewing offers to purchase the _____ operations.

- Spearheaded and supervised upgrading of the _____ companies' communications systems, including printing and copy machines, telecommunications systems, computer hardware and software systems, computer scanning system, computer filing system, and fax and modem transmission systems.

- Set up and implemented an auto and entry floor mat marketing program for _____ including pricing and product displays for retail sales outlets.

- Researched, purchased, and installed a bar code labeling program for the companies' products, including label set up and printing systems to allow them to sell their products to _____.

- Participated in the design and layout of a new logo for _____ division including specifications for all letterheads, forms, and printed communications materials.

- Provided major input for a factory-paid _____ point-of-sale system to display custom automotive floor mats.

Most of my projects should be wrapped up by the end of November, and so I will be looking for another company who could utilize my broad range of experience. Please let me know if you think you might have something for me.

Sincerely,

Cheryl Bloom

CB
enclosure

Follow-Up Letter (after telephone contact) (Manager)

Andrew T. Bestwick
653 Lassiter Drive
Lake Wylie, SC 29710
(803) 458-8004
managerpro@aol.com

(Date)

Bob _____
(Title)
Krieger, Skvetney, Howell
Executive Search Consultants
2426 Foundation Road
Columbia, SC 29753

Dear Mr. _____:

THANK YOU for allowing me to tell you a little about myself. I have just completed my MBA (December, 20–) and would appreciate the opportunity to talk with your client companies who are in need of an experienced and seasoned manager. Whether the need is for general (operational) management, products, marketing, or sales, my substantial background in management, marketing, and technical products should be very valuable to your clients.

I have enclosed two resumes (marketing-oriented and operational-oriented) with some other information which you may find useful. With eyes firmly welded to the bottom line, I offer: the ABILITY to manage, build, and quickly understand their business; EXPERIENCE in domestic and international corporate cultures; INTELLIGENCE and the capacity to grasp essential elements; and the WILLINGNESS to work hard, travel, and relocate.

Realizing that most of your clients aren't looking for VPs, I'm not necessarily looking for fancy titles (but I am promotable). What I am looking for is that special position which will offer not only a challenge but a career opportunity with long-range potential. I know my successes will bring them (and me) rewards.

Resumes and letters are brief by their very nature and cannot tell the whole story. I will be happy to discuss with your client and you how my commitment to them will help solve their needs or problems and will definitely make good things happen! After all, isn't that the bottom line?

May we work together?

Very truly yours,

Andrew Bestwick

Andrew Bestwick

AB
enclosures

Follow-Up E-Mail (after telephone contact) (General)

From: James Young [jyoung@earthlink.net]
To: hr@agcocorp.com
Cc:
Subject: Glad we finally caught up

Dear Ms. _____:

I appreciate the time you took yesterday to discuss the position at _____. I recognize that timing and awareness of interest are very important in searches of this type. Your comment regarding an attempt to contact me earlier this summer is a case in point.

Attached, as you requested, you will find an outline resume. I also believe that my experiences as a director of physical plant services are readily transferable to a new environment. I believe that I can contribute a great deal to the satisfaction of your client's needs.

Realizing that letters and resumes are not an entirely satisfactory means of judging a person's ability or personality, I suggest a personal interview to discuss further your client's needs and my qualifications. I can be reached directly or via message at (516) 555-1212, so that we may arrange a mutually convenient time to meet. I look forward to hearing from you. Thank you for your time and consideration.

Sincerely,

James Young
(516) 555-1212
jyoung@earthlink.net

Follow-Up E-Mail (after telephone contact) (Arts Management)

From: Jasmine Morgan [promotionspro@yahoo.com]
To: ewoods@maoriartspromos.com
Cc:
Subject: Thanks from a motivated flack!

Dear Ms. _____:

Per yesterday's conversation, I am forwarding a copy of my resume and am looking forward to our meeting in the very near future.

As we discussed, the positions that interest me are as follows:

Event/Arts Management
Promotions/Advertising/Public Relations
Corporate Training

I am a fanatic about image, excellence, and attention to quality and detail. As my academic and career background reveal, I have the tenacity of a rat terrier when it comes to task accomplishment.

I have never held an "eight-to-five" job and would most likely be bored to death if I had one. Therefore, I am looking for something fast-paced and challenging to my gray matter that will allow growth and advancement and an opportunity to learn. I am in my element when I am in a position to organize . . . the more details the better!

I'll give you a buzz on Tuesday, March 14th to try to set an appointment for further discussion.

Sincerely,

Jasmine Morgan
(516) 555-1212
promotionspro@yahoo.com

POWER PHRASES

Consider using adaptations of these key phrases in your follow-up letters after phone calls.

As you requested in our telephone conversation this morning, I am enclosing a copy of my resume for your review.

As you can see from my resume, I have some excellent secretarial experience.

I'll give you a buzz on Tuesday, March 15th, to set an appointment for further discussion.

In reference to our telephone conversation, enclosed is my sales and marketing resume; I believe the one you have is written toward a purchasing position.

I am a bright, articulate, and well-groomed professional with excellent telemarketing skills, sales instincts, and closing abilities. I am seeking a dynamic position with a reputable firm. I would like to meet with you in person to discuss how I could contribute to the effectiveness of your clients' operations.

Please remember me if something arises that would tie in with my background.

My many long-term professional relationships would benefit any employer in this area.

I'd like to meet with you to tell you more about my background and to show you some of the training and marketing materials I've developed. This would give you a better picture of my capabilities.

As you suggested when we spoke last week, I have enclosed my resume for your review and consideration. I contacted you on the recommendation of _____ of _____, who thought that you may have an interest in my qualifications for a position in the near future.

I have long admired _____ for its innovations in the industry, and I would consider it a tremendous career opportunity to be associated with your organization.

Follow-Up Letter (after face-to-face meeting) (Library System Director)

Victoria was genuinely impressed with the facility she visited, but also recognized she could help them improve by applying her management experience.

Victoria Leung

64 West Blossom Circle ▪ Brighton, New York 14618 ▪ (585) 586-5803

January 12, 20–

Ms. Louisa May Prescott, President
Orchard County Library Board
West View Library
One Orchard Parkway
MacIntosh, New York 14782

Dear Ms. Prescott:

Thank you for the opportunity to visit your facilities and discuss the Director's position with you. I enjoyed meeting you and the other trustees, as well as Sylvia Morrison and members of the library staff. I was impressed with your outline of the position and believe that I possess the capabilities to successfully lead the Orchard County Library system well into the 21st century.

My tour of three of your branches and my conversations with several staff members made it easy for me to understand how you have achieved your national ranking. As someone with over 20 years in the library field, and experience visiting literally hundreds of library branches in the course of a year, I was favorably impressed with the design and space utilization of your branches. The cordiality of your staff members and the fine way in which the facilities are maintained are also quite impressive. Your "Friends" organization and Foundation also appear to be real assets to the library.

Some key talents that I can bring to this leadership position include:

- *Establishing a strategic vision and motivating staff to pursue that vision.*
- *Maintaining productive rapport with advisory boards, and successfully interacting with governmental entities and the community at-large to achieve library goals.*
- *Developing information technology plans that have prepared libraries for the 21st century and that anticipate the changing technological landscape.*

I remain most interested in this position and am confident that my knowledge and expertise would allow me to exceed your expectations in this leadership role. I look forward to further discussing my candidacy with you soon.

Sincerely,

Victoria Leung

Victoria Leung

Follow-Up Letter (after face-to-face meeting) (Sales)

A two-point letter: (1) reinforces the point that he was successful in sales, even though he hadn't ever worked in pharmaceutical sales, and (2) moves the hiring official to make a decision.

NORMAN CORNFELD

75 Willow Street • Crenshaw, Alabama 36078 • 334.555.5555 • ncorn72@aol.com

Friday, July 20, 20—

Mark Pugh
Area Manager
Aventis Pharmaceuticals
609 Greenwich Circle
Birmingham, Alabama 35243

Dear Mr. Pugh:

Thank you for making time to meet with me this morning. Even during our interview, it struck me how good a match I think I am for Aventis. And on the way home, I began to formulate a plan to be productive for you from the first day, based on how I might meet your special needs. Here's what I've come up with so far:

Your needs	My capabilities
• Good track record	• Bringing in twice my sales quotas for four consecutive years. • Being my organization's top producer in those same four years.
• Communication skills that build sales	• Capturing sales with presentations before busy decision makers.
• Good work ethic	• Turning around a market that had been stagnant for 15 years. • Regularly overcoming strong sales resistance.

I can offer everything you see above because I show the benefit of what I sell—not just to the end user, but to the people who deliver those benefits. That's a direct parallel with an Aventis strength.

I've already spoken with your Dothan representative. And I'm looking forward to my "ride along."

At this point, most applicants would ask you to contact them if you have questions. I want to do something different. Please consider this question: What additional information do you need from me to choose me as the best candidate for the position?

Sincerely,

Norman Cornfeld

Follow-Up Letter (after face-to-face meeting) (Loan Processor)

Richard had to overcome the effects of a prolonged slowdown in his industry—portfolio management—and convince the decision maker that his skills were transferable and he could master the intricacies of new product lines he had never worked with before.

RICHARD WEIGMAN

1100 Apartment A	[334] 555-5555 (Home)
Patton Street	[334] 555-8888 (Office)
Montgomery, Alabama 36100	rweigman@hotmail.com

Wednesday, 13 June, 20–

Malcolm S. McLeod
Vice President
Alabama Home Mortgage Lending
1200 17th Street, South
Birmingham, Alabama 35205

Dear Mr. McLeod:

Thank you for meeting with me this afternoon. I think Alabama Home Mortgage Lending and I are a good match if I can be your newest loan processor.

In fact, as I was driving back to Montgomery, I began to plan how I might be productive for you right from the start. My ideas are, of course, preliminary. But I would value your reactions to this tentative plan:

- I would start by introducing myself to every "player." I want them to think of me as Alabama Home Mortgage Lending. And I want to find out what their special needs are before any rush requirements come up. When they need answers, I want them to remember two things: my name and my phone number.

- I have already started my plan to master FHA requirements. As first step, I'm jotting down the kinds of questions I must have the answers to so I can process FHA loans fast and right the first time. I want Alabama Home Mortgage to be the "provider of choice" in the eyes of buyers, agents, closing attorneys—in short, anyone who wants quality loan processing services. If I am successful, I hope our percentage of revenue for FHA loan processing grows steadily.

As you asked me to, I plan to call on Friday. And I've already thought of the question I would most like to ask. Here it is: Will the plan I've outlined above work for Alabama Home Mortgage faster and better than any plan suggested by the other candidates you've interviewed?

Sincerely,

Richard Weigman

Follow-Up Letter (after face-to-face meeting) (Concierge Associate)

Lacking professional experience as a concierge, Olivia was sure to remind her interviewers of her related volunteer work, enthusiasm, education, international travel experience, and multilingual communication skills. Notice how she copied ("cc") her interviewers.

Olivia Beth Copperfield

2 Jenkins Place
Brentwood, NY 11717
(631) 455-2344
worldtraveler@sky.net

February 19, 20–

Ms. Janet Berlinger
Human Resources Specialist
The Marriott Wind Watch Hotel
1717 Motor Parkway
Hauppauge, NY 11788

Dear Ms. Berlinger:

Thank you for the opportunity to participate in a follow-up interview with you and your supervising managers, Mr. Sean Johnson and Mrs. Rita Bronson, to further discuss the possibility of my joining your hospitality team as Concierge Associate.,

As discussed during our meeting, The Marriott Wind Watch Hotel is the ideal work environment for me to express my enthusiasm for working with people as well as put to use my education in psychology and business administration. I feel strongly that my volunteer work experience at The New York Hilton and my personal experiences acquired over the years while traveling worldwide will prove especially valuable in this highly visible position. Combined with an ability to communicate effectively in Spanish, French, and Italian, I feel I would make a significant contribution to The Marriott Wind Watch Hotel.

Please note that my availability is immediate. If you need to contact me, I can be reached at the above telephone number. Thank you again for your time and consideration. I hope to speak with you soon.

Sincerely,

Olivia Beth Copperfield

Olivia Beth Copperfield

cc: Mr. Sean Johnson
     Mrs. Rita Bronson

Follow-Up Letter (after face-to-face meeting) (Merchandise Manager)

This thank-you letter capitalizes on reinforcing the "fit" between the potential job and her qualifications, as well as introducing some areas overlooked in the interview.

DEBORAH DEVEREAUX

555 MAIN STREET, LAWRENCEVILLE, NJ 08648
(609) 771-5555 HOME • EMAIL: DDEVE@BOL.COM

November 9, 20–

Ms. Melinda Newby, Director
Human Resources
Universal Stores
1700 Primary Place
Princeton, NJ 08540

Dear Ms. Newby,

Thank you for the opportunity to interview for the **Merchandise Manager** position. You were extremely generous with your time and I was impressed with the warmth and efficiency of your office, and your genuine interest in acquainting me with the company's concepts and goals.

My background is unique – it does not fit into a traditional career mold – yet it encompasses a very diverse exposure in Home Furnishings and Ready-to-Wear. As we discussed, my extensive experience with the type of clientele your company targets has prepared me to quickly "come on board" your team. My sales record of $279,000 (20–) demonstrates that I can produce immediate value, as well as train new sales reps in highly effective merchandising and closing techniques.

What I did not stress is that I also have built an arsenal of skills around quantitative, technical processes involved in merchandising dollar planning. For example, I have developed six-month dollar merchandising plans for the RTW division of Chic Apparel, and classification planning which established the focus on merchandise categories, prices, styles, sizes, and colors.

I have always strived to achieve high quality results by knowing the customer well, anticipating profitable market trends and never forgetting the store image. Offering wide, but well-edited, assortments of multiple classifications so that one-stop shopping can easily occur has been my hallmark. Such high standards have been central in all of my work, whether with a major retail department store, New York City wholesale showroom, or upscale home furnishings boutique. Your corporate environment and company goals appear to reflect those same high standards and I am eager to join your team.

I am very interested in this position and would like to touch base with you next week to check on the progress of your search. Thanks again for the opportunity to interview.

Sincerely,

Deborah Devereaux

Follow-Up Letter (after face-to-face meeting)
(Manufacturer Representative)

Anthony Ruggerio

4 Edgewood Court   Dover, NJ 00000

Home Phone: (555) 555-5555 • Cell Phone: (555) 555-5555

February 28, 20–

Ms. Kathleen McMann
General Manager
Panoramic Imaging
975 17th Street
Morris, NJ 00000

Dear Ms. McMann:

Thank you for allowing me to interview with you on Friday, February 23rd, for the Manufacturer's Representative position. Everything I learned from you about Panoramic Imaging leads me to believe that this is a progressive company where I could fully utilize my skills and make a valuable contribution. In fact, I have not been this determined or excited about a job since I started my business 25 years ago.

As I mentioned to you, I am sales oriented and have a solid technical background in printing. I relate well to printers at any level, from pressmen to owners. In my sales activities with John Watkins when he was a printing buyer at Dart Industries, I found him to be very demanding and hard to please. One of the reasons why I was successful in acquiring and retaining his business was my constant commitment to customer service. Whenever there were any questions, I never failed to answer them promptly.

During our discussion, you seemed to express a concern about my lack of experience with dealers. Although I had not mentioned it at the time we spoke, I have had long-term relationships with dealers like Arvine, and have bought approximately $1 million worth of equipment from them, starting with my first press and expanding to 20 over the years. I am certain that with my persistency and follow-through, I know I can handle dealers at the sales and service end. Rest assured that I would keep you informed of my progress on a daily basis. Nothing would be done without you knowing about it. My first priority will be to make you look good.

Among my major strengths, I am goal-driven, self-motivated, have a strong work ethic, and an ability to learn quickly. My training period would be brief, and I would use my own time to familiarize myself with your equipment and product line. In addition, I am accustomed to long hours and have no objection to the travel requirements throughout the Middle Atlantic states or being away from home four days a week.

Coming from a medium-sized company, it would be an honor to work at Panoramic Imaging, and I am hopeful that I would have the chance to be a member of your team. Please do not hesitate to call me if you have any further questions or need additional information from me.

I look forward to your positive decision about my candidacy.

Sincerely,
Anthony Ruggerio

Follow-Up Letter (after face-to-face meeting) (General)

MARCY SMITH

222 East Ninth Street – Maryland Heights, MO 63146

999-555-4444 – marcysmith@msn.com

(Date)

Phillip _____
(Title)
ABC Corporation
1 Industry Plaza
St. Louis, MO 63141

Dear Mr. _____:

Thank you very much for taking the time to meet with me today. I enjoyed our discussion, and I'm now even more excited about the possibility of working for ABC and with your team.

It was great to learn that you are embracing technology as it relates to your business—both in terms of day-to-day operations and the future delivery of ABC's programs (e.g., on-the-spot training). I am very interested in, and have an affinity for, computer technology and would love to be a part of your efforts in this area.

I am confident that I could make a strong contribution to the continued growth of ABC. As we discussed, I have related experience in all of the required areas for the position. In addition, I look forward to taking a project management approach to establishing the new system for the delivery of the assessment workshops to your key client. This process would allow me to ensure that I am meeting your objectives and getting a system "up and running" within an established time frame. Having done this, I would continually review for improvement and focus on managing the enhancement of customer service.

I remain very interested in the position, and I look forward to hearing from you soon. If you require additional information in the meantime, I may be reached at (999) 555-4444.

Sincerely,

Marcy Smith

Marcy Smith

MS

Follow-Up Letter (after face-to-face meeting) (Librarian)

The interview in this case was by a committee and very structured, leaving the candidate with the feeling that there was more she would have liked to have said. This thank-you letter conveys some of these ideas. The result: the candidate was hired for this high-level position.

··· **Mary Kelner**

(date)
Mr. Philip _____
(Title)
ABC State Librarian
State Library of ABC
Wichita, KS 66627

Dear Philip:

Thank you for the opportunity to meet with you and the selection committee on Monday. I enjoyed our discussion of the Associate State Librarian for Library Development opening. I was impressed with your vision for this individual's role.

Based on our conversation, I believe that I possess the capabilities to successfully meet your expectations for this key position with the State Library.

To reiterate the experiences I bring to this opportunity, please note the following:

- Promoting programs and fostering working relationships with over 1,000 member libraries in all major segments of the field. These activities also encompass extensive community outreach.

- Providing strategic vision and mission, and motivating staff to pursue visionary goals. In two leadership assignments, I have recognized staff for their efforts and given them the guidance and direction that has delivered exceptional program results.

- Managing capital projects and spearheading information technology initiatives. These encompassed upgrades to comply with ADA access requirements, renovations that improved space utilization, and leading efforts to incorporate technology into library settings.

- Supervising departments in urban and suburban settings to address a broad range of competing priorities. Among these experiences was the supervision of an Interlibrary Loan department serving 100 individual branches in a five-county area.

I am most interested in this position and am confident that my track record at Ledgerock demonstrates my capacity to "hit the ground running," and apply my leadership, enthusiasm, and expertise to furthering the mission of state libraries in this development role. I look forward to continuing our discussions in the near future.

Sincerely,

Mary Kelner

Mary Kelner

···

113 Normal Avenue, Topeka, Kansas 66612
(785) 757-5555 Home • librarianspecialist@optonline.com

226

Follow-Up Letter (after face-to-face meeting)
(Construction Manager)

Leonard Curtis

123 Circle River Drive • Littleton, CO 81579
555.555.5555 • constructionmanager@msn.com

Emily _____ (Date)
(Title)
ABC Corporation
1 Industry Plaza
Craig, CO 81625

Dear Ms. _____:

We had the opportunity to speak briefly at last week's Chamber of Commerce meeting concerning the Construction Management position you are seeking to fill in Vancouver. I appreciate you filling me in on the details of the project and have enclosed my resume as you suggested.

As we discussed, I am well acquainted with ABC Corporation's brand and store concept, and I am excited to learn of the company's expansion plans over the coming decade. With my background in construction, maintenance, and project management as well as operations and strategic leadership, I believe I am primed to play a key role in this growth.

As Chief Executive Officer of Superior Landscape Design, I have been instrumental in leading the company to phenomenal success within a very short time, building the organization from start-up into a solid revenue generator reputed throughout the Pacific Northwest as an aggressive competitor in markets crowded by multimillion-dollar, nationally recognized companies.

I am currently in the process of selling the company and have been exploring opportunities with dynamic, growth-oriented organizations like yours that could benefit from my broad-based expertise in operations, organizational management, finance, and business development. Complementing my diverse leadership background is expertise in all the fundamentals of construction management, including the ability to see projects through to completion while exceeding quality standards.

Perhaps one of my strongest assets is my ability to cultivate long-lasting relationships with clients through attentive, direct communication. I have been highly successful at defining complex project plans, establishing budgets, outlining scope of work, and directly soliciting qualified contractors utilizing the bid process. I also offer extensive experience navigating through the paperwork and bureaucracy, forging productive alliances with key regulatory agencies to streamline permitting and licensing and to facilitate expedited project starts.

I would enjoy the opportunity to speak with you again in greater detail. Could we meet for lunch on Friday? I'll call your assistant in a few days to confirm the appointment.

Best regards,

Leonard Curtis

Leonard Curtis

Follow-Up Letter (after face-to-face meeting)
(Executive Assistant)

Janice Moss
55 Cherrytree Circle
Ashland, KY 41101
(606) 555-5555

(Date)

Phillip _____
(Title)
ABC Corporation
1 Industry Plaza
Lexington, KY 41235

Dear Phillip _____ :

The time I spent interviewing with you and Sandra gave me a clear picture of your company's operation as well as your corporate environment. I want to thank you, in particular, Phillip, for the thorough picture you painted of your CEO's needs and work style.

I left our meeting feeling very enthusiastic about the scope of the position as well as its close match to my abilities and work style. After reviewing your comments, Phillip, I think the key strengths that I can offer your CEO in achieving his agenda are:

- Experience in effectively dealing with senior level staff in a manner that facilitates decision-making.
- Proven ability to anticipate an executive's needs and present viable options to consider.
- Excellent communication skills—particularly, the ability to gain feedback from staff and summarize succinctly.

Whether the needs at hand involve meeting planning, office administration, scheduling, or just serving as a sounding board, I bring a combination of highly effective "people skills" and diversified business experience to deal with changing situations.

With my energetic work style, I believe that I am an excellent match for this unique position. I welcome an additional meeting to elaborate on my background and how I can assist your CEO.

Sincerely,

Janice Moss

Janice Moss

Follow-Up Letter (after face-to-face meeting)
(Management Information Systems)

CHRISTOPHER FALK

5555 VALLEY VIEW AVENUE • RESEDA, CALIFORNIA 91335 • (818) 555-5555

(Date)

Bob _____
(Title)
Krieger, Skvetney, Howell
Executive Search Consultants
2426 Foundation Road
San Jose, CA 95113

Dear Mr. _____:

Thank you for meeting with me this morning. Our associate, _____, assured me that a meeting with you would be productive, and it was. I sincerely appreciate your counsel, insight, and advice.

I have attached my resume for your review. I would appreciate any feedback you may have regarding effectiveness and strength. I understand you may not have any searches under way that would be suitable for me at this time, but I would appreciate any future considerations.

As we reviewed this morning, I seek and am qualified for senior MIS positions in a medium to large high-tech manufacturing or services business. I seek compensation in the $150,000-and-above range and look to report directly to the business CEO. These requirements are somewhat flexible depending on a number of factors, especially potential, of a new position. My family and I are willing to relocate to any area except New York City.

Please consider any associates, customers, or friends who may have contacts that would be useful for me to meet with. I have learned how important networking is, and will really appreciate some assistance from a professional like you.

Thanks again, Mr. _____, and please let me know if I can be of service to you. I wish you and your colleagues continued success and look forward to a business relationship in the future.

Best regards,

Christopher Falk

Christopher Falk

CF
enclosure

Follow-Up Letter (after face-to-face meeting) (Assistant)

MELANIE SHREVE
34 Oakwood Road
Provo, Utah 84062
(801) 555-3443

(Date)

Emily _____
(Title)
ABC Corporation
1 Industry Plaza
Salt Lake City, UT 84037

Dear Ms. _____:

Thank you for the opportunity to discuss the position of Assistant.

ABC Corporation is involved in one of the most pressing concerns of today: environmentally safe methods of disposing of solid waste materials. The challenge of creating proper disposal systems is paramount. I look forward to being a part of an organization that is focusing on furthering the technology needed to enhance our environment.

At ABC Corporation I would be able to:

- Be a productive assistant to management
- Be a part of a technologically developing industry
- Be in a position to learn and grow with the opportunities presented by your company
- Be involved in the excitement of a new, expanding company

The skills that I have to offer ABC Corporation are:

- Professionalism, organization, and maturity
- Excellent office skills
- Ability to work independently
- A creative work attitude
- Research and writing skills
- Varied business background
- Willingness to learn

Again, thank you for considering my qualifications to become a part of your organization.

Sincerely,

Melanie Shreve

Melanie Shreve

Follow-Up Letter (after face-to-face meeting) (Sales)

A follow-up on a meeting Carol arranged with a targeted employer. While there was no position currently available, she nevertheless wants to "sell" her suitability.

CAROL ANN CONASTA

43 Meadow Lane ~ Ludlow, MA 01056
(413) 589-2222 ~ salespro@comcast.net

(Date)

Philip _____
(title)
ABC Company
1 Industry Plaza
Boston, MA 01059

Philip,

First of all, thank you. I thoroughly enjoyed our meeting last Wednesday, and greatly appreciate your insight and the time taken to discuss where I might best fit in to the ABC team. Your professionalism and willingness to share what you know put me instantly at ease, and I am now even more motivated to be part of ABC's success.

Let me begin by restating how flattered I am that you saw such potential in me. I likewise feel confident that I have the management and leadership expertise, marketing skills, and business development experience to be successful, and I see tremendous opportunities for ABC in the future.

However, as we discussed, I understand that my first step is to make my mark as a member of the Road Crew and am equally excited at the opportunity to make an impact on the front line. I realize that you are not currently in the position to make such an offer, but I want to re-emphasize my enthusiasm to join the ABC team wherever you feel I could add value.

If you will, I'd like to take a moment of your time to re-state a few key points:

- I possess the drive, commitment, and strong people skills required to make an impact in this industry.

- I offer proven business development, sales, and revenue building experience.

- I know what it takes to get results, both out of myself and from others, and have proven again and again to be the "go to" person when results are expected.

I hope that you and I have the opportunity to continue our discussions and, once again, I appreciate the time you spent to meet with me. I wish you continued success in all your efforts and look forward to seeing you at the Sales Excellence seminar at the end of July.

Sincerely,

Carol Ann Conasta

Carol Ann Conasta

CC

Follow-Up E-Mail (after face-to-face meeting) (General)

From: William Long [w_long@hotmail.com]
To: jones@alphavax.com
Cc:
Subject: Great meeting! Can we talk again Tuesday?

Dear Mr. _____:

I appreciate the time you took today interviewing me for the position. I hope our 2-hour meeting did not throw off the rest of the day's calendar. I trust you will agree that it was time well spent, as I sensed we connected on every major point discussed.

Your insight on e-commerce was intriguing. My history in hi-tech, manufacturing, and bio-medical industries and background in technology solutions seems to be a good match with the opportunities available in your company. As I mentioned, at Continuum Biomedical I initiated the marketing stratagems that opened our markets to Latin America. What I failed to mention is that I also have contacts with some e-commerce investors developing online portals targeted to Latin Americans.

I am very interested in the position and would like to touch base with you on Tuesday to see where we stand.

Sincerely,

William Long
(516) 555-1212
w_long@hotmail.com

Follow-Up E-Mail (after face-to-face meeting) (Sales Manager)

From: Damien Chavez [salespro@aol.com]
To: mgabor@lds.com
Cc:
Subject: Thanks for an exciting meeting. Next steps?

(date)

Mr. Philip _____
(title)
ABC Corporation
1 Industry Plaza
Anytown, NY 12096

Dear Mr. _____:

I thoroughly enjoyed our meeting on Wednesday. After learning more about the ABC Corporation and its goals, the prospect of joining the organization as the Western Region Sales Manager is even more exciting.

One of the most important things I have learned in my 20+ years in sales is to listen to what the customer needs. I have always taken pride in designing customized solutions that not only meet the clients' objectives, but also are competitive in price. This philosophy has enabled me to exceed corporate expectations for 17 consecutive years. In addition, I have managed to convert about 65% of my clients to "repeat order" accounts, an objective you indicated was a high priority for your sales team in ensuring the company's continued growth.

ABC Corporation's Western Region Sales Manager position is an important cornerstone in the company's overall growth plans for the new fiscal year. The company is poised to make significant strides to gain ground on the competition and the West Coast territory will be instrumental in making the corporate goals a reality. I am excited about contributing my expertise, meeting ABC's customers, and building long-term client relationships.

Thanks again for your time. I am certain that I can be a valuable asset to your sales team, and I look forward to having the opportunity to contribute to ABC's growth.

Sincerely,

Damien Chavez
(516) 555-1212
salespro@aol.com

Follow-Up E-Mail (after face-to-face meeting) (Senior Counselor)

This e-mail shows how her skills and experience in counseling matched this particular job opening and would be an asset to the agency and its clients.

From: Susan Goodman [skilledcounselor@earthlink.net]
To: cpatterson@couns.edu.msu
Cc:
Subject: Looking forward to next week

Dear Ms. _____:

I would like to thank you for affording me the opportunity to meet with you to discuss the Senior Counselor position with your organization. I have long been an admirer of your services and commitment to the community. I am very confident that my education, experience and counseling skills will enable me to make an immediate and long-term contribution to your mental health program.

The position we discussed seems well suited to my strengths and skills. My counseling and teaching background includes an emphasis on the family unit and its influence and relationship to each client's needs and therapy.

I am looking forward to seeing you, again, next week. If you require any additional information before then, please feel free to call. Thank you for your time and consideration.

Sincerely,

Susan Goodman
(516) 555-1212
skilledcounselor@earthlink.net

Follow-Up E-Mail (after face-to-face meeting)
(Management)

From: Henry Jacobs [hjacobs@yahoo.com]
To: jjordan@forman.com
Cc:
Subject: The right choice for program development

Dear Mr. _____:

The position we discussed Friday is a tremendously challenging one. After reviewing your comments about the job requirements, I am convinced that I can make an immediate contribution toward the growth and profitability of ABC Corporation.

Since you are going to reach a decision quickly, I would like to mention the following points, which I feel qualify me for the job we discussed:

1. Proven ability to generate fresh ideas and creative solutions to difficult problems
2. Experience in the area of program planning and development
3. Ability to successfully manage many projects at the same time
4. A facility for working effectively with people at all levels of management
5. Experience in administration, general management, and presentations
6. An intense desire to do an outstanding job in anything which I undertake

Thank you for the time and courtesy extended me. I will look forward to hearing from you.

Sincerely,

Henry Jacobs
(516) 555-1212
hjacobs@yahoo.com

Follow-Up E-Mail (after face-to-face meeting)
(Corporate Graphic Design)

From: Melissa Harris [graphicdesignpro@earthlink.net]
To: rmatthews@redgraphic.com
Cc:
Subject: Let's keep in touch

Dear Mr. _____:

It was a pleasure speaking with you regarding my search for a position in Corporate Graphic Design. Thank you for your initial interest.

The position I am looking for is usually found in a corporate marketing or public relations department. The titles vary: Graphic Design Manager, Advertising Manager, and Publications Director are a few. In almost every case the job description includes management and coordination of the corporation's printed marketing materials, whether they are produced by in-house designers or by an outside advertising agency or design firm.

I would like to stay in the _____ area; at least, I would like to search this area first. My salary requirement currently is in the $_____ range.

My professional experience, education, activities, and skills uniquely qualify me for a position in Corporate Graphic Design. My portfolio documents over eight years of experience in the business, and includes design, project consultation, and supervision of quality printed material for a wide range of clients.

I hope you will keep me in your files for future reference. I will telephone your office next week to discuss my situation further.

Sincerely,

Melissa Harris
(516) 555-1212
graphicdesignpro@earthlink.net

Follow-Up E-Mail (after face-to-face meeting)
(General)

From: Joseph Winger [jwinger@hotmail.com]
To: hr@banacorp.com
Cc:
Subject: I listened . . . here's the result!

Dear Ms. _____:

It was a pleasure meeting with you last week in your office. I appreciate the time you spent with me, as well as the valuable information you offered. As we discussed, I have adjusted my resume in regard to my position with _____. I have attached the new resume with this e-mail so that your files can be updated.

_____, please allow me to thank you again for the compliment on my ability to present a strong interview. Please keep this in mind when considering me for placement with one of your clients.

Sincerely,

Joseph Winger
(516) 555-1212
jwinger@hotmail.com

Follow-Up E-Mail (after face-to-face meeting)
(Entry-Level)

From: Dana Sorrensen [dsorrensen@mindspring.com]
To: djackson@allianz.com
Cc:
Subject: Thanks from a quick study

Dear Mr. _____:

I would like to take this opportunity to thank you for the interview Wednesday morning at _____, and to confirm my strong interest in an entry-level position with your company.

As we discussed, I feel that my education and background have provided me with an understanding of business operations which will prove to be an asset to your company. Additionally, I have always been considered a hard worker and a dependable, loyal employee. I am confident that I can make a valuable contribution to your Group Pension Fund area.

I look forward to meeting with you again in the near future to further discuss your needs.

Sincere regards,

Dana Sorrensen
(516) 555-1212
dsorrensen@mindspring.com

Follow-Up E-Mail (after face-to-face meeting)
(Auditing)

From: Alex Davis [auditpro@earthlink.net]
To: hr@sunstar.com
Cc:
Subject: Very motivated by meeting you

Mr. _____:

Thank you for allowing me the opportunity to meet with you to discuss the IT Audit position currently available at Wilde Manye. The position sounds very challenging and rewarding, with ample room for growth. I feel my background and qualifications prepare me well for the IT Audit position we discussed.

I am committed to the ongoing development of my audit skills and feel I could work well with your focused audit staff at Wilde Manye. I look forward to hearing from you.

Sincerely,

Alex Davis
(516) 555-1212
auditpro@earthlink.net

POWER PHRASES

Consider using adaptations of these key phrases in your follow-up letters after face-to-face meetings.

Thank you for meeting with me this morning. Our associate, _____, assured me that a meeting with you would be productive, and it was. I sincerely appreciate your counsel, insight, and advice.

I have attached my resume for your review. I would appreciate any feedback you may have regarding effectiveness and strength. I understand you may not have any searches under way that would be suitable for me at this time, but I would appreciate any future considerations.

Please consider any associates, customers, or friends who may have contacts who would be useful for me to meet with. I have learned how important "networking" is and will really appreciate some assistance from a professional like you.

Thanks again, _____, and please let me know if I can be of service to you. I wish you and your colleagues continued success and look forward to a business relationship in the future.

In addition to experiencing a very enjoyable and informative interview, I came away very enthusiastic about the position you are seeking to fill.

I hope _____'s consideration of candidates will result in our being together again soon.

During my drive home I savored the possibility of working for _____ in the _____ area, and I must say it was an extremely pleasing thought.

I look forward to meeting with you again and hope our discussion will precede a long-term working relationship.

I am looking forward to meeting _____ on August 16 at 10:00 A.M.', at which time I will convince her of my abilities and prove I am the most qualified person for the position.

It was a pleasure meeting with you last week in your office. I appreciate the time you spent with me, as well as the valuable information you offered.

I hope you will take a few moments to review my resume and place it in your files for future reference. I will telephone your office next week to discuss my situation further.

Gone but not forgotten ...

Thank you for our time together this afternoon. What I lack in specific experience in your business I more than make up for with my people power and my proven record of achievement, energy, and just pure tenacity.

Given the opportunity, I can succeed in your office. That makes you and me both successes. Is that worth the investment in training me?

I would like to take this opportunity to thank you for the interview this morning, and to express my strong interest in the position with _____.

I would welcome the opportunity to apply and to further develop my talents within your company.

Through my conversations with you and Mr. _____, I felt that the company provides exactly the type of career opportunity that I am seeking, and I am confident that I will prove to be an asset to your organization.

I trust our meeting this morning helped you further define the position. First and foremost, however, I hope that you came away from our meeting with a vision that includes my filling one of the many offices in _____. I certainly did.

I would like to take this opportunity to thank you for the interview on Thursday morning. I was very impressed with the operation, and I am enthusiastic about the prospects of joining your team.

Since we spent so much time discussing the subject, I have enclosed ...

I look forward to hearing from you again to further discuss the position. Through my conversations with you and _____, I felt ...

After reviewing your comments about the job requirements, I am convinced that I can make an immediate contribution toward the growth and profitability of _____ .

Since you are going to reach a decision quickly, I would like to mention the following points, which I feel qualify me for the job we discussed:

The position in the _____ area is very attractive to me.

The interview confirmed that I want this career opportunity. Specifically, I want to work in the _____ department for you and _____ . That is the simplest way to say it. I will call you this week to see what the next step is in the process.

Again, thank you for your time and interest.

It was indeed a pleasure to meet with you after working with you by telephone several years ago.

Thank you for taking time out of your busy schedule to meet with me on Tuesday, December 10, 20–. I left the interview with an extremely favorable impression of your company.

I would like to take this opportunity to thank you for the interview on Friday morning, and to confirm my strong interest in the _____ position.

A career opportunity with _____ Corporation is particularly appealing because of its solid reputation and track record in research and development. I am confident that the training program and continued sales support will provide me with the background that I need to succeed in a _____ career.

I look forward to discussing my background and the position with you in greater detail.

I want to take this opportunity to thank you for the interview on Tuesday afternoon, and to confirm my strong interest in the position of _____ with XYZ Health Care Agency.

From our conversation, I feel confident in my ability to reach and exceed your expectations.

I am looking forward to spending a day in the field with a _____ representative. I will telephone you later this week to set up an appointment for my second interview.

Thank you for the time during my visit to _____ yesterday. I enjoyed our conversation at lunch and learned more about personal trust and investment services.

Thank you for your time and interest today. As I indicated, I am very new to this game of searching for employment and it is nice to start this effort on a positive note.

I am eager to hear from you concerning your decision; I know that you have several other candidates to meet with, so I will wait patiently. Good luck to you in your interview process; I know it must be difficult. Again, thank you so much for your time and consideration. I would welcome the opportunity to work for your company.

_____, the visit with you left me feeling positive about the possibility of working for _____. I would appreciate an opportunity to join your staff, and look forward to hearing from you.

"Resurrection" Letter (HR Position)

Kenyon knows this decision maker personally. Although he didn't get the job, he wants to keep the lines of communication open and hopes to be considered for other positions in the town government.

.... **KENYON P. STEWART**

January 13, 20–

Mr. Eric Pedersen, Supervisor
Town of Winterland
One Municipal Parkway
Winterland, New York 14528

Dear Eric:

Congratulations on the selection of your new Director of Human Resources! I hope this new person meets your expectations and I wish you every success.

I appreciate the chance to apply for the position and am grateful for the consideration you have given me throughout this process. Although I am obviously disappointed at not being the successful candidate, I remain interested in potential opportunities with the Town of Winterland. If for any reason you decide it is necessary to reopen the search at any time, please be aware that I am still interested in the position on either an interim or permanent basis.

In the meantime, should there be openings for support positions within the HR Department, or positions in other departments of the Town government, I would like to be considered for such opportunities.

Eric, as we have discussed in the past, I am a team player and believe that I have a contribution to make. At this stage of my career, I would be happy to accept something other than a managerial position and am convinced that my organizational skills, communication skills, and flexibility would make me an asset to any organization. If you know of other openings, either within governmental agencies or the private sector, I would be most appreciative if you could pass that information on to me.

Thank you for all your time and consideration. I look forward to speaking with you again soon.

Sincerely,

Kenyon

....
98 Meadowlark Lane • Penfield, New York 14526 • 585-388-5712

"Resurrection" Letter (Lift Line Driver Position)

After interviewing with the hiring authority and complying with their requests, this candidate is having trouble getting them on the phone. This letter is meant to get their attention.

Percival T. Morgan

3918 Calkins Road
Pittsford, New York 14534
585-555-5555
PercyMorgan@rochester.rr.com

January 2, 20–

Mr. Jefferson A. Bertram
Bureau of Human Resources
Genesee Regional Transit Authority
One Main Place
Rochester, New York 14692

Dear Mr. Bertram:

You may recall that we met on December 23rd regarding opportunities for Lift Line Operators. Following our meeting, I obtained a **CDL-B Learner's Permit with Passenger and Air-Brake endorsements.**

I am writing to reiterate my sincere interest in a **Lift Line Driver** position and hope to speak with you soon to learn what my next steps would be in order to further my candidacy.

Please contact me at **585-555-5555**. I look forward to talking with you soon.

Sincerely,

Percival T. Morgan

Percival T. Morgan

"Resurrection" Letter (Community Empowerment Team Director Position)

Another candidate was selected for the position that Madison interviewed for. Because he remains a city employee and hopes for other opportunities, he wants to both thank the mayor for the interview and keep his name (and qualifications) at the top of the mayor's mind for future consideration.

Madison P. Aldridge

45 Northern Crescent
Syracuse, New York 13081
315-286-4952

January 12, 20–

Hon. Michael Anderson, Jr., Mayor
City of Syracuse
City Hall
Syracuse, New York 13288

Dear Mayor Anderson:

Thank you for the opportunity to interview for the Community Empowerment Team Director position. I genuinely appreciated the chance to discuss your vision for the CET program.

Although another candidate was ultimately selected for this important position, I was pleased to be among the short list of applicants under consideration.

As we have discussed, I believe that my nine years' experience with the City of Syracuse provide me with a wealth of knowledge and expertise that can be beneficial to the City. I continue to be committed to the mission of the CET program, but also wish to offer myself as a candidate for other roles where my capabilities can further the objectives of the City.

To briefly reiterate, some of the qualities that I can bring to a new position include:

- **Strategic vision, creative energy, and strong leadership skills.**
- **Capacity to build collaborative teams across public, private, and government sectors.**
- **Excellent project management capabilities.**
- **Ability to build employee morale and inspire team members to strive for excellence.**
- **Innovative problem-solving skills.**

Please keep me in mind if other opportunities should arise where my talents would be an asset, particularly as you move ahead with implementation of The Syracuse Renaissance Vision. I would enjoy speaking with you further to discuss how I can best serve the City of Syracuse's needs.

Thank you, again, for your consideration.

Sincerely,

Madison P. Aldridge

Madison P. Aldridge

"Resurrection" Letter (Stevedore)

This is a follow-up letter to several telephone conversations with the best contact within the target company, the company president.

CASEY SMITH

1234 Main Street, #4 • Honolulu, Hawaii 96813
Home: (808) 555-5555 • Cellular: (808) 555-5551

November 14, 20–

Mr. Gregory Roberts
President, Roberts Line Shipping, Ltd.
P.O. Box 5555
Honolulu, Hawaii 96855

Dear Mr. Roberts:

First, I want to thank you for the time you spent with me in recent telephone conversations. I know you are a very busy person.

On August 4 I attended the stevedore recruiting event at the Oahu Convention Center. I submitted my résumé and spoke very briefly with a representative. In the short time I chatted with her I did my best to communicate my interest in, and qualifications for, the job. However, due to the overwhelming number of applicants there just wasn't sufficient time to convey how qualified I really am.

With that in mind, I have enclosed my brief résumé for your review. To summarize:

- I have an extensive history of working safely around heavy equipment.
- I am in outstanding physical condition.
- I am a very reliable and dedicated employee.
- I have received first aid, CPR, and terrorism awareness training.

This résumé is only a hint of who I am—words on paper cannot replace a personal conversation. Therefore, would you please consider my request for a face-to-face interview so that you may evaluate my qualifications, abilities, drive, and enthusiasm for yourself?

I will make myself available for any time that you can take out of your schedule. Thank you for your consideration, and I look forward to possibly meeting with you in the near future.

Respectfully,

Casey Smith

Casey Smith

Enclosure: résumé

"Resurrection" Letter (Social Worker)

Having already interviewed with Mr. Thornson, Beth started the letter in an upbeat, informal manner to re-establish a rapport. The indication that he thought she was well suited at the time of their initial interview was an effective way to sell herself.

BETH ANDERSEN
77-42 Gateway Circle
Bay Shore, NY 11706
(631) 665-9992
BAndersen@4kidsake.net

February 16, 20–

Mr. William Thornson
Foster Care and Adoption Coordinator
Little Lamb Foster Care & Adoptive Services
290 Brentwood Road
Brentwood, NY 11717

Dear Mr. Thornson:

Talk about small coincidences. I bumped into Father O'Brien at church this past Sunday and learned that St. Mary's is opening a new foster care division this coming March. One word led to another, and he informed me that Little Lamb Foster Care & Adoptive Services is in desperate need of social workers and foster/adoptive care counselors to fill several positions.

You might not recall my name, but hopefully I can help you to remember our meeting. I participated in an interview with you in early May of 20– for the position of Foster Care Counselor with Little Lamb's Brentwood facility. We discussed my involvement with St. John's Youth & Family Counseling Program at great length, and agreed I would be well suited for a similar position with Little Lamb as an Adoptive Care Counselor. Unfortunately, the lack of state and federal funding was reduced that month leaving Little Lamb with no other choice but to put a freeze on hiring.

As you can imagine, I am thrilled to learn of Little Lamb's new foster care program, and would welcome the opportunity to meet again to pick up where we left off. For your convenience, I am enclosing my updated resume for your review.

Thank you for your reconsideration. I look forward to speaking with soon.

Sincerely,

Beth Andersen

Beth Andersen

"Resurrection" Letter
(Wholesale Market Manager)

Leanne K. Boardman
617 Van Winkle Drive ▪ Keller, IN 46185 ▪ (888) 449-2200 ▪ marketmanager@email.com

(Date)

Phillip _____
(Title)
ABC Corporation
1 Industry Plaza
Indianapolis, IN 46222

Dear Mr. _____:

I understand from _____ of _____ that the search is continuing for the Wholesale Market Manager position at _____ Bank & Trust. As you continue your search, I would like to ask that you keep in mind the following accomplishments and experiences that I would bring to the job:

1. Maximized relationships and increased balances through the sale of trust and cash management products.

2. Captured largest share of public funds market in _____ within three years and captured a disproportionate market share of insurance companies in _____.

3. Developed cash management and trust products tailored to the needs of my target market.

4. Marketed services through mass mailings and brochures, through planning and conducting industry-specific seminars, and through active participation in target market's industry professional organization.

5. Direct experience in all phases of wholesale commercial banking, including: market segmentation, prospecting, building and maintaining customer relationships, lending, and the sale of non-credit products and services.

Sincerely,

Leanne Boardman

Leanne Boardman

LB

P.S. I will call you next week, after you have seen the other candidates, to continue our discussion. In the meantime, please be assured of both my competency and commitment.

"Resurrection" Letter (Construction Manager)

(Date)

Alice _____
(Title)
Krieger, Skvetney, Howell
Executive Search Consultants
2426 Foundation Road
Atlanta, GA 30605

Dear Ms. _____:

I am writing to you to follow up on the initial inquiry I wrote to you on July 11th, 20–. At that time I forwarded you a cover letter and resume. I am in the construction management and business management fields. Since I have not had a response I can only assume that you do not have any currently active searches that meet my qualifications in process or that my file has been deactivated.

I am still in the market for an executive position that matches my qualifications and abilities. I am open to relocating throughout the United States and overseas. If any positions become available, I would be interested in hearing from you. If you need an updated resume, please write or call me and I would be most happy to forward you any information required.

Sincerely,

Eric L. Ross

Eric L. Ross

ER

P.S. I'll call in a couple of days to follow up on this letter.

250

"Resurrection" Letter (Entry-Level)

Elizabeth A. Andrews

307 West Ivy Lane • Meridian, Idaho 83642

(Date)

Bob _____
(Title)
Krieger, Skvetney, Howell
Executive Search Consultants
2426 Foundation Road
Boise, ID 83712

Dear Mr. _____:

I feel I should more thoroughly explain why I am willing to take even an entry-level position considering all my past experience. And that's just it—past experience.

For the past three years I ran my own small business, which, of course, kept me out of the job market. Meanwhile, computers took over the world! Fortunately, since moving here and doing temp jobs, I have gotten hands-on experience in data entry. I have also taken and finished a private course in Microsoft Word. So I guess that makes me computer literate, if not entirely experienced.

Nevertheless, I'm in no position to be proud or disdainful of clerical jobs, as I realize I must start somewhere. Fortunately, I enjoy all facets of office work (even filing), so that would not be a problem. I have enough faith in myself and my ability to learn quickly to know that some form of upper movement would be possible for me ... eventually.

Incidentally, even though I am on a temp job this week and possibly next, I do have an answering machine I check every couple of hours during the day. So please leave a message and I'll return your call soon after.

Thank you, and I look forward to hearing from you. I have enclosed another copy of my resume for you.

Sincerely,

Elizabeth Andrews

Elizabeth Andrews

EA
enclosure

"Resurrection" E-Mail (Account Executive)

From: Katherine Knockwood [accountexecutive@aol.com]
To: hr@incentivedepot.com
Cc:
Subject: Thanks from Katherine, I'll be the next one

Mr. _____:

I wanted to thank you for the interview we had on March 13th, 20–. The position that was being offered sounds like something I would be interested in. However, I do understand your reasons for not choosing me for the position, and I thank you very much for your honesty.

Perhaps when you are looking for an account executive with five years of experience instead of ten, you will bear me in mind. I am determined to be your choice. I hope the fact that I came in a close second to someone with twice my chronological experience will help you keep me in mind.

I look forward to hearing from you, and thank you again for your time. With your permission I will stay in touch.

Sincerely,

Katherine Knockwood
(516) 555-1212
accountexecutive@aol.com

"Resurrection" E-Mail (Programmer)

From: Robert Zelinski [programmerpro@yahoo.com]
To: hr@jitmfg.com
Cc:
Subject: Oh the software we could create!

Dear Ms. _____:

I must have been one of the first people you spoke with about the job posting, because at the time you seemed very interested in me. However, when I called you back, you had received so many calls for the position, you didn't know one from the other. That's understandable, so I hope I can stir your memory and, more importantly, your interest.

When I spoke with you I got the feeling we could both benefit from working together. I am a computer enthusiast, always looking for new applications and ideas to implement on the computer. I have a solid programming and project development background in both the Windows and Macintosh worlds. What's even better is my hobby: my work. I spend countless hours in one way or another doing things which concern computing.

You had asked if I had children and I do: a four-and-a-half-year-old daughter and a four-and-a-half-month-old daughter. You had some ideas for children's software and thought having kids would help when working on such software. My oldest uses _____ on my Macintosh at home and double-clicks away without any assistance from my wife or myself. She has learned a great deal from "playing" with it and is already more computer literate than I ever expected. We need more software like _____ to help stir the minds of our kids.

I have attached a resume for your perusal. But in case you don't want to read all the details, here it is in short:

- I have 6 years programming and development experience in Windows.
- I have 3 years programming and development experience on the Macintosh.
- I am currently the Senior Developer for Macintosh programming here at _____ Corp.

I look forward to speaking with you again, so please don't hesitate to call me, either at home (516-555-1212) or at work (516-555-1213) anytime.

Regards,

Robert Zelinski
(516) 555-1212
programmerpro@yahoo.com

"Resurrection" E-Mail (Product Manager)

From: Amanda Jones [ajones@hotmail.com]
To: jkline@activeproducts.com
Cc:
Subject: We will work together!

Dear Ms. _____:

Four months ago you and I discussed an opportunity at Active Products, and you were kind enough to set up meetings with _____ and _____. Shortly thereafter, as you know, I accepted a position with _____, where I am now.

For reasons I will go into when we meet, I would like to reopen our discussions. If you think such a conversation would be mutually beneficial, I hope we can get together. I'll call next week to see when you have a half hour or so of free time.

Sincerely,

Amanda Jones
(516) 555-1212
ajones@hotmail.com

POWER PHRASES

Consider using adaptations of these key phrases in your resurrection letters.

I turned down your job, but for reasons I will go into when we meet, I would like to reopen our discussions. If you think such a conversation would be mutually beneficial, I hope we can get together. I'll call next week to see when you have a half hour or so of free time.

As you continue your search, I would like to ask that you keep in mind the following accomplishments and experiences that I would bring to the job.

I am still in the market for an executive position that matches my qualifications and abilities. I am open to relocating throughout the United States and overseas. If any positions become available, I would be interested in hearing from you.

I look forward to hearing from you, and thank you again for your time. With your permission I will stay in touch.

I hope I can stir your memory and, more importantly, your interest.

I look forward to speaking with you again, so please don't hesitate to call me either at home or at work anytime.

Rejection of Offer Letter (Public Library Director)

Tamara has decided to take another position. As a courtesy, she wants to tell Blossom City that she's no longer interested in the position, while keeping her name alive for any future opportunities.

Tamara L. Salinger
622 Cromwell Drive • Pittsford, New York 14534 • (585) 248-7042

January 12, 20–

Mr. Henry O. Felix, President
Blossom City Public Library Board of Trustees
447 South Avenue
Blossom City, New York 13901

Dear Mr. Hastings:

Thank you for taking the time to meet with me recently to discuss the position of BCPL Director. I genuinely appreciated the opportunity to meet with the Board and the Search Committee to learn about the position. I was very favorably impressed with the Blossom City Library System and believe that if selected, my contributions would have significantly enhanced your organization's success.

However, I am writing to ask that my name be withdrawn from further consideration for the Director's position at this time. I have recently been offered another challenging and rewarding opportunity. The relative time frames involved have made it necessary for me to render a decision without further delay, and I have chosen to accept the offer.

Had circumstances permitted, I believe that it would have been productive to continue our discussions and am confident that we could have arrived at a mutually beneficial arrangement. I would be most interested in applying and interviewing for the position should there ever be another search for a Director at some future date.

I wish you the best of luck in your current search, and much success in the future. Thank you, again, for your time and consideration.

Sincerely yours,

Tamara L. Salinger

Tamara L. Salinger

Rejection of Offer Letter (Team Supervisor)

This candidate interviewed for a position that turned out to be below his level of experience and at a salary well below his expectations. He didn't want to slam the door shut on other opportunities, but couldn't accept the position offered.

Ms. Lucretia A. Selander
Program Director
Salinas Group, Ltd.
443 Electronics Parkway
Liverpool, New York 13088

Dear Ms. Selander:

Thank you for your e-mail message updating me on the status of the telecommunications project we discussed in our recent telephone conversation.

Although I genuinely appreciate your consideration for the Team Supervisor position, at this time, I feel it is in my best interest to seek a position more closely aligned with my level of experience and demonstrated managerial skills.

I remain most interested in opportunities with Salinas Group, and would ask that you keep my name in consideration for other positions that would more fully capitalize on my knowledge and expertise.

Thank you for your time and interest.

Sincerely,

Christopher J. Franz

Christopher J. Franz

Rejection of Offer Letter (General)

AUDREY M. LAURENCE

968 PLEASANT AVENUE • ROCHESTER, NEW YORK 14622
(585) 248-9917 • ALAURENCE@ROCHESTER.RR.COM

(Date)

Phillip _____
(Title)
ABC Corporation
1 Industry Plaza
Buffalo, NY 14657

Dear Mr. _____:

It was indeed a pleasure meeting with you and your staff to discuss your needs for a _____. Our time together was most enjoyable and informative.

As we have discussed during our meetings, I believe a purpose of preliminary interviews is to explore areas of mutual interest and to assess the fit between the individual and the position. After careful thought, I have decided to withdraw from consideration for the position.

My decision is based upon the fact that I have accepted a position elsewhere that is very suited to my qualifications and experiences.

I want to thank you for interviewing me and giving me the opportunity to learn more about your facility. You have a fine team, and I would have enjoyed working with you.

Best wishes to you and your staff.

Sincerely,

Audrey Laurence

Audrey Laurence

AL

Rejection of Offer E-Mail (Department Manager)

From: Allen Meriden [managementpro@earthlink.net]
To: hr@seatoncorp.com
Cc:
Subject: With regret for the present and sincere hope for the future

Dear Ms. _____:

I would like to take this opportunity to thank you for the interview on Thursday morning, and to express my strong interest in future employment with your organization.

While I appreciate very much your offer for the position of Department Manager, I feel that at this stage of my career I am seeking greater challenges and advancement than the Department level is able to provide. Having worked in _____ management for over four years, I am confident that my skills will be best applied in a position with more responsibility and accountability.

As we discussed, I look forward to talking with you again in January about how I might contribute to ABC Corporation in the capacity of Unit Manager.

Sincere regards,

Allen Meriden
(516) 555-1212
managementpro@earthlink.net

POWER PHRASES

Consider using adaptations of these key phrases in your rejection of offer letters.

It was indeed a pleasure meeting with you and your staff to discuss your needs for a _____.

Our time together was most enjoyable and informative.

After careful thought, I have decided to withdraw from consideration for the position.

As we discussed, I look forward to talking with you again in _____ about how I might contribute to _____ in the capacity of _____.

Acceptance Letter (Marketing Research Manager)

JULIE GREGORIO
3339 Elldin Street
Portland, ME 04412
(207) 555-5555

(Date)

Ms. Emily _____
ABC Financial Services Group
1 Industry Plaza
Bangor, ME 04401

Dear Ms. _____:

Thank you for your positive response to the Marketing Research Manager position. I am delighted to accept your offer of employment and look forward to "jumping in head first" into the various projects we discussed during our meetings, especially sales forecasting and strategic market planning for ABC's core product line.

I am honored that your organization feels that I am the right person to lead your marketing research efforts, and am confident that I can deliver the results Radiant wants. As I mentioned in our telephone conversation yesterday, I am constantly in touch with what the competition is doing with the goal of placing my team's effort higher in the market place to yield maximum results.

Per your instructions, I will contact Mary Smith, Human Resources Manager, on Monday morning to arrange an orientation appointment. I look forward to meeting with you after that to discuss in detail my ideas for meeting the objectives we explored in our interviews.

Sincerely,

Julie Gregorio

Julie Gregorio

JG

Acceptance Letter (Managing Consultant)

Jacqueline Mains

788 Port Republic Road ▪ Port Republic, NJ 08241

(609) 652-5555 Residence ▪ managingconsultant@comcast.com

(Date)

Dear Philip,

I want to thank you for the privilege of joining your staff as Managing Consultant. Your flexibility and cooperation in the counter negotiations was encouraging. Thank you for making every effort to make the pending transition a smooth one.

Per your requests, I am providing this letter, for my official file.

"In that your organization is a competitor of my previous employer, and in that this organization seeks to maintain goodwill and high levels of integrity within the industry, it should be duly noted, that neither you nor any representative of your organization, sought me as a prospective employee. It was my identification of a possible position, and solely my pursuits toward your company, that resulted in my resignation as Senior Director, to join your firm as Managing Consultant."

If I can provide additional clarification on this matter, or assist in protecting the ethics of your company, notify me at your convenience. I look forward to starting with your team on the 15th of July. Until then . . .

Respectfully yours,

Jacqueline Mains

Jacqueline Mains

JM

Acceptance Letter (Vice President)

.... **Victor L. Williams**
555 Hillcrest Circle
Dearborn, Michigan 48121

(Date)

Emily _____
(Title)
ABC Corporation
1 Industry Plaza
Detroit, MI 48227

Dear Ms. _____:

This letter will serve as my formal acceptance of your offer to join your firm as Vice President of _____. I understand and accept the conditions of employment which you explained in your recent letter.

I will contact your personnel department this week to request any paperwork I might complete for their records prior to my starting date. Also, I will schedule a physical examination for insurance purposes. I would appreciate your forwarding any reading material you feel might hasten my initiation into the affairs of _____.

Yesterday I tendered my resignation at _____ and worked out a mutually acceptable notice time of four weeks, which should allow me ample time to finalize my business and personal affairs here and be ready for work at _____ on schedule.

You, your board, and your staff have been most professional and helpful throughout this hiring process. I anxiously anticipate joining the ABC team and look forward to many new challenges. Thank you for your confidence and support.

Yours truly,

Victor L. Williams

Victor L. Williams

JS

Acceptance E-Mail (General)

From: George Keller [gkeller@mindspring.com]
To: pwalters@raytheonco.com
Cc:
Subject: Yes! Absolutely! I accept!

Dear Mr. _____:

I would like to express my appreciation for your letter offering me the position of _____ in your _____ Department at a starting salary of $53,000 per year.

I was very impressed with the personnel and facilities at your company in Dallas and am writing to confirm my acceptance of your offer. If it is acceptable to you I will report to work on November 20, 20–.

Let me once again express my appreciation for your offer and my excitement about joining your engineering staff. I look forward to my association with ABC Corporation and feel my contributions will be in line with your goals of growth and continued success for the company.

Sincerely,

George Keller
(516) 555-1212
gkeller@mindspring.com

POWER PHRASES

Consider using adaptations of these key phrases in your acceptance letters.

I am delighted to accept _____'s generous offer to become their _____. All of the terms in your letter of October 13th are amenable to me.

My resignation was submitted to the appropriate managers at _____ this morning, but we are still working out the terms of my departure.

I am eagerly anticipating starting my new position, particularly at a firm with _____'s reputation. During the interim, I will stay in direct contact with _____ to assure a smooth initiation at _____. Thank you again for this opportunity.

We are still working out the terms of my departure from _____, but it is safe to say that I will report to _____ no later than November 9th. It should be possible to confirm a starting date early tomorrow morning. I will telephone you directly when my erstwhile managers and I have a departure schedule completed.

_____ has scheduled my pre-employment physical for _____, and I do not expect any problems to arise. I have found several possible housing alternatives that I will be investigating and I do not expect any problems here, either.

I appreciate the confidence you demonstrated by selecting me to be _____.

I am confident that you made an excellent choice.

I feel that I can achieve excellent results for your firm, and I am looking forward to working with you. I am also anxious to get to know you and your corporation better.

This letter will serve as my formal acceptance of your offer to join _____. I understand and accept the conditions of employment that you explained in your recent letter.

I will contact your personnel department this week to request any paperwork I might complete for their records prior to my starting date. Also, I will schedule a physical examination for insurance purposes. I would appreciate your forwarding any reading material you feel might hasten my initiation into the affairs of _____.

Yesterday I tendered my resignation at _____ and worked out a mutually acceptable notice time of four weeks, which should allow me ample time to finalize my business and personal affairs here, relocate my family, and be ready for work at _____ on schedule.

You, your board, and your staff have been most professional and helpful throughout this hiring process. I anxiously anticipate joining the _____ team and look forward to many new challenges. Thank you for your confidence and support.

I look forward to making a contribution as part of your team.

I look forward to the challenges and responsibility of working in this position.

Negotiation Letter (General)

Betsy Kimble
121 Eight Mile Drive   555-555-4567
Haddenville, VT 05600   bkimble@aox.com

(date)

Mr. Philip _____
(Title)
ABC Corporation
1 Industry Place
Montpelier, VT 05602

Dear Philip,

I want to thank you for your invitation to join the ABC family. I have reviewed the offer of position and compensation, as presented in your letter dated _____. I would like to ask for clarification on a few items prior to providing you with a "formal acceptance." While none of these items are necessarily "deal breakers," I believe they will enable both parties to begin the partnership more informed of mutual goals and expectations.

Per the breakdown provided:

- I accept the 401(K) plan as proposed
- I accept the paid holiday and personal days plan as proposed
- I accept the educational reimbursement plan as proposed
- I accept the Direct Payroll Deposit plan as proposed (if elected)
- I accept the Medical, Dental, Vision, Pharmacy, and Life Insurance benefits as proposed, contingent on factors clarified below.

Points of Clarification:

- What is available in regard to "Stock Options"?
- What are the "standard hours of operation" for ABC employees?
- Would it be possible to have a "Performance Evaluation" at the end of 6 months?
- I would like to structure the vacation days as follows: 3 days in remainder of year 20–, One week during calendar year 20–, Two weeks during calendar years 20– to 20–, Three weeks beginning January of 20–.
- In light of the "out of pocket expenses" anticipated correspondent to the medical benefits, how might we agree to get the annual base salary to $35,000? I am open to a number of different options to achieve this goal, including profit sharing, commission, or 5% annual bonus arrangement.

Page 1 of 2

I am excited about the long-term possibilities that exist at ABC. As you can see by my level of interest, I intend to partner with you for a long tenure of success. I believe my skills will be an enhancement to the existing leadership. My presence will enable you and others to focus on new aspects of business development and achieve corporate goals and objectives that will be beneficial to us all. Again, I want to thank you for the gracious offer. I look forward to finalizing these minor details very soon.

Sincerely yours,

Betsy Kimble

Betsy Kimble
BK

Negotiation Letter (Sales)

Eden Miller

67 Walden Road • Somers, TX 89776 • (555) 555-5555 • e-mail: salespro@aol.com

(Date)

Dear Mr. _____,

I have reviewed your letter and the specific breakdown regarding compensation. I believe there to be a few items to clarify, prior to providing you with a formal acceptance. I do not consider any of the items to be "deal breakers" in any way. I also do not perceive them to be issues that cannot be discussed, as we are in fact, moving ahead.

The primary concern has to do with the commission structure, as opposed to salary plus commission, to which I have grown accustomed. I am therefore asking for a one-time initial payment to me in the amount of $5,000. I am trying to diminish some of the "exposure" that I may experience in the transition from one office to another. I also believe exposure will be felt as a shift occurs from receipt of compensation on a monthly basis, when I am currently accustomed to a biweekly format. Lastly, I am hoping to afford your company the opportunity to share some of the "risk" in this process and show some "short-term good faith" toward what I hope will be a long-term relationship of success, productivity, and increased profitability.

The second clarification revolves around the 401K program; the percentages, time frames, and terms. This is something we can discuss over the course of the next two weeks. You may even be able to pass something specific on to me in writing.

With these two concerns articulated, I want you to know that I will be meeting with the owner of our company tomorrow morning, to discuss my plans for departure. In fairness to him and to my current client load, I could not start full-time with you for 21 days.

I would like to set a time for us to have dinner one evening next week, so you can meet my wife and we can talk a bit less formally.

Looking forward to what lies ahead,

Eden Miller

Eden Miller

EM

Negotiation Letter (Senior Lab Specialist)

MITCHELL T. NORDSTROM

621 SAWMILL ROAD • HAMLIN, NEW YORK 14464

(585) 964-1298 (DAYS) / (585) 964-45201 (EVENINGS) • LABSPECIALIST@CS.COM

(date)

Philip _____
ABC
1 Industry Plaza
Jamaica, NY 11434

Dear Philip:

I want to thank you for the time that we were able to spend together last week. I was encouraged by the invitation to join the ABC family as Senior Lab Specialist. The position, responsibility, and geography are consistent with my career goals and objectives. Based on the information that you gave to me, there are a number of items for clarification, prior to providing you with a formal acceptance. None of the items listed are necessarily "deal breakers," but they are essential to us beginning this tenure with full disclosure of mutual expectations and responsibilities. Items for clarification are as follows:

- Detailed description of insurance benefits
- Realistic analysis of the corporate stock and 401(K) plans
- Written explanation of educational reimbursement allowance
- The mobility plan seems very reasonable, but would like specifics on the Permanent Work Relocation (Is it an allowance or reimbursement of actual expenses incurred in the move?)
- Detailed explanation of the Variable Pay Plan

This final item is significant, as it will impact the "full compensation potential" and modify the suggested salary. In our conversations, I communicated to you that I was making $32K while working part-time and going to school. The salary offer is substantially lower and represents a pay cut. My goal is to discern how feasible it will be for me to meet my financial obligations.

I am interested in your company and this position, but am finding it difficult to give serious consideration to anything less than $40K salary plus benefits. I am hoping to discover a variety of vehicles that will enable you to help me achieve that goal, so that I can help you accomplish your growth and profit targets.

I look forward to discussing these issues with you in the very near future and trust that we will soon be working together in the best interest of Philip _____, Mitchell Nordstrom, and ABC Incorporated.

Respectfully Yours,

Mitchell Nordstrom

Mitchell Nordstrom

MN

Negotiation Letter (Product Specialist)

MARY A. MARTIN

717-755-1369 (Cell) • 717-845-5856 (Home)
productspecialist@email.com
202 Springhill Street • Greenville , SC 29681

(Date)

Philip _____
(Title)
ABC Corporation
1 Industry Plaza
Columbia, SC 29170

RE: Product Specialist/ABC Team

Dear Philip:

Thank you for your offer of employment with ABC Corporation. Your state-of-the-art company would afford me the opportunity to make a contribution while continuing to grow professionally in an ever-evolving industry. I am confident that my strong work ethic would enhance the ABC Team.

As you know from our previous conversations, I have outstanding skills and abilities that I can bring to ABC. First and foremost is my hands-on experience in the medical field. I have a proven track record of relating well to other medical professionals and accommodating their needs. It is my understanding that as Product Specialist, my expert communication skills will be tantamount to performance success. With my experience in troubleshooting technical problems, I know that technology can be learned but becomes utilitarian only when it can be translated into user effectiveness. My expertise integrates both of these critical components that are key in the Product Specialist role.

The Product Specialist position promises challenge and a high level of professional commitment that I am prepared to embrace. However, based upon the value I can bring ABC, plus the knowledge that the annual salary range for this type of position in our industry normally falls between $34,000 and $46,000, I must request that you reconsider your starting offer of $35,000. I am more than happy to assume all of the responsibilities necessary to meet the expectations of the Product Specialist position at a starting salary of $40,000. Of course, I appreciate the generous benefits package that you provide.

I look forward to your response, and hope that we can reach an agreement that will enable me to begin my career with ABC on June 4.

Sincerely,

Mary Martin

Mary Martin
MM

Resignation Letter (CCU Nurse)

This situation was sensitive. A lot of names and dates were needed to explain the events leading to the decision to resign. Notice how Elizabeth apologizes so she doesn't burn her bridges.

Elizabeth Dixon, RN

33 Leo Street ▪ Brentwood, NY 11717 ▪ (631) 555-0220 ▪ criticalcare@med.net

April 26, 20–

Ms. Dorothy Powell
Director of Special Care
Good Health Hospital
1024 Montauk Road
Brentwood, NY 11717

Dear Ms. Powell:

As requested by Joan Larson, Nursing Manager, I am submitting this letter as written confirmation of my resignation as a per-diem on-call CCU nurse with Good Health Hospital.

My employment with Good Health was scheduled to begin April 7th as a permanent part-time CCU nurse; however, in the interim, I accepted a permanent full-time position with Long Island Hospital to begin May 1st. On April 3rd I met with Gretchen Miller, Human Resources Administrator, to inform her of my decision. I expressed a desire to honor my commitment with the understanding that the need for flexibility in my schedule would be taken into consideration. Ms. Miller contacted Joan Larson to discuss an alternative employment arrangement. Subsequently, my status from permanent part-time was changed to per-diem on-call.

Immediately upon completion of the mandatory two-week orientation period, I was faced with a schedule conflict. As a result of an apparent miscommunication, I was scheduled to do my floor orientation from April 21st through 25th. I approached Diane Willis, Nursing Manager, to resolve the conflict and learned that she was completely unaware of both my situation and agreement between Joan Larson, Human Resources, and myself. As a result, my resignation seemed to be the logical solution.

Ms. Powell, it was never my intention to cause problems within your administration; therefore, please accept my apology for any inconvenience experienced. Thank you for the opportunity to be a part of your staff.

Sincerely,

Elizabeth Dixon

Elizabeth Dixon

Resignation Letter (Care Coordinator)

Marilyn was offered a new position with another organization, and this letter helped her make a positive exit from her current employer.

Marilyn Cummings

19 Blueberry Circle
Valhalla, NY 06077
(914) 776-3455

April 9, 20–

Ms. Karen Lawrence, R.N.
Patient Care Manager
Community Care Center, Inc.
56 Murray Lane
Valhalla, NY 06077

Dear Karen:

This letter will confirm my resignation from the position of Care Coordinator. I have accepted a new position as Supervisor of Client Services at a growing medical center in New Jersey.

My last day of employment will be on Friday, May 9, 20–, which should provide sufficient time to complete existing projects and assist with the transition to a new coordinator

The past 10 years at the Center have been both professionally and personally rewarding. Thank you for your trust and support over the years. I have appreciated the opportunity to expand my skills and work with many talented individuals.

Thank you, sincerely,

Marilyn Cummings

Marilyn Cummings

Resignation Letter (Management)

A very firm resignation, where a company needs encouragement to live up to obligations.

ROBERT McINTYRE
9803 Clinton Avenue
Lubbock, TX 79424

home: 806.783.9900
cell: 806.698.0451
robertmcintyre@crpn.com

November 11, 20–

Tim Johnson, President
XTC, Inc.
500 Indiana Avenue
Lubbock, TX 79314

Dear Mr. Johnson:

I am writing this letter as a follow-up to the resignation notice I submitted on Wednesday, November 5, 20–. Given the sensitive nature of the events leading to my resignation, I feel it is in everyone's best interest to resolve any issues remaining as quickly as possible.

In this respect, I hope that you will demonstrate swift compliance in delivering to me the management severance package guaranteed as a result of my employment with your firm. I wish to move ahead in my career and put the past several months behind me, as I am sure you can understand; therefore, I am certain you will act upon this request in a professional and forthright manner.

Please be advised that, in the event there is an attempt to withhold or deny this severance package to me, I will have no other alternative but to seek legal remedy for this situation. **Again, I believe that you will act as a man of integrity concerning this issue**, and I only mention the possibility of legal action in the unlikely event that my request is rejected or delayed.

I can assure you that I, like you, would like for this to be resolved without further complications or additional steps—and as quickly as possible.

Mr. Johnson, I thank you in advance for your swift attention and cooperation in this matter.

Sincerely,

Robert McIntyre

Robert McIntyre

Resignation Letter (Sales Representative)

.... **Gerard Carlisle**

(Date)

Phillip _____
(Title)
ABC Corporation
1 Industry Plaza
Idaho Falls, ID 83726

Dear Mr. _____:

Please accept my resignation of my position as Sales Representative in the _____ area, effective January 25, 20–. I am offering two weeks' notice so that my territory can be effectively serviced during the transition, with the least amount of inconvenience to our clients.

While I have enjoyed very much working under your direction, I find now that I have an opportunity to further develop my career in areas that are more in line with my long-term goals. I thank you for the sales training that I have received under your supervision. It is largely due to the excellent experience I gained working for ABC Corporation that I am now able to pursue this growth opportunity.

During the next two weeks, I am willing to help you in any way to make the transition as smooth as possible. This includes assisting in recruiting and training my replacement in the _____ territory. Please let me know if there is anything specific that you would like me to do.

Again, it has been a pleasure working as a part of your group.

Best regards,

Gerard Carlisle

Gerard Carlisle

GC

.... 5555 State Street • Boise, Idaho 83701 • (208) 555-5555 ....

Resignation Letter (Vice President)

David R. Chang
_____

2491 Goodman Street, San Francisco, CA 94080 / (650) 258-6911

changvp@earthlink.com

(Date)

Emily _____
(Title)
ABC Corporation
1 Industry Plaza
San Francisco, CA 94082

Dear Ms. _____:

As of this date, I am formally extending my resignation as _____. I have accepted a position as Vice President of _____ at a university medical center in _____.

My decision to leave ABC Corporation was made after long and careful consideration of all factors affecting the institution, my family, and my career. Although I regret leaving many friends here, I feel that the change will be beneficial to all parties. My subordinate staff is readily able to handle the institution's operations until you find a suitable replacement. I intend to finalize my business and personal affairs here over the next several weeks and will discuss a mutually acceptable termination date with you in person.

Finally, I can only express my sincere appreciation to you and the entire board for all your support, cooperation, and encouragement over the past several years. I will always remember my stay at ABC Corporation for the personal growth it afforded and for the numerous friendships engendered.

Yours truly,

David Chang
David Chang

DC

Resignation E-Mail (General)

From: John Billingsly [systemsoperator@hotmail.com]
To: nbraun@mis.augsburg.edu
Cc:
Subject: With regrets but many thanks

Dear Mr. _____:

This email is to notify you that I am resigning my position with ABC Corporation effective Saturday, March 26, 20–.

I have enjoyed my work here very much and want to thank you and the rest of the MIS Department for all the encouragement and support you have always given me. In order to achieve the career goals that I've set for myself, I am accepting a higher level Systems Operator position with another company. This position will give me an opportunity to become more involved in the technical aspects of setting up networking systems.

Please know that I am available to help with any staff training or offer assistance in any way that will make my departure as easy as possible for the department. I want to wish everyone the best of luck for the future.

Sincerely,

John Billingsly
(516) 555-1212
systemsoperator@hotmail.com

POWER PHRASES

Consider using adaptations of these key phrases in your resignation letters.

I am offering two weeks' notice so that my territory can be effectively serviced during the transition, with the least amount of inconvenience to our clients.

While I have enjoyed very much working under your direction, I find now that I have an opportunity to further develop my career in areas that are more in line with my long-term goals. I thank you for the sales training that I have received under your supervision. It is largely due to the excellent experience I gained working for ABC Corporation that I am now able to pursue this growth opportunity.

During the next two weeks, I am willing to help you in any way to make the transition as smooth as possible. This includes assisting in recruiting and training my replacement in the _____ territory. Please let me know if there is anything specific that you would like me to do.

Again, it has been a pleasure working as a part of your sales force.

I have thoroughly enjoyed the work environment and professional atmosphere at _____. Your guidance and counseling have been the source of great personal and career satisfaction, and I am grateful.

These _____ years have made a considerable contribution to my career and professional development and I hope that I have likewise contributed during this time to the growth and development of ABC Corporation. I am grateful for the kind of associates I have had the opportunity to work with and the substantial support I have consistently received from management.

Thank-You Letter (after hire) (General)

Matilda Vixard
310 Sweetwater Lane ▪ Milwaukee, WI 53172 ▪ (414) 555.3471

(Date)

Phillip _____
(Title)
ABC Corporation
1 Industry Plaza
Madison, WI 53182

Dear Mr. _____:

I want you to be among the first to know that my job search has come to a very successful conclusion. I have accepted the position of _____ Director at _____, Inc., located in _____.

I appreciate all the help and support you have provided over the last several months. It has made the job search process much easier for me. I look forward to staying in contact with you. Please let me know if I can be of any assistance to you in the future. Thank you.

Sincerely,

Matilda Vixard

Matilda Vixard

MV

Thank-You E-Mail (after hire) (Software Manager)

From: Shane Franklin [softwarespecialist@yahoo.com]
To: hr@surrex.com
Cc:
Subject: Great News! Thanks for the help ;-)

Dear Ms. _____:

I am happy to inform you that I received and accepted an offer of employment just after Thanksgiving. I am now employed by the _____ Corporation.

I would also like to thank you for all your help the past several months not only in my search for employment but also by your understanding and friendly words of encouragement.

My duties include responsibility of all Dun & Bradstreet software (General Ledger, Accounts Payable, Accounts Receivable, and Fixed Assets) for _____ worldwide plus the first-year training of several entry-level employees.

I am enjoying my new responsibility and being fully employed again, although at times I feel overwhelmed with all I have to learn.

If there is ever anything I can do for you please call me. I hope you and your family have a wonderful holiday season and much luck and happiness in the new year.

Sincerely,

Shane Franklin
(516) 555-1212
softwarespecialist@yahoo.com

POWER PHRASES

Consider using adaptations of these key phrases in your thank-you letters.

I am writing to share this good news with you and to thank you for your efforts on my behalf. If there is ever anything that I can do for you, please do not hesitate to call on me.

Thank you for all your help. I have accepted a position as a _____ for _____.

I want you to be among the first to know that my job search has come to a very successful conclusion.

I appreciate all the help and support you have provided over the last several months. It has made the job search process much easier for me. I look forward to staying in contact with you. Please let me know if I can be of any assistance to you in the future.

I would like to extend my sincere thanks to you for your kind help and encouragement during my job search. If I can be of any assistance to you in the future, please do not hesitate to contact me. I was often reminded during the past few months that we too easily lose contact with old friends. Let's try to stay in touch.

If you ever get a chance to visit _____, on business or pleasure, please be sure to let me know.

If there is ever anything I can do for you please call me. I hope you and your family have a wonderful holiday season and much luck and happiness in the new year.

Just a quick note to bring you up to date with what I am doing.

CAREER CONSULTANTS AND RESUME WRITING SERVICES

As part of your job search, you might feel the need to look into getting extra help from a professional resume writer and/or a career counselor. A professional in the field might be able to help you develop a more polished layout or present a particularly complex background more effectively.

As in any other profession, there are practitioners at both ends of the performance scale. I am a strong believer in using the services of resume writers and career consultants who belong to their field's professional associations. They tend to be more committed, have more field experience, and have an all-around higher standard of performance, partly because their membership demonstrates their commitment to the field and partly from the ongo-ing educational programs that these associations offer to their members.

The three major associations in the resume-writing field are: the Professional Association of Resume Writers (PARW, *parw.com*), the National Resume Writers Association (NRWA, *nrwa.com*), and Career Masters Institute (CMI, *www .cminstitute.com*). All three associations have hundreds of members and provide ongoing opportunities for members to gain mentoring experience and additional training. They all offer resume-writing certification and operate e-mail list servers for members with access to e-mail.

Two important smaller organizations are CertifiedResumeWriters. com and CertifiedCareerCoaches. com. These two Web sites are designed to connect job seekers with certified career professionals who meet specific resume writing and career coaching needs. All of the resume writers on these two sites are active members of one or more of the above associations and have taken the time to achieve accreditation in different aspects of the resume writing and career coaching process.

Finally there is the Phoenix Career Group *(www.phoenixcareergroup.com)*, a small group of highly qualified and exceptionally credentialed career management consultants and resume writers spread all over North America.

This is a by-invitation-only marketing consortium of independents who all know each other through membership in other groups. Although I do not offer these one-on-one services myself, I am a member of Phoenix solely for the camaraderie and value I receive from rubbing shoulders with a select group of mature and committed professionals.

The following is a list of career consultants and professional resume writers. All of these have contributed to the *Knock 'em Dead* books and are members of one or more of the above groups.

Martin Yate, Executive Career Strategist

E-mail: *martin@knockemdead.com*

Martin Yate, CPC

Typically works with C-level and C-level-bound professionals facing challenges in the areas of Job Search, Interviewing, and Career Strategy.

Phoenix Career Group

www.phoenixcareergroup.com

Debbie Ellis, CPRW, CRW

Serving career-minded professionals to senior executives, the Phoenix Career Group is a one-of-a-kind consortium of 15 industry-leading professionals specializing in personal branding, resume writing, career management coaching, research, and distribution.**A First Impression Resume Service**

www.resumewriter.com

Debra O'Reilly CPRW, CEIP, JCTC, FRWC

Debra provides job-search and career-management tools for professionals, from entry level to executive. Areas of specialty include career transition and the unique challenges of military-to-civilian conversion.

A Resume For Today

www.aresumefortoday.com

Jean Cummings M.A.T., CPRW, CEIP, CPBS

Distills complex high-tech careers into potent, memorable, and valuable personal brands. Provides resume writing and job search services to executives and managers seeking to advance their careers in high tech.

A Word's Worth Resume and Writing Service

www.keytosuccessresumes.com

Nina K. Ebert CPRW/CC

Serving clients since 1989, A Word's Worth is a full-service resume and cover letter development / career coaching company with a proven track record in opening doors to interviews.

A+ Career & Resume, LLC

www.careerandresume.com

Karen M. Silins CMRS, CCMC, CRW, CECC, CEIP, CTAC, CCA

Expertise includes career document development, career exploration and transition, assessments, job search methods, networking, interviewing, motivation, dressing for success, and career management strategies.

Abilities Enhanced

www.abilitiesenhanced.com

Meg Montford MCCC, CMF, CCM

Helps enable radical career change, as from IT trainer to pharmaceutical sales rep and technical writer to personal trainer. Career coaching and resumes by a careers professional since 1986.

Advanced Résumé Services

www.resumeservices.com

Michele Haffner CPRW, JCTC

Resumes, cover letters, target mailings, interview coaching, and search strategy/ action plan development. Specialty is mid- to senior-level professionals earning $75K+. Complimentary critique. Over 10 years of experience. Guaranteed satisfaction.

Advantage Resume & Career Services

www.CuttingEdgeResumes.com

Vivian VanLier CPRW, JCTC, CCMC, CEIP, CPRC

Full-service resume writing and career coaching serving clients throughout the U.S. and internationally at all levels. Special expertise in Entertainment, Management, Senior Executives, Creative and Financial Careers.

Arnold-Smith Associates

www.ResumeSOS.com

Arnold G. Boldt CPRW, JCTC

Offers comprehensive job search consulting services, including writing résumés and cover letters; interview simulations; career assessments and coaching; and both electronic and direct mail job search campaigns.

Brandego LLC

www.brandego.com

Kirsten Dixson CPBS, JCTC

Creates Web Portfolios for executives, careerists, authors, consultants and speakers. Includes experts in branding, career management, multimedia, copywriting, blogging and SEO to express your unique value.

Career Directions, LLC

www.careeredgecoach.com

Louise Garver JCTC, CPRW, MCDP, CEIP, CMP

Career Directions, LLC, is a full-service practice specializing in resume development, job-search strategies and career-coaching services for sales and marketing executives and managers worldwide.

Career Ink

www.careerink.com

Roberta Gamza JCTC, JST, CEIP

Offering career marketing and communication strategy services that advance careers. Services include precisely crafted resumes and customized interview training sessions that persuade and motivate potential employers to action.

Career Marketing Techniques

www.polishedresumes.com

Diane Burns CPRW, CCMC, CPCC, CFJST, IJCTC, CEIP, CCM

Diane is a career coach and resume strategist who specializes in executive-level military conversion resumes and federal government applications. She is a careers industry international speaker and national author.

Career Solutions, LLC

www.WritingResumes.com

Maria E. Hebda CCMC, CPRW

A certified career professional, Maria helps people effectively market themselves to employers and position them as qualified candidates. Provides writing and coaching services in resume and cover letter development.

Career Trend

www.careertrend.net

Jacqui Barrett MRW, CPRW, CEIP

Collaborates with professionals and executives aspiring to ignite their careers or manage transition. The owner is among an elite group holding the Master Resume Writer designation via Career Masters Institute.

Cheek & Cristantello Career Connections, LLC

www.cheekandcristantello.com

Freddie Cheek M.S. Ed., CCM, CPRW, CRW, CWDP

Resource for resume writing and interview coaching with 25 years' experience satisfying customers and getting results. Creates accomplishment-based resumes that help you achieve your career goals.

Create Your Career

www.careerist.com

Joyce Fortier CCM, CCMC

Company collaborates with clients as a catalyst for optimum career success. Services include résumé & cover letter services, and coaching services, including job search techniques, interview preparation, networking, and salary negotiation.

ekm Inspirations

www.ekminspirations.com

Norine T. Dagliano FJST, Certified DISC Administrator

More than 18 years of comprehensive and individualized career transition services, working with professionals at all levels of experience. Specializes in federal job search assistance, assisting dislocated workers and career changers.

Executive Essentials

www.career-management-coach.com

Cindy Kraft CCMC, CCM, CPRW, JCTC

Prepares professionals and executives to outperform the competition. Top-notch marketing documents, a focused branding strategy, and job search coaching result in a multifaceted, effective, and executable search plan.

Executive Power Coach

www.ExecutivePowerCoach.com

Deborah Wile Dib CPBS, CCM, CCMC, NCRW, CPRW, CEIP, JCTC

Careers-industry leader helps very senior executives stand out, get to the top, and stay at the top. Executive brand development, power resumes, and executive power coaching services since 1989.

Guarneri Associates

www.Resume-Magic.com

Susan Guarneri NCC, NCCC, LPC, MCC, CPRW, CCMC, CEIP, JCTC, CWPP

Comprehensive career services—from career counseling and assessments to resumes and cover letters—by full-service career professional with top-notch credentials, 20 years of experience, and satisfied customers.

JobWhiz

www.JobWhiz.com

Debra Feldman B.S., M.P.H.

Personally arranges confidential networking appointments delivering decision makers inside target employers. Engineers campaign strategy, innovates positioning, and defines focus. Banishes barriers accelerating job search progress. Relentless follow-up guarantees results.

The Loriel Group - CoachingROI :: ResumeROI

www.ResumeROI.com

Lorie Lebert CPRW, IJCTC, CCMC

A full-service career management provider, offering personalized, confidential support and guidance; moving client careers forward with focused customer service.

The McLean Group

yourcareercoach@aol.com

Don Orlando MBA, CPRW, JCTC, CCM, CCMC

Puts executives in control of the career they've always deserved. Personal, on-demand support that helps busy managers get paid what they are worth.

Mil-Roy Consultants

www.milroyconsultants.com

Nicole Miller CCM, CRW, IJCTC, CECC

Creates the extra edge needed for success through the innovative design of dynamic résumés and marketing tools that achieve results.

Partnering For Success, LLC

www.resumes4results.com

Cory Edwards CRW, CECC, CCMC

Resume writer and career coach currently achieving 98% success rate getting clients interviews. Specializing in all resumes, including federal, SES, Postal, and private sector from entry-level to executive.

Resume Suite

www.resumesuite.com

Bonnie Kurka CPRW, JCTC, FJST

Career coach, resume writer, speaker, and trainer with more than 11 years' experience in the careers industry. Specializes in mid- to upper-level management, IT, military, and federal career fields.

The Resume Writer

www.theresumewriter.com

Patricia Traina-Duckers CPRW, CRW, CEIP, CFRWC, CWPP

Fully certified career service practice offering complete career search services, including personalized civilian/ federal resume development, business correspondence, web portfolios, bios, CVs, job search strategies, interview coaching, salary research, and more.

Resume Writers

100PercentResumes

www.100percentresumes.com

Daniel J. Dorotik, Jr. NCRW

Global career development service specializing in the preparation of resumes, cover letters, and other associated career documents. In addition to traditional formats, prepares online-compatible documents for Internet-driven job searches.

ResumeRighter

www.ResumeRighter.com

Denise Larkin CPRW, CEIP

A mount-a-campaign, market-yourself, total-job-search support system. They promise to: Present your qualifications for best advantage. Write an attention-grabbing cover letter. Coaches you to ace your interview.

Write Away Résumé and Career Coaching

www.writeawayresume.com

Edie Rische NCRW, JCTC, ACCC

Creates targeted resumes and job search correspondence for clients in every vocation, and specializes in helping others discover their "Authentic VocationTM," shift careers, and resolve issues using "QuantumShiftTM" coaching.

INTERNET RESOURCES

These are really Knock 'em Dead Internet resources, with links to Web sites in twenty-two job search and career-management categories.

You'll find the big job banks, profession specific sites for eighteen major industries, association, entry level, executive, minority sites, and more. You'll discover tools that help you find companies, executives and lost colleagues, plus sites that help you choose new career directions or find a super qualified professional resume writer, job, or career coach.

To save time, you can come to the *knockemdead.com* Web site, where you can click on each of these resources and be connected directly—no more typing in endless URLs!

Association Sites

www.ipl.org
The Internet Public Library. Lots of great research services of potential use to your job search. This link takes you directly to an online directory of professional associations.

www.weddles.com
Peter Weddle's employment services site also offers a comprehensive online professional association directory.

Career and Job Coaches

www.knockemdead.com
Martin Yate CPC Executive Career Strategist
E-mail: martin@knockemdead.com

Martin typically works with C-level and C-level bound professionals facing challenges in the areas of Job Search, Interviewing, and Career Strategy.

www.phoenixcareergroup.com
A private, by invitation only, association of seasoned and credentialed coaches, of which I am a member. I know all the Phoenix consultants professionally, and I'm proud to know most of them personally; they're the finest you'll find.

www.certifiedcareercoaches.com
A Web site that features only certified career coaches.

www.certifiedresumewriters.com
A Web site that features only certified resume writers.

Career Assessments

www.assessment.com
A career choice test that matches your motivations against career directions. I've been using it for a number of years.

www.crgleader.com
careerplanning.about.com
Links to career planning and choice tools. The first free career choice test listed wasn't very helpful, but the site has other good resources.

www.analyzemycareer.com
A well-organized and comprehensive career choice online testing site.

www.careerplanner.com
Affordable RIASEC oriented career choice testing by an established online presence.

www.careertest.us

www.college911.com
Helps you find colleges based on your interests. No career choice tests; rather, a site you might want to visit after you have a general sense of direction.

www.livecareer.com
Home page says it's free, and the free report is okay as far as it goes, which is not very far. To get a full report you will pay $25 and there are also premium options, but you don't know this until you have spent 30 minutes taking the test! Despite this sleight of hand, a good career choice test with comprehensive reports.

www.princetonreview.com
A $40 online test; this is a good solid test and the site is easy to navigate.

www.rockportinstitute.com
Excellent career choice tests for all ages. Although priced on a sliding scale dependent on income, they start at $1,500 for someone earning 40K a year or less.

www.self-directed-search.com
This is the famous SDS test developed by John Holland. An extremely well-regarded test, and at just $9.95 it's a great deal.

Career Choice and Management Sites

www.acinet.org
A site that offers career choice and advancement advice via testing for job seekers at all levels. Has good info on enhancing your professional credentials.

www.phoenixcareergroup.com
A premier site featuring deeply experienced and credentialed career counselors available for consultation on an hourly basis.

www.quintcareers.com
Career and job search advice.

www.rileyguide.com
Excellent site for job search and career management advice. It's been around for years and is run by people who really care.

Career Transition
Military Transition

www.destinygroup.com
A great site for anyone transitioning out of the military. The #1 post-military careers site.

www.corporategray.com

www.taonline.com
Military transition assistance.

Other Transition

www.careertransition.org
For dancers once their joints go.

College and Entry Level Job Sites

www.a1education.com
Directories and links for colleges and graduate schools, test prep, financial aid, and job search advice.

www.aboutjobs.com
Links and leads for student jobs, internships, recent grads, expats, and adventure seekers.

www.aftercollege.com
Internships and co-ops, part-time and entry level, Ph.D.s and post-docs, teaching jobs, plus alumni links.

www.backdoorjobs.com
Short-term and part-time adventure and dream jobs.

www.blackcollegian.com
Premier site for black college students and recent graduates; help and sensible advice in areas of concern for the young professional.

www.campuscareercenter.com
Job search, career guidance, and advice on networking for transition into the professional world.

www.careerfair.com
Career fair directory.

www.collegecentral.com
A networking site for graduates of small and medium-size community colleges.

www.collegegrad.com
A comprehensive and well-thought-out site full of good information for the entry-level job seeker; probably the best in the entry-level field.

www.collegejobboard.com
A top job site for entry-level jobs; includes jobs in all fields.

www.collegejournal.com
Run by the Wall Street Journal, it's a savvy site for entry-level professionals, with lots of resources.

www.collegerecruiter.com
One of the highest traffic sites for students and recent grads with up to three years' experience. Well-established and comprehensive job site.

www.ednet.com
Reports on college aid, college selection, career guidance, and college strategy.

www.entryleveljobs.net
It's been around since 1999, and it does have jobs posted, though much is out of date.

www.graduatingengineer.com
A site for graduating engineers and computer careers.

www.internshipprograms.com
A good site if you are looking for an internship.

www.jobpostings.net
The online presence of one of the biggest college recruitment magazine publishers in North America; includes jobs across U.S. and Canada.

www.jobtrak.com
Now owned by Monster, it's their presence in the entry level job market.

www.jobweb.com
Owned and sponsored by the Association of Colleges and Employers. It's a great way to tap into the employers who consistently have entry level hiring needs.

www.snagajob.com
For part time and hourly jobs.

College Placement and Alumni Networks

www.mcli.dist.maricopa.edu
Resource for community college URL's.

www.utexas.edu
Resource for locating college alumni groups.

Diversity Sites

janweb.icdi.wvu.edu
Job Accommodation Network: a portal site for people with disabilities.

www.bilingual-jobs.com
Like the name says: a site for bilingual jobs in America and around the globe.

www.blackcollegian.com
Premier site for black college students and recent graduates; help and sensible advice in areas of concern for the young professional.

www.business-disability.com
Run by the National Business and Disability Council, job search through listings of member organizations, post resumes, career events, and internships.

www.bwni.com
Business women's network

www.christianjobs.com
Full-featured employment Web site focusing on employment within the Christian community.

www.diversitylink.com
Job site serving women, minorities, and other diversity talent.

www.eop.com
The online presence of the oldest diversity recruitment publisher in America. For women, members of minority groups, and people with disabilities.

www.experienceworks.org
Training and employment services for mature workers, 55 and older.

www.gaywork.com
A job site featuring a resume bank and job postings for gay men and women.

www.hirediversity.com
Links multicultural and bilingual professionals with both national and international industry sectors. Clients primarily consist of Fortune 1000 companies and government agencies.

www.imdiversity.com
Communities for African-Americans, Asian-Americans, Hispanic-Americans, Native-Americans, and women. No jobs or overt career advice, but lots of links for members of minority communities on issues that affect our lives.

www.latpro.com
The number-one employment source for Spanish- and Portuguese-speaking professionals in North and South America. The site can be viewed in English, Spanish, or Portuguese. Features both resume and job banks.

Executive Job Sites

www.netshare.com
Been around since before the Internet with tenured management; really understands and cares about the executive in transition. Job banks, resources, etc.

www.6figurejobs.com
Solid and well-respected site; includes job banks, resources, etc. A warning: some of their career advice seems very non-specific and geared to selling services.

www.careerjournal.com
Run by the *Wall Street Journal* with all the bells and whistles, this is an excellent executive transition site.

www.chiefmonster.com
Monster's site aimed at the executive area, though it's difficult to differentiate from the rest of the brand. Comprehensive job postings.

www.execunet.com
One of the top executive sites (along with Netshare, 6 Figure, and the WSJ site). Job banks and resources. Founder Dave Opton has been around a long time and runs a blog with interesting insights.

www.futurestep.com
Korn Ferry is the search firm behind the site. You can put your resume in their database, which is not a bad idea.

www.spencerstuart.com
Executive site for eminent search firm Spencer Stuart. You can put your resume in their database.

www.theladders.com
Like pretty much all the executive sites, you pay for access. Good job board and aggressive marketing means this site has become a player in the space very quickly.

Finding Companies

flipdog.monster.com

www.corporateinformation.com
In addition to having an alphabetical listing of over 20,000 companies, you can also research a country's industry or research a U.S. state. Also, if you register with the site, it will allow you to load the company profile. Within the address section, you will find a link to the company's home page.

www.eliyon.com

www.goleads.com

www.google.com

www.infospace.com

www.searchbug.com

www.superpages.com

www.wetfeet.com

General Job Sites

flipdog.monster.com

hotjobs.yahoo.com

www.4jobs.com

www.americasjobbank.com

www.bestjobsusa.com

www.career.com

www.careerboard.com

www.careerbuilder.com

www.careerhunters.com

www.careermag.com

www.careers.org

Good one-stop site for job search resources.

www.careershop.com

www.careersite.com

www.directemployers.com

www.employment911.com

www.employmentguide.com

www.employmentspot.com

www.job-hunt.org

Excellent site with sensible in-depth advice on job search and career management issues.

www.job.com

www.jobbankusa.com

www.jobfind.com

www.jobwarehouse.com

www.jobweb.com

www.localcareers.com

www.mbajungle.com

Site for current entry level-ish and future MBAs.

www.monster.com

www.nationjob.com

www.net-temps.com

www.quintcareers.com

Diversity Job-Seeker Career, Employment, Job Resources

www.snagajob.com

www.sologig.com

www.summerjobs.com

www.topusajobs.com

www.truecareers.com

www.vault.com

www.wetfeet.com

www.worklife.com

Job Posting Spiders

www.indeed.com

www.jobbankusa.com

www.jobs.just-posted.com

www.jobsearchengine.com

www.jobsniper.com

www.worktree.com

International Sites

www.ukjobsnet.co.uk

UK Jobs Network: the easiest way to find vacancies throughout the UK.

www.4icj.com

www.careerone.com.au

www.eurojobs.com

www.gojobsite.co.uk

www.jobpilot.com

www.jobsbazaar.com

www.jobserve.com

www.jobstreet.com

Asia-Pacific's #1 job site.

www.monster.ca

Monster Canada

www.monster.co.uk

Monster UK: England's #1 job site.

www.overseasjobs.com

www.reed.co.uk

www.seek.com.au

Australia's #1 job site.

www.stepstone.com

www.topjobs.co.uk

www.totaljobs.com

www.workopolis.com

Canada's #1 job site.

Job Fairs

www.careerfairs.com

CareerFairs.com is the fastest one-stop internet site for locating upcoming job fairs and employers. In some cases you can even find the specific positions you desire and the specific positions you are trying to fill.

www.cfg-inc.com

Career Fairs for all levels: Professional & General, Healthcare, Technical, Salary, Hourly, Entry to Senior Level.

www.preferredjobs.com

www.psijobfair.com

www.skidmore.edu

Networking Sites

network.monster.com

socialsoftware.weblogsinc.com

This blog maintains a comprehensive listing of hundreds of networking sites. If you want to check out all your networking options, this is the place to start.

www.40plus.org

Chapter contact information.

www.alumni.net

www.distinctiveweb.com

www.eliyon.com

Helps you find people and companies.

www.execunet.com

An extensive network of professionals with whom you can interact for advice, support, and even career enhancement through local networking meetings. To locate meetings near you (U.S. and the world), check under "Networking" on their Web site.

www.fiveoclockclub.com

National career counseling network.

www.fiveoclockclub.com

Network with members, and alumni database.

www.rileyguide.com

www.ryze.com

Ryze helps people make connections and expand their networks. You can network to grow your business, build your career, and find a job. You can also join networks related to your industry for free.

www.tribe.net

www.womans-net.com

www.linkedin.com

Newspaper Sites

newsdirectory.com
Links to newspapers (global).

Profession-Specific Sites

Advertising, Public Relations, and Graphic Arts

www.adage.com

www.adweek.com
Adweek Online

www.amic.com
Advertising Media Internet Center

www.creativehotlist.com

Communication Arts

www.prweek.net
PR Week

Aerospace and Aviation

www.aerojobs.com

www.avcrew.com

www.avjobs.com

www.spacejobs.com

Agriculture and Horticulture

www.agricareers.com
www.fishingjobs.com
www.hortjobs.com

Broadcast, Communications, and Journalism

www.b-roll.net

www.cpb.org
Corporation for Public Broadcasting
www.crew-net.com

www.journalismjobs.com

www.telecomcareers.net

www.womcom.org
AWC Online

Business, Finance, and Accounting

www.accounting.com

www.bankjobs.com

www.brokerhunter.com

www.businessfinancemag.com

www.careerbank.com

www.careerjournal.com

www.cfo.com

www.efinancialjobs.com

www.fei.org

www.financialjobs.com

www.jobsinthemoney.com

Education

www.aacc.nche.edu
American Association of Community Colleges
www.academic360.com

www.academiccareers.com

www.chronicle.com

www.higheredjobs.com

www.petersons.com

www.phds.org

www.teacherjobs.com

www.ujobbank.com

www.wihe.com

Women in Higher Education

Engineering

www.asme.org

www.chemindustry.com

www.engineeringcentral.com

www.engineeringjobs.com

www.engineerjobs.com

www.enr.com

Engineering News Record Magazine
www.graduatingengineer.com

www.ieee.org

www.mepatwork.com

www.nsbe.org

National Society of Black Engineers

www.nspe.org
National Society of Professional Engineers

www.swe.org
Society of Women Engineers

Entertainment, TV, and Radio

www.castingnet.com

www.eej.com

Entertainment Employment Journal
www.entertainmentcareers.net

www.showbizjobs.com

www.themeparkjobs.com

www.tvandradiojobs.com

www.tvjobs.com

Health Care

www.accessnurses.com
Travel nursing jobs

www.allnurses.com

www.dentsearch.com

www.healthcaresource.com

www.healthjobusa.com

www.hirehealth.com

www.jobscience.com

www.mdjobsite.com

www.medcareers.com

www.nurses123.com
Nurses can use this site to find nursing jobs across the USA.

www.nursetown.com

www.nursing-jobs.us
Nursing jobs in the USA.
www.nursingcenter.com

www.nursingspectrum.com

www.physemp.com

Human Resources

www.hrjobnet.com

www.hrworld.com

www.jobs4hr.com

www.shrm.org

www.tcm.com

IT and MIS

www.computerjobs.com

www.computerjobsbank.com

www.dice.com

www.gjc.org

www.mactalent.com

www.tech-engine.com

www.techemployment.com

www.techies.com

Legal

www.emplawyernet.com

www.ihirelegal.com

www.law.com

www.legalstaff.com

www.theblueline.com

Nonprofit

www.execsearches.com

www.idealist.org

www.naswdc.org

www.nonprofitcareer.com

www.opportunityknocks.org

Real Estate

www.realtor.org

Retail, Hospitality, and Customer Service

www.allretailjobs.com

www.chef2chef.net

www.chefjobsnetwork.com

www.coolworks.com

www.hcareers.com

www.leisurejobs.com

www.resortjobs.com

www.restaurantrecruit.com

www.supermarketnews.com

Sales and Marketing

www.careermarketplace.com

www.jobs4sales.com

www.marketingjobs.com

www.marketingmanager.com

www.marketingpower.com

www.salesheads.com

www.salesjobs.com

Science, Chemistry, Physics, and Biology

www.biocareer.com

www.biospace.com

www.bioview.com

www.bmn.com

www.eco.org

www.hirebio.com

www.medzilla.com

www.microbiologistjobs.com

www.pharmacyweek.com

Recruiter Sites

www.kellyservices.com

www.kornferry.com

www.manpower.com

www.napsweb.org

A job seeker can search the online directory by state, specialty, or by individual. Be sure to check out the headhunters who are designated C.P.C's—the few but the best.

www.randstad.com

www.recruitersonline.com

www.rileyguide.com

www.snelling.com

www.spherion.com

www.staffingtoday.net
Search the database by state, skills, and type of services you need (temporary/permanent/profession) and it will tell you about staffing services companies in your area.

www.therecruiternetwork.com

Reference Checking

www.allisontaylor.com

Researching Companies

bls.gov

iws.ohiolink.edu
A place for getting started with company research.

iws.ohiolink.edu
Helpful in understanding industry research.
newsdirectory.com

www.competia.com

www.fuld.com

www.industrylink.com

www.learnwebskills.com

A business research tutorial that presents a step-by-step process for finding free company and industry information on the Web. This online course will enable you to learn about an industry, and locate company home pages.

www.quintcareers.com
The quintessential directory of company career centers.

www.quintcareers.com
Guide to researching companies, industries, and countries.
www.thomasregister.com

www.vault.com

Company research

www.vault.com
Industry list

www.virtualpet.com
Teaches you how to learn about an industry or a specific company.

Resume Creation

Knockemdead.com
E-mail: martin@knockemdead.com
www.phoenixcareergroup.com
certifiedresumewriters.com
parw.com

Resume Distribution

www.resumemachine.com

Salary Research

www.jobstar.org

www.salary.com

www.salaryexpert.com

Telecommuting

www.homeworkers.org
www.jobs-telecommuting.com
www.tdigest.com
www.tjobs.com

Web Resumes / Portfolios

www.brandego.com
www.qfolio.com

INDEX

For More Information

You can send me your comments and questions about any of the *Knock 'em Dead* books through my Web site at *www.knockemdead.com*, or by:

E-mailing me at *martin@knockemdead.com*

Or writing to me at:
Martin Yate
c/o Adams media
57 Littlefield Street
Avon, MA 02322

The best of luck to you in your job search, and throughout your career!

The bestselling job-search series that will help you land the job you want!

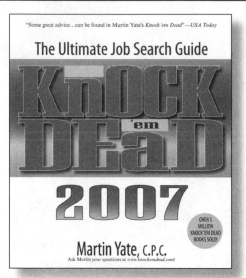
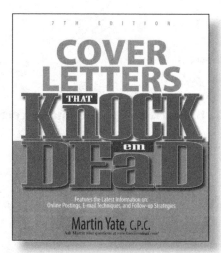